Secretaries Talk

Secretaries Talk

Sexuality, Power and Work

ROSEMARY PRINGLE

VERSO

London · New York

First published in 1988 by Allen & Unwin, Australia Pty Ltd
This edition published by Verso 1989
© Rosemary Pringle 1988

Verso
UK: 6 Meard Street, London WIV 3HR
USA: 29 West 35th Street, New York, NY 10001-2291

Verso is the imprint of New Left Books

British Library Cataloguing in Publication Data available

ISBN 0 86091 234 5

ISBN 0 86091 950 1 Pbk

Produced by SRM Production Services Sdn Bhd

Contents

Tables

Illustrations

Abbreviations

AA	affirmative action
ABS	Australian Bureau of Statistics
ACTU	Australian Council of Trade Unions
AFR	*Australian Financial Review*
APSA	Australian Public Service Association
ACOA	Administrative and Clerical Officers Association
ASCO	Australian Standard Classification of Occupations
CA	clerical assistant
CCLO	Classification and Classified List of Occupations
CES	Commonwealth Employment Service
CAE	college of advanced education
DT	*Daily Telegraph*
EDP	electronic data processing
EEO	equal employment opportunity
IPSA	Institute of Professional Secretaries (Australia)
MBC	Metropolitan Business College
NT	*National Times*
PEP	Participation and Equity Program
PSA	Public Service Association
RSI	repetitive strain injury
SMH	*Sydney Morning Herald*
ST	*Sunday Telegraph*
TAFE	Department of Technical and Further Education
TEAS	Tertiary Education Allowance Scheme
2IC	Second in command

Preface

Studies of work have traditionally focused on archetypal *male* work experiences. Socialist accounts have emphasised degradation, deskilling, and struggles for control between capital and labour. Feminists responded by making *female* workers more visible but concentrated on similar themes. They have either dealt generally with the issues of how women combine motherhood and domestic work with being in the paid workforce, or concentrated on the experience of factory workers. The cover of Kaye Hargreaves' major Australian survey of *Women at Work* (1982) featured a woman in overalls standing outside a factory. Though by 1979 83 per cent of women worked in the tertiary or service sector, office workers appear only very briefly in the book, under health and safety, and again as unemployment statistics. Clerical work has been of interest mostly in so far as it seemed to have become more like factory work and could therefore be understood in terms of deskilling and proletarianisation. When treated at all, secretaries tend to be subsumed under the general heading of 'women office workers' rather than looked at in their specificity. Most studies of women's work have been based on quite small samples or on one single workplace.

Recently there have been a number of attempts to do more than 'add women' to the existing framework. Rather than just making women 'visible' there has been a concern with gender as an organising principle of work relations. This has included accounts of masculinity and sexuality in the workplace (Cockburn, 1983, 1986; Hearn and Parkin, 1987); the realisation that gender is not merely created at home and that work is one of a number of important sites of its construction; and the understanding of the importance of the ideological and the symbolic in constructing the 'economic'. My own earlier book with Ann Game, *Gender at Work* (1983), was shaped by these concerns.

Yet feminists still tend to treat sexuality and work as entirely separate areas of analysis. The main meeting ground so far has been in accounts of 'sexual harassment'. There is a vast gulf between feminist debates on psychoanalysis, discourse theory, cultural production and semiotics, and the frameworks of political economy and industrial sociology within which most studies of work are situated. Veronica Beechey has noted that 'people writing about work have tended to avoid the new forms of "deconstructionist" feminist theory and, with a few exceptions, the field of work has become a rather atheoretical area of feminist intellectual enquiry' (1987: 13). This book is an attempt to bridge the gap by locating 'work' in the context of debates concerning culture, sexuality and subjectivity.

This is not a work of political economy. On the contrary, it offers a critique of existing labour market and labour process theories. Since I am concerned with processes and relations rather than with digging out the concrete details of companies, organisations or industries, the actual names of individuals or organisations are not important. Since secretaries are located in every part of the economy it was necessary to sample a wide range of workplaces in order to be in a position to make generalisations. The book is based on a very large number of interviews. But it attempts to offer more than an empirical account of secretaries. It is equally concerned with broader theoretical questions as they are emerging in a variety of countries.

I have organised the material around discourses of power rather than analyses of the labour process. Issues such as the labour process and proletarianisation, technological change, occupational health and sexual harassment, which have featured in many accounts of clerical work, are not the centre of attention here. While all these things are important, I have wanted to avoid a framework that latches onto them as the 'tangibles' and instead bring to the centre issues that have less frequently informed studies of 'work'. The focus here is on the relationship between secretaries as an identifiable social group and the discursive construction of secretaries as a category; on the relationship between power structures and the day-to-day negotiation and production of power; on the connections between domination, sexuality and pleasure. I am concerned with what is involved in the deconstruction of present structures of class, status and gender. The boss—secretary relationship is presented not as an archaic remnant of the past but as an archetype of the workings of contemporary bureaucracy and the system that we might call 'liberal patriarchy'.

Rather than taking 'woman' or 'secretary' as unitary categories I look at the ways in which they are constructed. This involves a consideration of the unconscious processes, the repressions and the fantasies that structure 'consciousness', of the precariousness of 'identity' and of the ways in which 'experience' is interpreted through existing discourses. The early chapters argue for the centrality of sexuality, family and personal life in the organisation of work and the production of power. I go on to consider some of the more traditional 'work' themes in the light of this. I argue that class, status and occupational prestige should be placed in the context of wider patriarchal relations and the series of dichotomies associated with them: between home and work, production and consumption, public and private and so on. The central theme throughout is the relationship between subjectivity, sexuality, work and culture. I hope, therefore, that the book will be read, not just as a study of 'work', but as a contribution to feminist theory more widely.

It has not been an easy book to write. It raises questions about all the areas that have been difficult for feminism: work, sexuality, language and discourse, representation and culture, gender and class, technology and the labour process—the list is never-ending. If it raises difficult theoretical questions it also raises difficult personal questions. For the most part feminists and secretaries come from different subcultures and are somewhat suspicious of each other. Feminists have often ignored or patronised women who work as secretaries; secretaries often have stereotypical notions of feminists. The starting point of this book was that secretaries and feminists should take each other more seriously. In a real sense the secretary is Everywoman, and feminism needs to recognise that.

Studying secretaries presents not just a theoretical challenge but, I believe, an emotional and political challenge. Speaking for myself, I grew up being told that when I left school I was to go to a 'good' business college and become a very superior sort of secretary. My mother, after not expecting she would have to work for a living, did clerical work for more than thirty years, and wanted me to do better than she had done. She hoped such a start would lead eventually to marriage with a lawyer or businessman. This scenario is not very different from the one that many secretaries described to me. At the last minute I jacked up, decided that I wanted to go to university and sweated it out waiting to see if I would get a scholarship. What was going on for me then was complex. I suppose that part of me liked academic work and wanted to continue. But also motivating me was a fear of what was involved in becoming a secretary. For me university looked a great deal easier than business college! It was not that I regarded secretarial work as inferior. On the contrary, being a secretary implied a sophistication and self-confidence that I did not think I could muster. Going to university meant I could stay a gawky schoolgirl! It is hard to say whether my choice was an act of resistance or of panic!

I suspect that many feminists have had similar experiences. Secretaries represent something from which we ran away. They perhaps represent a part of ourselves which we denied or feared. To me they represent all sorts of unresolved questions about what it means to be a woman in a patriarchal society such as ours. I certainly did not resolve them in 1962. I ran! This study has for me therefore, an element of wanting to cast some light on my own past and present, as a necessary part of political thinking in a wider sense. The secretaries I have spoken to have shown me the extent and limitations of the choices we all make. While I cannot speak as one of them there were many times when the gap between researcher and researched all but disappeared.

Given my emphasis on subjectivity and 'fragmented' identities, and my shift away from any kind of 'us' and 'them' model of the labour process, it is difficult to claim a particular 'standpoint'. Nevertheless my strongest identification is with feminist secretaries and the book is written 'for' them. It is not a 'blueprint for action' and it presents no shopping list of demands. I hope it throws light on power relations in the workplace and beyond as well as offering a challenge to those theories of power and work in which gender relations are suppressed or marginalised.

The book is part of a research project carried out with Ann Game and funded by the Australian Research Grants Scheme 1985−87. The research was carried out primarily in Sydney, with brief excursions to Adelaide and to country areas of New South Wales for comparative material. Historical and statistical information was collected for the period since 1890. Media representations of 'secretary' were analysed. And more than 400 interviews were carried out with a range of managerial, clerical and secretarial workers as well as with teachers and students. While the book is Australian the theoretical debates with which I am engaging are being carried out internationally. While on study leave in 1987 I had the opportunity to talk with representatives of secretaries' organisations Nine to Five in the United States and Typecaste in London. These meetings left me in no doubt that there are greater similarities than there are differences in the experiences of secretaries in all the advanced capitalist countries.

Many people have contributed to the outcome of this book. Without Ann Game the project would never have got off the ground. We set it up together, shared various aspects of it for three years and generated a mass of research material from which I have drawn. Some of the early ideas developed here were first articulated in joint papers—to the 4th Women and Labour Conference, University of Queensland, July 1984 and the Women's Studies Conference, Sydney University, September 1985. The latter paper is a starting point for Chapter 4. An impetus for this book was a joint critique (Game and Pringle, 1986) of our earlier publication, *Gender at Work* (1983). From this joint critique our interests have diverged somewhat and Ann Game has used material from the project for a variety of public lectures, papers and publications of her own.

Marie Flood, Judy Messer, Julienne Vennard worked as research assistants on this project at various time, collecting and analysing data, setting up and conducting interviews, writing reports and contributing much to the framework and direction. It was frequently through their ingenuity that organisations agreed to participate and individuals agreed to interviews. Gary Dowsett helped interview the men and Pip Martin did a valuable literature search. David Tait and his colleagues at Social Facts collected and analysed statistical information and quizzed the ABS on their classification criteria. Jan O'Leary put in an inspired burst in the closing stages and I am particularly grateful for her help in selecting illustrations.

A number of people read, criticised and commented either on the entire manuscript or parts thereof: Judith Allen, Michele Barrett, Clare Burton, Bob Connell, Jean Curthoys, Anne Edwards, Jim Gillespie, Anne Phillips, Deena Shiff, Sophie Watson and Viv White. June Crawford talked to me about statistics. I thank them all. I should also like to thank the following for their encouragement and practical help: Patricia Bellamy, Maria Hall, Annette Hamilton, Mildred Holman, Brenda Morse, Julie McGlone and Hester Watson. My particular thanks go to Judith Allen for her sharp feminist insights, and to Bob Connell, not only for his sharing of ideas and his detailed and careful comment on the entire manuscript, but for his loyal support throughout the years I have been at Macquarie.

I have guaranteed that individuals and workplaces remain anonymous and so names and, where necessary, minor details have been changed. Sadly, the anonymity prevents me thanking directly the many organisations and individuals who contributed to this study. It goes without saying that without their participation there would be no book. I thank everyone who agreed to be interviewed and in particular those people who took the time and the care to schedule groups of interviews for me and to make suggestions about where to go next. Women at Allen & Unwin and at Macquarie University set the ball rolling by participating in a series of pilot interviews and made suggestions about how to conduct the interviews. The TAFE Women's Co-ordination Unit gave advice on which colleges to visit and feedback on our progress.

For typing I thank myself, my faithful word processor, and my mother, who long ago persuaded me that typing was a 'useful thing for a girl to fall back on'.

For reproductions I thank the following: NEC Australia Pty Ltd, Computer Associates, Peter Isaacson Publications Pty Ltd, Componere, Intelligence, Sigma Data Corporation, GBC Australia Pty Ltd, ICL Australia Pty Ltd, Stott & Underwood Ltd, Voca,

Adler Business Machines Pty Ltd, Sanyo Office Machines, Australian Business Magazine.

My greatest debt is to Sophie Watson, who convinced me I could write this book and lived with me through much of it. She explored ideas, put up with my anxieties and got me to express myself when my thoughts seemed permanently locked inside. She read and commented on the 'pre-first drafts' as well as all of the later ones. Without her love and friendship this book would not have been finished.

·1· What is a secretary?

> I think the word 'secretary' means a girl or a woman
> that works for another man in the company, no
> matter what she does.

> We have a problem as secretaries that nobody knows
> what to call us. A secretary could be a typist or it
> could be a full-blown personal assistant or
> administrative officer. No one can say that they are a
> secretary without doing certain tasks but even typists
> seem to say they do those tasks regardless of whether
> they have got a business qualification or whether
> they have done anything like the HSC...

There is nothing straightforward about defining secretaries or identifying them as a group. The first speaker, a senior executive in a large Sydney-based company, gives a very broad definition which makes no reference at all to specific tasks or skills. Instead he stresses that secretaries are *women*, and that they work *for* bosses (who are presumed to be men). In doing so he voices the conventional assumptions first, that 'secretary' is a gendered category and second, that it takes its meaning from its *relation* to another category, namely bosses. Pushed further, he said that a secretary is an 'appendage' of the boss's function. To understand the meaning of 'secretary' produced here it is helpful to consider the unconscious elements that underlie this man's conscious definition. If, as the psychoanalysts suggest, 'woman' is perceived as 'lacking' what it takes to be a 'man', so are secretaries defined as 'lacking' the qualities that make a successful boss. Our executive defines secretaries in negative terms as representing everything that bosses are not. His answer to the question 'what is a secretary' is effectively 'not a boss'. This understanding, widely shared by both men and women, goes some way to explaining the general 'vagueness' about what a secretary is, the trivialisation of her work, and the reluctance to acknowledge secretarial skills as a path into management.

That these ideas are largely unconscious means that they are accepted as 'natural' and rarely articulated. The equation of secretary with woman or 'wife', and boss with man, is important in establishing the normative versions of what a secretary is. It creates problems, not only for female secretaries but for female bosses and male secretaries. Not only can a woman not have a wife, but the discourse casts doubt on whether any woman can fully be a 'boss'. Can a boss take up the 'feminine' position and still be a boss? In our culture these unconscious meanings go deep. They are present in the reservations that secretaries have about working for women and, more openly, in the ridicule that male secretaries receive and the deep unease that they have with the title.

The second speaker, a representative of the Institute of Professional Secretaries (IPSA), indicates the kinds of problems secretaries have had in asserting the importance of skills in their self-definition. She is operating at a conscious, rational level and seeking to ignore or play down the deeper levels at which meanings are generated. It will not be sufficient merely to assert that secretaries have skills if the current sexual meanings are not acknowledged and challenged. An important part of the struggle to improve the conditions of secretaries is the deconstruction of existing meanings.

There is no single answer to the question 'what is a secretary?'. There is not even agreement about what the question 'means'. Statisticians, work analysts and industrial sociologists answer it by attempting to describe what a secretary *does*. But secretary is one of the few employment categories for which there has never been a clear job description. Secretaries do a wide variety of things and there is not even one task which we can confidently say they all perform. We cannot simply point to a place in the labour process and say, *that* is occupied by secretaries. The meanings that derive from job definitions and the labour process offer only one kind of answer to the question of what a secretary is.

We come to know about secretaries, and to identify them as a group, through the ways in which they are represented. This is true of all groups but in most cases the emphasis is on the actual work and the social relations surrounding it. A plumber or, for that matter, a stenographer or typist does not have a particularly strong cultural presence. By contrast, the secretary is constructed in popular culture in a way that plays down the importance of what she *does*, in favour of discussion of what she *is*. The ambiguity about what constitutes a secretary's work makes it easily 'available' for cultural redefinition. Secretaries are part of folklore and popular culture and are represented in stereotypical ways in advertising and the media, even in pornography.

The nature of secretarial work and its relation to other categories has changed over time. New technologies continually transform the skills and tasks involved. In census and labour force analyses, statisticians have generally abandoned the category in favour of more 'precise' alternatives. As a result 'secretaries' have disappeared into more amorphous groups such as 'typists and stenographers' and 'other clerical' workers. Some 'professional' or 'career' secretaries, like the IPSA representative quoted above, would prefer a narrow definition. Others, like the boss quoted, are happy to use the term broadly. That way they can avoid acknowledging the skills of 'top' secretaries and maintain a clear division between secretaries and management. While the senior or career secretaries are the main focus of this book, they need to be situated in relation to the larger group of 'secretarial' workers and the cultural meanings attached to 'secretary'. I am concerned not with tracing the evolution of a pre-given category but with the ways in which the category is itself constituted.

Though men retained a presence in the area until World War II, secretarial work is currently presented as quintessentially feminine. Moreover, all women are assumed to be capable of secretarial work. As one secretary put it, 'typing is seen as something every woman can do—like washing up!'. There is still a widespread belief that it is a 'good thing' for girls to learn shorthand and typing as something 'to fall back on', whatever else they might do. Men may perceive any woman in an office as the secretary or expect her to perform secretarial services in the absence of a secretary. A male friend insisted I should go and see *Prick Up Your Ears* because, he said, there was a wonderful secretary in it. It turned out to be Vanessa Redgrave playing, not a secretary, but Joe Orton's literary agent! Even if they have not started off as secretaries, women managers know what it is like to be treated as one. They often go to some lengths to dress in a way that will distinguish them from secretaries. The meanings given to 'secretary' and to 'woman' are mutually dependent. The qualities of 'good woman' are encapsulated in the 'good secretary'. Representations of secretaries thus have a direct relevance to all women, whether or not they have worked in the occupation.

If secretaries are represented as women they are also represented almost exclusively in familial or sexual terms: as wives, mothers, spinster aunts, mistresses and femmes fatales. The emphasis on the sexual has made it easy to treat the work itself as trivial or invisible. We experienced the inside of this when we visited workplaces to do our research. Everywhere people cracked jokes about whether we were going to harass them, whether we were perverts and what we had found out about their sex lives. They would often ask 'how's 'secs' going?' basing the joke on the phonetic identity of 'secs' and 'sex'. At every workplace at least some people assumed that studying secretaries meant unravelling sexual scandals. As sociologists we became aware that we too might be perceived as trivial or frivolous, not dealing with work in a 'serious' way. The interviews seemed to contrast with earlier ones we had done, in factories, banks and retail stores, where we had asked workers to describe in detail their place in a particular production process. It was impossible to talk to secretaries about what they do without the talk running fairly quickly onto questions about coffee-making, personal services, clothes, femininity and sexuality. These themes are central to their self-definition and their working relations.

Everybody has something to say about secretaries, makes jokes about their sexuality or their relationship with the boss. For secretaries the boss is often supposed to be a highly sexualised being, representing a kind of sex-power that may be desired or repudiated or both. For him the sexual is presented as a piece of light relief, a diversion from his real business. The boss—secretary relationship is the subject of fantasy, both in a general way and in specific office situations. At the back of most people's minds is the question of whether any kind of sexual relationship is taking or might take place. It provides the subject matter for office gossip as well as affecting the expectations or anxieties that bosses and secretaries may have about each other. Driving to work one morning I listened to a news item on the administrative arrangements for the new Child Support Agency whose task is to collect maintenance payments. The minister for social security and the shadow minister were interviewed about what should be done in 'tricky' situations where the woman may not wish to reveal the father of her child. The example which both singled out was the secretary who may have to 'dob in' her boss ('AM', 29 October 1987).

If the boss—secretary relationship is the subject of humour and gossip it is also constructed as intimate, intense, emotionally powerful, a source of both strength and vulnerability for both parties. Secretaries may either save or destroy their bosses. In England we think of Sarah Keay's near-destruction of Cecil Parkinson when he reneged on his promise to leave his wife and marry her, following the birth of their child; in America of Richard Nixon's secretary destroying some of the Watergate tapes, and of Oliver North's shredding the evidence of 'Irangate'; in Australia the image of Justice Lionel Murphy's secretary weathering hostile questioning during his trial on charges of conspiracy to pervert the course of justice. Secretaries often come to the fore in courtroom dramas, whether actual or fictitious. Just as we construct our 'knowledge' of the law from the likes of Perry Mason, so we turn to the same sources for our understandings of secretaries. Mason's secretary, Delys Street, is the idealised 'office wife'.

Stereotypes do not simply distort or reflect 'reality'. As Perkins suggests, their strength lies in a 'combination of validity and distortion' (1979: 154). All typologies are simplifications in so far as they select common features and exclude differences. But stereotypes go further than this, for rather than merely classifying people they draw on broader associations. Stenographers or typists may have certain things in common as groups but they do not elicit stereotypes. On the other hand it is virtually impossible to talk about secretaries without making a set of sexual associations. Images of secretaries sitting around filing their nails or doing their knitting reinforce the idea that they do little work, that their work is of secondary importance or that their interests and priorities are in a sphere 'outside' work. If they are idle it is linked to their femininity and blamed on them rather than on poor management. They are acknowledged as 'real' workers. Discussion of what a secretary *does* seems inseparable from popular images and expectations of what a secretary *is*.

'Secretary' has not one but a variety of meanings. These meanings are not fixed for they have to be continually produced and reproduced. Herein lie the possibilities for transformation and change. However, the alternative meanings are not infinite. The prevailing images and representations operate in the context of structures which, if not fixed, do have a certain longevity. Structures of patriarchy and capitalism, gender and class, the labour process and psycho-sexuality provide a context and a set of limitations to the transformations that are possible at any point in time. They have been produced for so long, and in such a variety of contexts, that alternative positions may be literally unthinkable or relegated to the political wilderness. The relation between 'discourses' and 'structures' is a recurrent theme of this book.

The question of 'what is a secretary' may be answered with reference to three discourses which have coexisted, at times peacefully and at others in open competition with each other. The first of these, the 'office wife', is strongly middle-class and may be found in 'serious' journals, teaching manuals, the ideas and practices of a good many secretarial studies teachers as well as the more 'traditional' bosses and secretaries. The second, the 'sexy secretary', became the dominant one in the 1950s and 60s and is predominantly working-class. It relates to folklore and popular culture, particularly the tabloids, as well as some soft-core pornography. It rests on stereotyping and caricature and its central theme is the mindless Dolly bird. Women who refuse this image may be lampooned as asexual spinsters or dragons who will never be attractive to men. The third discourse, the 'career woman', derives from a variety of approaches that may be described as 'modernist' in the sense that they seek to extend the principles of bureaucratic rationality and efficiency to all those parts of life that are still seen to be governed by the personal, the familial or the arbitrary. It is within the modernist context that attempts to measure secretarial skills become relevant. There is no place here for familial or sexual definitions. Nevertheless it has not been at all easy to shake them off and a number of compromises have been reached.

The office wife

'Office wife' has its origins in debates in the early part of the century, about whether (middle-class) women should work outside the home. It signified that women's primary place was in the home, that her other tasks would be defined in relation to this and would be restricted to lower-level and support roles. 'Office wife' distinguished the secretary from other clerical workers, notably stenographers, and represented the highest position to which members of these groups could aspire. Benet suggests that it also embodied male fantasies. The office is a mirror image of family life, but slower to change since it represents what men would still like the family to be. Men have a nostalgic desire to be paterfamilias in the large Victorian family and use their authority at work to recreate something of this situation (1972: 66—69). By the 1930s when women began to predominate in secretarial work, the term was well established. Though its content has changed somewhat it remains an important reference point for talking about secretaries. The discourse creates clearly gendered positions: the possibility of bosses taking a feminine, or secretaries a masculine, position is all but excluded.

The two main requirements of the office wife were (and still are) that she be deferential and that she be ladylike. Marriage services still speak of a couple becoming, not husband and wife, but man and wife. Men are never referred to, even in secretaries' discourse, as 'office husbands', though secretaries will at times make comparisons between their husbands and bosses. Bosses do not take their identity primarily from their relationship with their secretaries but from relations with equals and superiors in their own and other organisations. As 'wives' secretaries are positioned as subordinates who are defined in relation to their bosses rather than having separate identities. On one occasion I sat with some senior secretaries while they planned their week's work. They made arrangements for 'relieving Mr P' this week and 'Mr Q' next week. This meant not getting Messrs P and Q's work done but relieving their secretaries who were going to be away in the said weeks. Boss and secretary were so conflated that 'Mr P' could be used as a shorthand for 'Mr P's secretary'.

The office wife is portrayed as the extension of her boss, loyal, trustworthy and devoted. She is expected to 'love, honour and obey', relieving him of the routine and the trivial, creating the conditions for his detachment from the mundane rituals of everyday life. She is the gatekeeper, protecting him from those who would waste his time or want to know his private business, mediating his relations with the outside world and even with himself. In folklore she may either rival the wife or liaise with her in order to 'organise' him. A university professor mentioned as an aside that 'My wife rings up sometimes and they sort out my problems together'. The relationship between the wife and the secretary is not always an easy one. One secretary said, 'It is a lot better now because a lot of them work—the wives I mean. But twenty years ago they didn't...and they would ring you up and expect you to go and do messages for them in your lunch hour...' while suitably deferential the secretary must have enough initiative to anticipate, to work unsupervised and to act on the boss's behalf. This requires that she be thoroughly aware of the business, and in tune with his moods, his thought processes and his ways of working.

While thoroughly subordinate to her boss, as 'wife' the secretary is allocated considerable power. She acts on his behalf, determines who gets to see him and, through having his ear, has considerable influence. Since in some sense she participates in his class position she is expected to look, sound and behave like a lady. It was the task of the business colleges to produce these characteristics rather than a set of merely technical skills, hence the emphasis on what was called 'grooming and deportment'. Texts of the 1950s and 60s were full of pious cliches about how secretaries should behave. Corish's widely used *Tomorrow's Secretary* (1960) gave the following advice:

> As a secretary, you are a kind of co-partner with your employer. It is your duty to save him a great deal of detail and as much purely routine work as you can. Think for him, and anticipate his needs...Learn his preferences and obey them even if you do not always agree with his ideas or methods. Assume that he is always right. (p. 12)

> In the office be on the conservative side in your dress—quiet, simple and neat. Do not call attention to your clothes in any way, either in extremes of colour or style. Avoid sleeveless frocks or overdainty blouses, or low-cut neck lines...You should also avoid fixing your hair or 'making up' your face in the office. Remember, your desk is not a dressing table...All this does not mean that you should be dowdy or unattractive. It merely means that you should look like a secretary.
> People unconsciously are noticing you all the time—other people in your office, your employer and also callers. Careless walk and posture give the impression of slackness. There should never be any slouching...Even when you go to the files or sit at your typewriter or approach your employer's desk, somebody is always noticing your posture and being either impressed or otherwise by it. (p. 32–33)

> There are some things which you will not do in public...When you see a girl walking down the street eating, you can safely assume that she is not

somebody's secretary. The chewing of gum is, of course, considered an unforgivable sin. (p. 35)

> To succeed in the position you must *like* being a secretary and be keenly interested in the work. It is necessary that you should look on it as a career and not merely as the necessary filling in of a few years before marriage...Make yourself fit to hold the top secretarial position in the firm...There always has been, and probably always will be, a shortage of first-class secretaries. (p. 47)

Solly, in *The Secretary at Work*, counselled that: 'A secretary should be particularly aware of her hands since they are on constant display. Yet, all too often, it isn't until she receives an engagement or wedding ring that she gives her hands the attention they deserve' (Solly et al. 1970: 13).

It would be tempting to relegate this to a bygone age, were it not still a big part of secretarial studies teaching. Bosses continue to speak in similar terms about their 'ideal' secretary. Most demur from the overt master—slave implications of the discourse but they accept that the relationship is analagous to a marriage and see marriage in fairly 'traditional' terms with a clearcut division of labour. The secretary's task, like the wife's, is to manage the details of their lives so they can get on with 'business'. The relationship is less formal than it used to be and the boss is more likely to be on first-name terms with his secretary. But he still wants his needs anticipated and met, his instructions carried out without question, and his secretary always available to him. He wants her to like both him and his work, to do his bidding not purely out of fear of the sack but because she cares about him.

John Morley, a senior financial controller, says 'I couldn't have a secretary who worked 9 to 5'. He believes his secretary understands 'exactly what I am trying to do' and is totally committed to his own career goals. 'I have absolutely no secrets from her whatsoever.' Though her job is to save him 'wasting' his own time, he describes it in terms of managing, organising, even 'controlling' his day, just as his wife 'controls' household matters: 'In fact my wife is complaining about my increased distance from reality in day to day cares. I don't have any. I get out of my car in the company garage, walk into my office and everything is organised for me so I don't have to do anything but think about business.' He considers her not as an individual but an extension of himself. When he says her job is a 'career' job he actually means, 'if I got promoted then I would take her with me because I am satisfied with her'. Morley's secretary conforms outwardly to his expectations but does not endorse them. To her it is 'just a job' and she does what she is told. She finds the work tedious and him bombastic and hard to get on with: 'I sometimes think when I leave the office and go home to my son and he starts on about something, which is worse, the office or home?'

While it is open to different meanings, 'office wife' continues to structure work arrangements. Bosses and secretaries are still perceived as operating in 'pairs'. Although most secretaries work for more than one person there is always a 'boss' with whom they have a special relation; bosses often do not admit to sharing a secretary: she is still 'their' secretary who happens to work for other people as well.

Debate about changes in secretarial work is frequently cast in terms of how far office marriages are changing. Are traditional marriages based on deference being transformed into more companionate and egalitarian relations, where the wife might have other interests or refuse to do certain aspects of the housework? 'Deference' and 'respect' have been replaced by 'friendship' and 'team-work'. While this may enable the secretary to exercise more power, she may also lose some of the respect and distance she had in the old relationship, find it harder to resist emotional or sexual demands, or she may allow herself be drawn in more deeply through her emotional involvement. Informality in itself is no guarantee of a more reciprocal relationship. It may serve to disguise the operations of power.

In the 'office wife' discourse secretaries tend to be represented as lower middle class. They are the social inferiors of the boss but only by a sufficient amount to maintain an appropriate deference. This raises the question of whether the secretary can actually marry the boss. Before World War II secretaries were likely to be single, and in their late twenties at the youngest, having started as stenographers and worked their way up to positions of responsibility. Conventionally women were expected to resign on marriage so most had left the workforce before they reached the position of secretary. To be a secretary was, by implication, to have chosen a career instead of marriage. It was not very difficult therefore to represent her as devoting herself to her boss as a substitute for the absent husband. Such women often appear in Agatha Christie's stories. In *Ordeal By Innocence* (1958), for example, we have:

> Gwenda...the perfect, helpful secretary, working for him, always at hand, kind, helpful. There was something about her than reminded him of what Rachel had been when he first met her. The same warmth, the same enthusiasm, the same warm-heartedness. Only in Gwenda's case, that warmth, that warm-heartedness, that enthusiasm were all for him...But suddenly one day—he had known that he loved her. And that as long as Rachel lived, they could never marry.

Secretaries come from similar social backgrounds to their bosses and not surprisingly many marry business and professional men.

THE NEW SIERRA RANGE OF TYPEWRITERS

FROM

STOTT + UNDERWOOD

You can't go wrong with the second biggest selling typewriter in the USA.

* Golf ball Electric Typewriter for professional and executive use. Includes correction key!
* Stationary carriage
* Takes foolscap sideways
* Golf ball element interchangeable with IBM Selectric II
* 6 months warranty on parts & service
* Maintenance agreement available
* Prices start from only $495.

STOTT + UNDERWOOD
LIMITED (INC. IN N.S.W.)

SYDNEY (02) 929 0566
MELBOURNE (03) 329 5366
BRISBANE (07) 391 8144
ADELAIDE (08) 223 3700
PERTH (09) 328 7851

Secretaries get asked all the time.

Plate 1   Pornographic codes carry over to images of secretaries in advertising as the top two examples show. The one on the left is conservative in its layout, but the 'look' signifies sexual availability. The one on the right is an advertisement for telephone equipment but it is the explicit sexual message of both text and image that attracts attention. The image below is part of an advertisement for typewriters. But it is clear that it is sexual favours that secretaries are asked for; and the exchange of looks hints that they say, yes.

Plate 2 Standard cartoon images of the 'sexy secretary' as the blonde bombshell. The one above is part of an advertisement for filing systems, but the chaos in the office is caused by more than an overflowing filing cabinet. The secretary signifies chaos along with sexuality.

Since the 1950s a growing proportion of secretaries have been both younger and married. It became less feasible, even bigamous, to represent married women as 'office wives', but it was possible to represent them more openly as mature sexual beings. Both of these factors were significant in the moves to represent secretaries in sexual terms. The 'office wife' was the dominant representation of secretaries from the 1930s to the 1950s or 60s when it came under challenge, first from the more explicitly sexual stereotypes and then from what I have described as modernism.

Sexy secretaries

The postwar period saw the rapid expansion of all sectors of the economy. As companies grew and diversified, their management structures became larger and more complex and the demand for different types of secretaries increased. There was an expansion of mass consumption and the mass media, the emergence of a sophisticated advertising industry, the commodification of sex and its use to sell a range of other commodities, the preoccupation with glamour and sex appeal and wider participation in clothes, fashion, make-up and so on. In the office, unlike the factory, women could dress in ways that evoked desire. So the growth of offices provided a central site for 'sexuality'. Secretaries were targeted for this treatment, becoming a metaphor or a euphemism for sex. They were a focal point in new discourses about 'sexuality' as identity, adventure, recreation, commodity.

Elements of this discourse had been present, along with the 'office wife', from the 1920s and 30s, but remained subordinate. Members of the typing pool, being low down on the social scale, had previously been regarded as sexually available to men of the executive class. Working-class women who would otherwise have been domestic servants or shop assistants had traditionally provided sexual entertainment for 'respectable' men (Benet, 1972: 52–69). This was not publicly celebrated nor was it applied to the private secretary, who was either male or, as office wife, a respectable woman with shared social connections.

From the 1950s there was a qualitative change and women came to be discussed in terms of their femininity and their sexual attractiveness and in particular their bodies. Secretaries were singled out for this treatment. Agatha Christie (1953: 5–6) noted the change:

> Miss Grosvenor was an incredibly glamorous blonde. She wore an expensively cut little black suit and her shapely legs were encased in the very best and most expensive black-market nylon.
> She sailed back through the typists' room without deigning to give

anyone a word or a glance. The typists might have been so many blackbeetles. Miss Grosvenor was Mr Fortescue's own special personal secretary; unkind rumour always hinted that she was something more, but actually this was not true... Miss Grosvenor was to Mr Fortescue just a necessary part of the office decor—which was all very luxurious and very expensive.

The earlier image of the secretary as a prim, bespectacled, mousy-looking woman in her late thirties was now displaced by the blonde bombshell: not very smart but long-legged, big-bosomed and above all young. In the popular press she is usually perched on the boss's knee taking shorthand while he is winking back at the viewer. This image was obsessively reiterated in the 1950s and 60s and has since receded somewhat. But it is still the one most readily produced in casual conversation and in tabloids.

Newspaper articles of the 1950s and 60s contain a curious mixture of sexual banter and discussion of wage levels and productivity, technology and office rationalisation. In popular culture, the office was as a kind of erotic war zone in which men were constantly on the prowl and women were presumed to enjoy their advances or advised how to control them. This appealed particularly to working-class men, unfamiliar with office environments. Bosses, it was suggested, were basically wolves: 'Quite a few bosses, it seems, think that the salary they pay their stenographers includes activities that are not part of the normal office curriculum. And many of them at least feel that it gives them the right to all sorts of little familiarities' (*SMH* 1 April 1956). The sexual overtones of the boss—secretary relation, already present in the 'office wife' metaphor, now took over completely:

> ...one must mention the side effects of today's sex-conscious advertising and public relations techniques. Perhaps its most long-standing joke has been the good-looking secretary...The good-looking girl may feel that her legs are her main qualification. The plain ones will feel insecure. Both ways, secretarial work loses caste as something that has to be worked at before one is qualified (*AFR* 25 September 1958).

Not until the 1980s would wolf-like behaviour be named 'sexual harassment'. In the earlier period it was regarded as natural and inevitable, a subject of jokes and something that added excitement to the working day.

That 'bosses' could be written and spoken about in this way is interesting and indicates a changed usage of the term. The boss was originally the owner, with the power to hire and fire. As companies grew and diversified, their administrative structures became larger and more complex and new categories of middle management emerged, almost entirely male. These men were essentially employees who were answerable to those more senior.

It has often been suggested that such people suffer considerable anxiety about their worth and status and look for tangible signs that they have 'made it'. They were able to appropriate the name of 'boss' and build up their masculinity by acquiring a secretary of their own, often the only employee over whom they had direct power. Their status was enhanced by having a sexually attractive secretary (*Sun Herald* 10 November 1957). The existence of the crude sexual stereotypes legitimated the evaluation of secretaries in physical terms and implied that sex appeal rather than skills was the key to success. Fashion writers advised on how to become 'a Rolls-Royce type secretary' (*SMH* 19 March 1960), while in London, Lucy Clayton's college for secretaries taught how to get in and out of an E-type Jaguar in a mini skirt without showing a thigh.

The 1950s saw the expansion of the soft-core pornography of popular girlie magazines like *Pix* and *Post* where boss—secretary jokes were weekly fare. As Hearn & Parkin (1984) point out, the office is also a common setting for pornography—'girls are shown studiously taking dictation in owlish glasses and severe hairstyles, quite unconscious that their neat white blouse is completely open down the front and the boss is absent-mindedly playing with their breasts. Office girls cannot open a filing cabinet without revealing that they have nothing on under their respectable grey skirts...' The pornographic codes carry over into advertising and other representations of secretaries. These images have a 'to be looked at' quality signifying sexual availability (see Plate 1).

In contrast to the office wife, the 'Dolly' is the 'bad girl', a potentially disruptive presence in the office. While clearly the object of male fantasy, she has a certain power of her own. Where the office wife is subservient, passive and reserved, the Dolly is cheeky and loud and is represented as having an active sexuality and a degree of sexual power over her boss. Where the office wife is a drudge, the Dolly is represented as not doing any serious work at all, as taking the boss for a ride. In the cartoons he is made to look as silly as she is, his own pretensions to masculine power and status invariably being sent up (Plate 2).

Stereotypes do not exist because of their truth functions and they cannot be removed simply by being shown to be an inaccurate account of 'reality'. Whether or not the Dolly Bird exists as a referent, the stereotype affects the ways in which people think about secretaries. The Dolly signifies that secretaries/women are ranked in terms of heterosexual attractiveness and their ability to please a man. Men are always the subjects in these discourses, entitled to comment on women's attractiveness in terms of their own choosing. As with much popular romance the only subject position available for the woman is in advice on how to catch a man or marry the boss.

The Dolly lacks the respect allocated to the office wife as an extension of her boss; she is valued only as a sex object and thus when she loses her looks will become redundant. While she is at a structural disadvantage she is also represented as being on the prowl. Where the boss is prowling for casual sex, she is prowling for a husband, using her body to full advantage. As with 'office wives', grooming and deportment are stressed but the object is not simply to enhance the bosses' reputation. The executive secretary, for example,

> combines the best features of an executive's wife, his mother and his best friend, without any of their faults. That's a sobering thought for the starry-eyed junior who dreams some day of becoming, first, the boss's private secretary, and a little later, maybe, his wife or his daughter-in-law... Never lose any of your femininity in the battle to the pinnacle of success—you never know but the boss's next visitor may be your dream man (*Sun-Herald* 23 October 1966).

Secretaries were exhorted, not to become Dolly birds exactly, but to develop their femininity as their most valuable asset: 'She's 25—27 years old, her manner of dress is "conspicuously inconspicuous", she's the next best thing to a junior executive, she's a mature person, she knows a little of accounting, a little of economics, she's charming, poised and attractive...but not too attractive' (*Sun-Herald* 4 June 1961). Books like Helen Gurley Brown's *Sex and the Single Girl* and Pagrelin's *How to Make it in a Man's World* became popular for they explained to women how to use their bodies and sexual attractiveness to get on in the world. At the same time secretaries were berated for concentrating on femininity. The *Sunday Telegraph* (26 October 1969), for example, claimed that they only worked four hours a day because of 'nose powdering in excess, preening in the loo, gossiping, tea-making and titillating, and deciding which set of panti-hose was more attractive to the boss'.

Moving away from the cartoon images, a new term was becoming popular to describe secretaries. The number of advertisements for 'Girl Fridays' in the *Sydney Morning Herald* classified section leapt from one in 1966 to 57 on the equivalent Saturday in 1971. Though deriving from the UK, the Girl Friday had a distinctively Australian character. She was the 'girl' who was willing to turn a hand to anything, combining the skills of the private secretary with the range of mundane tasks including making the tea (she was also expected to be sexy). This was the dominant image of the secretary, in striking contrast to North America where a professional image had taken hold much earlier. North American visitors frequently expressed their surprise at the menial treatment of Australian secretaries (*AFR* 20 August 1970).

The stereotypes ensure that neither the secretary nor her work are taken very seriously. While lip-service is paid to the secretary as the person who actually runs the office, her true role is never realistically assessed. Either she does everything or she does nothing but adorn the office as a glamorous status symbol. All women workers, whatever their age, are put down as adolescent 'girls' and assessed in terms of their physical attributes. Secretaries still say it is harder to get jobs after 35, with 40 a definite cut-off point. Sexual desirability remains an important criterion for secretarial work.

Career women?

Struggling to emerge from the previous two identities is a third one, which emphasises skill and experience, resists the sexual and familial definitions and plays down the 'special' relationship between boss and secretary in favour of being an autonomous part of the management *team*: this is the career woman. Career 'woman' remains a contradictory term, for it implies questions about whether it is possible both to be a woman and to have a career. Can a 'career woman' maintain her femininity or does she have to give up her gender and become an honorary man? Is it possible to create new understandings of the feminine that are not inconsistent with careers? And is 'femininity' so implicated in our ideas about secretaries that the term 'secretary' would have to be dropped?

The secretary as 'career woman' shares the same origins as the 'office wife': being a 'wife' was itself portrayed as a 'career' for women. It is only since the 1970s that the 'career' secretary, in a larger sense, has gained much public recognition. This is often conceptualised as a transition 'from office wife to office manager' (e.g. ACIBS, 1985). A variety of factors have brought the 'office manager' identity to the fore. They include the struggles of secretaries themselves, supported by the wider women's movement; the more sophisticated communications and decision-making requirements of large corporate structures; severe shortages of people with skills and qualifications; technological change with its implications for the transformation of jobs and skills; and the arrival, in the 1980s, of Equal Employment Opportunity (EEO) and Affirmative Action (AA) legislation which has created at least the potential for a proper recognition of secretarial skills and the opening up of career positions.

A seminar on new roles for secretaries was held by the Australian Council of Independent Business Schools in Sydney in 1985. Entitled 'From Office Wife to Office Manager', its starting point was that new technology had made a bigger impact on secretaries

than on any other occupation and that there was a strong demand
for those properly qualified. It was argued that secretaries, far
from being reduced to routine word-processor operators, had
a strong role to play in sophisticated computer-based decision-
making. John Plummer, the managing director of Centacom,
argued that while all recent recessions had seen a brief drop in
demand for secretaries, the 1982 recession had brought a larger
shakeout with heavy cutbacks in middle management. This, he
suggested, had created opportunities for secretaries to take on
some of the middle management functions and work closely with
top management. (ACIBS, 1985: 16—19). In his view the 'modern'
secretary was part of the management team, participating in all
management meetings, and entitled to incentive payments as well
as a share of profits and bonuses (ACIBS, 1985: 23). While not all
participants at the conference shared Plummer's optimism, there
was a strong emphasis on the development of professional roles
for secretaries. Ann Kern, then deputy secretary of the Commonwealth Department of Health, made direct connections between
her own work and that of secretaries in the public service. Noting
the appointment of Helen Williams as the first departmental
head, she put forward the departmental or company secretary as
the career positions to which secretaries might realistically aspire
(ACIBS, 1985: 33—37). Such emphases on professionalism were
counterbalanced by many male managers who assumed that secretaries would continue to be women, that their role would be to
'assist' their boss, and that they would adjust their 'demeanour'
and skills to future trends.

The struggle for better conditions and for professional recognition got going in the 1960s, at a time when a higher proportion
of women were remaining in the paid workforce after marriage.
The Secretaries' Forum was established in Sydney in 1961 to
promote and improve the professional and educational standards
of secretaries and to challenge the stereotypes. The Institute of
Professional Secretaries (IPSA) was established in Melbourne a
year or two later and quickly became Australia-wide. Its national
executive rotates between the state capital cities every two years. It
draws much of its membership from tertiary-educated secretaries
and has been active in pushing for the expansion of graduate
courses.

The Secretaries' Forum initiated 'Secretary of the Year' and
'Secretaries' Week' to help increase public awareness of the vital
role played by secretaries in business, industry, education, government and the professions. Its members criticised the relentless
references to them as 'girls' and the undignified representations
of them as 'sex objects' rather than workers. The panel for the
first 'Secretary of the Year' competition actually voted 'trim suits

and dresses, neat hairdos, and one or two pieces of simple jewellery' as 'correct attire for a secretary' (*Women's Weekly* 22 May 1963). The Forum challenged the stereotype that secretaries are young, single, and sexually available, stressing that six of the eight finalists were married and three had young children. The media quickly coopted this new 'reality' into the stereotype. Bosses, they said, like the young, married woman, preferably childless. Both media and (male) bosses began to refer to her as a more graceful hostess, who understands how to please a man and is less 'touchy' than the single woman.

The Secretaries' Forum and IPSA promote secretarial work as a career and a profession rather than just a stopgap between leaving school and getting married. They are, of course, particularly keen to distinguish themselves from the range of quasi-secretarial workers beneath them, though the latter are welcome to join if they see themselves on a career path. Since the early 1960s secretaries' organisations have battled for professional recognition. In 1970 the Secretaries' Forum put pressure on the Sydney Chamber of Commerce to reintroduce its secretarial examinations after a lapse of 25 years. The chamber's system created three categories of examination and therefore three levels of secretary, junior, intermediate and executive. Feminist journalist Yvonne Preston wrote that the aim was to

> impress on the business mind that every girl who can do shorthand and typing is not a secretary and that the top-flight secretary is more valuable than to be used as a general office dogsbody...As long as she continues to be lumped together with thousands of others who have nothing more than stenographic skills and as long as business men continue to see secretaries as a homogeneous breed who merely type or take dictation, then the girl with the potential to make the ranks of the executive secretary will remain one of the most frustrated members of the whole business hierarchy. (*AFR* 20 August 1970)

The business community showed little interest in upgrading secretaries. Perhaps because of their own educational limitations, Australian managers have felt more comfortable with the 'Girl Friday' than with the career secretary. Their patronising references to their 'top girls' ensured that senior women would not be viewed as part of the management. Ever since the 1950s managers have complained about the shortage of 'top' secretaries, without giving much thought to the improvements in pay and conditions that may be necessary to attract and keep such staff. They have maintained a gap between secretaries and lower management and continued to deny secretaries any career aspirations. George L. Taylor, Chairman of the Commercial Education Section of the

● *What is a secretary?* ●

Melbourne Chamber of Commerce, replied to Yvonne Preston's article in the following terms:

> Valuable though the services of private secretaries may be to the executives they serve, their functions are not those of an executive with decision-making authority; nor are they professional consultants. Their work is essentially of a practical and procedural nature in assisting management to be more effective. They would be more accurately described as technicians of business rather than technologists of professional status.
>
> We feel they will not be well served by attempts to upgrade the status of their vocation beyond its true nature. (*AFR* 30 September 1970)

As the 1970s wore on these kinds of patronising comments would be contested both by secretaries' organisations and by the women's movement. However, it was not so easy to break away from the overall framework within which they were made. Lip-service to career women blended in with the older discourses in a rhetoric about changing roles for secretaries. Secretarial work was represented not as skilled but as 'glamorous'. This appealed to young working-class women for it was a means of social mobility.

From the 1950s the various state Departments of Technical and Further Education (TAFE) took over from the private business colleges as the main providers of secretarial training and attempted to make previously 'middle-class' skills and styles universally available. In 'democratising' grooming and deportment TAFE actually reinforced middle-class femininity as essential to secretarial success. This is nicely illustrated by the following:

> Learning to be the perfect secretary
> There was a time when you couldn't move from the typing pool unless you had trained at one of three private business colleges in Sydney. These were known by employers to produce nice young ladies. Today private secretaries are seldom heard of, and executive secretary is the status ambitious typists yearn to attain. As well as shorthand, typing and business procedures, they can now learn 'nice-young-ladyship' at several TAFE colleges. On Friday nearly 80 girls graduated from a deportment and grooming course introduced this year at Meadowbank Tech. It was an extension of the normal Day Secretarial Course—optional. Instruction was given 4—6, after normal hours. They had a quest 'The Image of the Secretary' judged by the state superviser of sec studies, Miss A. G. Coxhead, president of the Secretaries' Forum, Mrs J Boehm and the college principal. All candidates carried gloves. The winner wore them throughout the whole time of the judging. 'Gloves are still important,' said Mrs Boehm, 'especially for the initial interview'. She told them 'Your appearance is your greatest asset. You should look trim and well-dressed but should keep your taste simple at the same time. A career girl should keep up with the pace of fashion, but should never go to extremes'.
> (*Sun-Herald* 20 August 1972)

Feminists have fought a long battle in TAFE to replace 'grooming and deportment' with gender-neutral courses on 'preparation for work and life'. At the same time the top private colleges are promoting more sophisticated versions of femininity, linking it with assertiveness and clearcut career goals.

Besides making secretarial training more widely available, there have been moves to upgrade its quality. Ros Byrne and Elsie Solly from Canberra CAE have long been active in developing tertiary and postgraduate courses. These are now available, for example, at Canberra CAE, Caulfield Institute of Technology and Nepean CAE. Under current plans to reorganise the tertiary system there will be more movement between the universities, the colleges of advanced education and the TAFE network. Secretarial courses may then be credited as components of arts degrees. What is not clear is the extent to which tertiary-qualified secretaries are significantly advantaged on the job market (Vella, 1984). A further issue to be debated is whether 'secretarial studies' ought to retain its identity as a separate discipline or be integrated with business and computer studies. Those seeking to upgrade secretarial training argue that it should now include higher-level computer skills.

'Professionalisation' as part of the 'modernising' project comes into conflict with 'traditional' expectations. Is it professional to make the tea? There is a tendency to play this down as part of the job, part of the hostessing role, too trivial to make a fuss about. Yet it is of immense symbolic importance, to bosses no less than secretaries. How does a professional image sit with a continued requirement that they do 'office wife' duties? This dilemma is comparable to the one which nurses face. With professionalisation, who does the general nursing care? This is part of the question of the relation between professionalisation and femininity. How far does success for secretaries, or for that matter any woman, depend on the cultivation of a certain kind of femininity? And does this femininity in itself place limits on what they can achieve? While stereotypes of the doctor—nurse relationship also abound, nurses now have a stronger and more separate identity than do secretaries. Their work is more readily appreciated and their subordination to the doctors is counterbalanced by their power in relation to the patient.

While the secretaries' organisations were calling for professionalisation other secretaries were becoming more militant. The popularity of a film like *Nine to Five* was that it played with the fantasy of turning the tables on the bosses, allowing the audience vicariously to act out long-suppressed anger and frustration. The 'dolly' fights back in the person of Dolly Parton, making it clear that she is not to be fooled with: and secretaries are represented as skilled workers who are much more capable of running the office than their bosses.

• What is a secretary? •

In Australia, in 1969 O'Leary and Caldwell published *Girl Fridays in Revolt*, which was the first systematic demand in Australia for proper pay, recognition and career openings for secretarial work. It drew attention to the dismal role of the Arbitration Commission in maintaining women's lower wage rates and fed directly into the struggle for 'equal pay for work of equal value'. In the 1970s there were a series of strikes over rates of pay including strikes by secretaries at the Builder's Labourers Federation (BLF) in 1974 and the Amalgamated Metal Workers' and Shipwrights' Union (AMWSU) in 1981. There were also protests by individuals and groups about expectations of personal services. Typists and stenographers at the Corporate Affairs Commission, for example, refused to carry on making tea. They argued, with the support of the Public Service Association (PSA) that they were not hired for this. (*Australian* 25 July 1974). Later Helen Curtis, a private secretary, was to fight and lose a discrimination case over this issue before the Victorian Equal Opportunities Board.

In the United States organisations like Nine to Five and Women Office Workers developed a national presence, and there has been considerable militancy amongst secretaries (Cassidy and Nusbaum, 1983; Carroll, 1983). In Australia, by comparison, organisations like IPSA and the Secretaries' Forum represent only minimal demands for change. Activists among secretaries have preferred to rely on the trade unions, with their strong institutional links and women's caucuses. While the main union covering secretaries in the private sector, the right-wing Federated Clerks' Union (FCU) has done little for its members, the public sector unions have been active in struggles for improved pay and working conditions. They have also been assisted by Working Women's Centres supported by the unions in Sydney and Melbourne.

Describing what secretaries do

It is only in the context of struggles to improve the conditions of secretaries and to recognise them as skilled workers that it becomes feasible to answer the question 'what is a secretary' by developing a job description. The 1972 Equal Pay decision of the Federal Arbitration Commission required the phasing in, over three years, of the principle of 'equal pay for work of equal value'. The gap between the wages of male and female workers has narrowed since 1972 but it remains high. As Table 1.1 shows, it is over 20 per cent for full-time workers, rising to around 37 per cent when part-time and junior workers are included. A large proportion of this is due to the failure to develop adequate measures of women's skills or to adjust rates of pay accordingly.

Table 1.1   Earnings—May quarter 1987

Average weekly earnings	Female	Male	F/M ratio
Adult employees			
—Full-time, ordinary time earnings	$383.00	$461.70	0.83
—Full-time, total earnings	$393.20	$498.20	0.79
All employees weekly total earnings	$299.00	$451.70	0.66

Source: Women's Bureau *Women at Work* December 1987

The 1972 decision did not specify how 'equal value' was to be measured, and Australian 'work value' cases have traditionally been required to show that the nature of the work has actually *changed*, rather than that it was wrongly valued in the first place. Given these problems, there has been a lot of debate about the application of 'comparable worth' in the Australian context (Ryan, 1988). Comparable worth requires the development of 'neutral' measures of skill which make possible the direct comparison of men's and women's jobs. Secretaries and nurses were identified, by the unions and by women's organisations, as the key groups to whom the principle should be applied. 'Secretaries' are treated here as a group of workers whose skills are undervalued by comparison with equivalent groups of male workers. In the United States their skills were compared with those of truck drivers; the secretaries were shown to be more skilled than the truckies but paid considerably less. In order to bring 'comparable worth' or 'work value' cases before the Australian Arbitration Commission it is essential to have an 'objective' measure of the skills involved. An accurate job description thus takes on a primary importance. Yet it remains difficult to separate out the skills from more stereotypical expectations around personal service.

In considering how secretarial work may be defined, I have been mindful of Clare Burton's observation about the importance for a job profile of the order in which duties or tasks are presented (Burton et al, 1987: 95–98). Only the first four or five are taken much account of. If one says 'types, takes shorthand, answers the phone', then *that* is how the job is seen and whatever else one adds will be ignored. It is not simply a matter of describing the labour process but of exposing the assumptions behind existing descriptions. Women's use of equipment such as typewriters or telephones may be played down as in '...she just rings up'. In this phraseology the use of the telephone to coordinate is lost.

To describe secretarial work in professional terms it is important to stress communications and administration. A secretary's task is to facilitate communication between her section or department and the rest of the organisation as well as the outside world of clients, customers and suppliers. This takes both written and verbal forms. She may draft correspondence herself, or work from longhand copy, from shorthand or from a dictaphone. She may type and circulate letters, reports, papers or minutes, or pass all but the most confidential down the line.

Secretaries may spend a lot of time communicating by telephone. They deal with appointments, customer enquiries, enquiries from within the organisation. The monitoring of incoming calls is one of their most familiar roles. Not all managers use this facility. Some take all calls themselves while others place severe restrictions on the calls they will take. The secretary is usually expected, without it being spelt out, to develop a sixth sense of when to let calls through, when to deal with them herself and when to divert them or simply take a message. This requires high-level skills in listening and questioning. It often involves a sound knowledge of the organisation overall and delicate judgements about political priorities. Some secretaries are expected to dial telephone numbers for the manager, a task they universally hate. With automatic dialling, they see it as having little reference to the productive use of his time and much more with boosting his ego. If you can have your secretary say, 'Mr X is on the line', the recipient is forced to wait, and to recognise you rather than the reverse. Relations between bosses are mediated by secretaries in this way. Some secretaries spend a lot of time ringing out to track down people or information. Their work here overlaps with that of research as-sistants or journalists. The amount of time spent on the phone will vary with the job. If you are working for a busy newspaper editor the telephone may be primary. Medical secretaries act as receptionists and regularly have to tell people the results of tests, often giving them the first indications of serious illness. 'Word-processing' or 'correspondence' secretaries may not answer the telephone at all.

In some organisations secretaries arrange the agenda for meet-ings and take minutes; in others these tasks are left to an adminis-trative officer who takes minutes in longhand and passes them on to her to type. A secretary will be expected to copy and distribute papers and to file away copies. Even senior secretaries find them-selves spending time at the photocopier. Creating and maintaining an efficient filing system is a skilled task, however boring and mundane routine filing may be. Secretaries are responsible for ordering stationery, arranging maintenance and cleaning and all the things that are involved in the smooth running of the office. Most secretaries keep their boss's appointments diary and they are responsible for setting up and arranging meetings, booking meet-ing spaces, making travel arrangements and hotel bookings. This task involves complex juggling, since one changed appointment or rescheduled meeting could involve rescheduling the whole week or undoing days of careful organising work. This is 'behind the scenes' work which can easily be ignored.

At a certain point the description of secretaries' work shifts from an account of clearcut tasks to the more intuitive ones, and 'non-professional' considerations begin to creep in. Secretaries are reputed to be the 'ears' of their bosses, providing them with information they would not have access to, warning them about things they need to know. They are part of an informal communications system without which the formal bureaucratic structure would come grinding to a halt. One boss described this as 'having a feel for the place', another of those immeasurables that are not part of the pay scale. A secretary commented:

> It is very dangerous for him not to tell me something. . .He travels a lot and I spend fifty per cent of my time while he is away protecting his back. . .Another part of the role is being the ears, keeping awake up to what is going on. I am not saying that I tell him. . .but if it is something I think he should know, then yes, I will tell him. . .If I hear that there is going to be a big brawl at the partners' meeting and that this particular item has been asked to be put on the agenda at the next national council meeting. . .I think oh, who is behind that, and I have to try and find out if I don't already know.

Secretaries are expected to play hostess, welcoming visitors, arranging refreshments, lunches and dinners. They organise the catering for conferences, seminars and meetings. This may simply involve ordering some sandwiches or it may actually involve setting up tables, serving, clearing away and washing up. Hence the traditional concern that secretaries be trained in the 'feminine' arts of flower arrangements and correct table settings!

We have already moved into the area of 'office wife' functions and the fine line between what is 'part of the job' and what is 'extra'. Even shorthand can be treated less as a skill than a basis for companionship or fantasies about power and domination. The double meaning of 'dictating' is relevant here. The notion of 'dictating' evokes the boss—secretary as a master—slave relationship. Negotiations about what is part of the job and what is not can be ongoing and subtle.

A surprisingly frequent request is to chauffeur their boss around. An important part of men's sense of autonomy is never having to wait around for public transport, even for taxis. Chris recalled a workaholic boss, 'a little man. . .who used to drive a big car. . .I used to have to travel out to the airport with him taking shorthand. The first time I did it I got carsick! I saw the whole thing as a Hollywood movie set'. Janet, who works for the chairman of a corporation and frequently stays late says:'They don't seem to realise you know, that we've got to catch public transport...and after peak hour that's not always easy...My boss has got a chauffeur at his beck and call. There's no waiting time. He just goes and gets in the car and then he's home. I go over there and sit and wait perhaps half to three quarters of an hour for a bus.'

The issue of making tea and coffee came up in just about every interview. It provoked more passion than repetitive strain injury (RSI) or sexual harassment. It both mirrors and reproduces the power relationship—the more effectively because the issue is treated by most bosses as utterly trivial and beneath their notice. Most secretaries accept the role to some extent but try to define it in a way that is consistent with their self-image. For Marcia, making coffee is the classic expression of catering to a manager's personal needs which, she believes, distinguishes the boss—secretary relationship from all others. She hates being caught up in it, knowing that in her actions she is reproducing it, but she does it because 'one, he made it very clear that I didn't have to do it...Secondly, he will grab his own cup which I strategically place in his room on the bookcase...and make himself one, which he does sometimes...And thirdly, it's what I would do in my own home if I had visitors'.

The idea of making visitors feel 'at home' is important here. Secretaries are reluctant to do it purely for the boss and devise various strategies of manipulating him into getting his own at least some of the time. They will do it voluntarily but resent being asked or ordered to do so. They prefer to think of it as something that they can choose to do spontaneously, especially if the boss is busy or under pressure. They get angry if they have to clear the cups away and wash up, for this more clearly defines them as servants than the act of preparing and serving the coffee, which is perceived as an act of hospitality or friendship. Many claim it is a reciprocal arrangement, where the boss also (at least occasionally) brings *them* a cup of coffee, but mostly this seemed closer to fantasy than reality. Bosses were reluctant to talk about such a 'trivial' issue. They do not so much actively enforce it as take it for granted. That it *is* important to them is indicated by the following comment from a woman who had worked for a long time as a relieving secretary: 'You knew how all their jobs were done...even things like where the guy liked his cup of coffee put on his desk! You know, its incredible...Make sure his pencil was sharpened and the blotting paper was clean...I guess you can count that as secretarial...but really, to have to say that the cup of coffee went three inches from the left, it's a bit much!'

A lot of people define a secretary as someone who performs a set of personal services as distinct from shorthand, typing or administration. A word-processor operator comments: 'I don't really fit into the secretary mould so I don't look for secretarial work...I think that they have to look after somebody else. I just like to come in and get on with my own work and not have to worry about anybody else and if they need a cup of coffee and where they are and things like that.' And a secretary turned union organiser said: 'I don't get on with your average man...That's why I had to get out of secretarial work. It does involve sucking up to men—whether you do it because you believe that's the way to go or whether you do it for totally cynical purposes...Pleasure? Well, it's a mixture of real and feigned!' Despite the stereotype, secretaries are rarely expected to remember the wife's birthday or buy her a present though they may be required to write down birthdays and anniversaries in the diary. They are, however, asked to buy lunches, collect drycleaning, do minor errands, and get the car from the garage. One could produce a long list of occasional demands, such as taking the washing off the line, pressing a pair of trousers, stitching up a seam, cutting hair or applying a bandaid. Most of these have been the subject of jokes. They often have to do typing that is clearly of a personal nature or is unrelated to the job. The provision of emotional support is often acknowledged to be central to their job and to the 'success' of the working relationship.

Because secretaries tend to work up and across the hierarchy they don't score very well on points systems which measure skill in terms of motivating and controlling other people (Burton et al., 1987: 92). Their operational knowledge, developed through work and other experience, gains less attention in the job evaluation process than the formally acquired knowledge of many of their male counterparts. Skills learnt at home do not count though, as we have seen, bosses pay a lot of attention to 'home background' in choosing their secretaries. Even quantifiable skills such as short-hand and typing are rarely respected as qualifications. As subordinates, secretaries may be obliged to play down their knowledge or be subtle in their questioning of something in order to avoid threatening their superiors (Burton et al., 1987: 89). This makes it hard to acknowledge what they contribute to the organisation in reducing mistakes, getting changes in a directive from a superior, patching up arguments or getting unpleasant decisions implemented in the least disruptive way.

What then is a secretary? In attempting to describe what she does we have been driven back to stereotypical notions of what she *is*. We cannot answer the question by simply providing a description of tasks. Gender and sexuality continue to be extremely significant in the construction of secretaries. In the following chapters I look at the way in which images of 'office wives', 'sexy secretaries' and 'career women' structure relations between secretaries, managers and other office staff, and at the negotiation of power relations in the context of these stereotypes. While secretaries are at all sorts of structural disadvantages in relation to bosses they are not hapless victims: a variety of strategies of power and resistance are open to them.

·2· Office relations: male bosses and female secretaries

> ...a multiplicity of discursive elements...can come
> into play in various strategies. It is this distribution
> that we must reconstruct, with the things said and
> those concealed, the enunciations required and those
> forbidden... with the variants and different
> effects—according to who is speaking, his position of
> power, the institutional context in which he happens
> to be situated...We must make allowance for the
> complex and unstable process whereby discourse can
> be both an instrument and an effect of power, but
> also a hindrance, a stumbling-block, a point of
> resistance and a starting point for an opposing
> strategy. Discourse transmits and produces power; it
> reinforces it, but also undermines and exposes it,
> renders it fragile and makes it possible to thwart it.
>
> *FOUCAULT, 1980: 100–101*

The structural inequalities between bosses and secretaries are clear enough: differences in pay, conditions, opportunities, status and authority. But the power relation cannot simply be read off from these structures or be said to reflect them. Power refers to a complex strategic situation, always in flux. Tables can be turned, roles reversed, outcomes changed. Power relations have constantly to be reproduced in order to be maintained. However solid the 'structures' might look they are not set in stone. 'Bosses' for example, rarely have the arbitrary power to hire and fire or to lay down wages and conditions. They are generally employees themselves, part of a management hierarchy and subject to rules and regulations. There are important differences between senior executives in career positions and those more junior in the pecking order.

Bosses have a variety of ways of exercising power over secretaries, and secretaries may accommodate or resist. A variety of discourses contradict and cut across each other. Three are singled out here. First there is the 'master—slave' discourse in which the boss is typically subject and the secretary the object. Second, there is what I shall call the mother/nanny—son discourse, in which the secretary is the subject and the boss may be positioned as 'naughty boy'. And third, there is the team discourse which evokes equality and modernity. A number of cycles are set in motion as subjects and objects in the different discourses interact with themselves and each other. There are parallels with transactional analysis: once the psyche is divided into child/parent/adult it is possible that two people will have not one but nine different interactions going on between them.

I will focus here on male bosses and female secretaries and then go on to explore what happens when the 'normative' gender ascriptions are changed: female bosses with female secretaries and, less frequently, male secretaries with bosses of either sex. In so far as all discourses are gender-differentiated, the subject and object positions are not equally available to men and women. Since they have to be constantly reproduced by *specific* men and women there is room for change, play, experiment. My central concern is with the way in which power is associated with definitions of pleasure, and coercion itself is defined as pleasurable.

My information comes from interviews carried out separately with bosses and secretaries. The interviewer is inevitably caught up in the power plays, becoming a part of the interviewee's strategies as well as pursuing her own. No doubt if bosses and secretaries were interviewed together, or in groups, the strategies would be different again. My own act of writing about it contributes to the production of power in the sense that I am imposing a structure on what they have said. Who, if anyone, has the last word? (Perhaps it is the media, who have contributed so much to the boss—secretary stereotypes.) One can never have a 'complete' account of power because power is never complete. But it is possible to outline some of its major dimensions.

Bosses were, for the most part, harder to pin down but easier to interview than secretaries. Top managers place a high premium on their time, are harder to find and less likely to be in the office than their secretaries. The latter are there almost by definition, since part of the task is to manage the office in their boss's absence. I did not speak to the chairman of any major corporation, though I did interview some of their secretaries. Managers are more used to interviewing procedures than secretaries are and know how to use these to their advantage. Talking into a tape recorder is second nature to most of them now that they are accustomed to using dictaphones. The secretary's role is to transcribe what others say, not to speak herself.

Once they agreed to be interviewed the bosses, particularly the men, seemed to enjoy themselves. Having control of the 'secrets' of the office, they were at liberty to reveal as much or as little as they chose. The pattern of women interviewing men seemed to be sexually comfortable and they took for granted the importance of what they had to say. They could be funny, they could flirt, offer confidences or confess minor misdeameanours in their private or work lives. Given that the starting point for this research was a 'standpoint' sympathetic to secretaries, it was a shock to acknowledge that interviews with bosses, and male bosses at that, were often more pleasurable. I could have been talking to my uncles! What were these interactions about?

Many bosses had thought carefully about what they wanted to say to us, had prepared their jokes and their lines. The seemed generally respectful of academics, of the cultural and scientific standing of universities, and they aimed to impress. They wanted to demonstrate their control and they wanted recognition of some sort. They had therefore to hand over the power to recognise, which meant granting a degree of autonomy that they did not necessarily grant to their secretaries; they could do this because we were unlikely to meet again. It was the mutual recognition which made the interviews flow so well. They positioned us as 'independent' researchers, whether or not they viewed us as feminists.

The interviews with secretaries were never as expansive and rarely flowed as smoothly. Far from seeing us as their political allies, secretaries were likely to see us as a threat. What, after all, did we represent to them? We were more likely to be perceived as bosses than as fellow secretaries and, as we were to discover, there was considerable ambivalence about woman bosses. We could all be perceived as having 'made it' out of the secretarial ranks, making an implicit criticism of them for being there. We could not offer them 'recognition' but could only signify to them their own limitations. Why would they *not* be hostile? Their main comeback was to look down their noses at our 'failed' femininity, whether it was our dress, appearance, sexuality or 'masculine' position in relation to knowledge, technology and research. Where they were trapped in an office, working for someone, we were free to move about. 'We' were studying 'them'. Whether seen as sympathetic or not, we structurally had the upper hand.

Secretaries were often reluctant to shut the office down, to 'not be there' while they were talking to us. In extreme cases, they insisted on doing the interviews at lunch time, that is, in their own time, so they would not disturb the office. It was often a problem to find a private space to do the interview—sometimes it meant slinking into the boss's office while he was out. Secretaries do not have private space and interviews were frequently interrupted by people or phone calls. They were more guarded than their bosses, fearing we were going to prize out their secrets, wanting to protect the boss or show him in the best 'possible light. They were used, in their gatekeeper role, to deflecting questions, to dealing with people trying to get information or access, to charm their way into favour or make a place in the appointments book. So their tendency was to close up. They were reluctant to take us into their confidence and worried about preserving their anonymity. This meant the interviews were often 'hard work', less pleasurable than those with the managers.

From time to time I did meet secretaries with whom I 'clicked'. These were secretaries who exercised power in one way or another; sometimes they were personal assistants with a lot of power, sometimes secretaries lower down the scale who knew about strategies of resistance. They felt freer to speak, often joked about the hopelessness of their bosses or other staff, had negotiated a space for themselves and bowed and scraped to no one. Whatever the limitations they were proud of what they were. Because they had acquired autonomy, they were able both to give and seek recognition. They viewed us as potentially having something to offer them; they did not appear to be threatened by us. In one or two cases they had read our previous work and were waiting to tell us exactly what they thought was wrong with it! Were they the secretaries we might have been? Did they represent what we would like all secretaries to be? Something of these identifications contributed to the flow of these interviews, which sometimes extended into social activity.

What of women bosses? This ought to have been the group with whom we most closely identified. But they were not as easy to talk to as the men. They shared much of the ambivalence or reserve of the secretaries. What does this say about subjectivity and discourse? Being our 'equals'· they yet felt under scrutiny. How did they compare with us on the pecking order? Who earned the most? Who had most status? These implicit questions, on both sides, informed the interviews. While many were empathetic, they rarely had the openness, humour or sheer outrageousness of some of the men. They produced less pleasure. They were defensive about how they treated their secretaries.

I came away less certain of my 'standpoint'. What could it mean to side with secretaries? They are not a unified group and they do not face a unified opposition. I side with them here only in the most generalised sense of attempting to unravel the multitude of ways in which power relations are constructed. It is safe to assume that such an analysis benefits secretaries, given the way that power operates through masking and deception.

Richard Whittaker and Stephanie North

The first 'pair' have been chosen for their ordinary even stereotypical qualities. Richard is a senior advertising executive, in his mid-thirties, married with young children. Stephanie is in her late twenties and is single. On the face of it they do not have a 'master—slave' relationship. They see themselves as much more modern. In any case she works not only for him but for three or four account directors. 'No one can afford to have a secretary just for themselves any more, you've always got to share,' she says. He adds: 'I think we actively break down those boss/secretary sort of boundaries...Working as a team is much more efficient, much more conducive to a good working environment.' And she comments: 'I give them the respect that is their due but I also have this working rapport where there's no real hierarchy. It's an equal team and we're all part of the team, so...I mean, they would yell at me if I stuffed things up and I do the same.' Richard's idea of a good boss is someone who cares, understands, respects and is able to communicate with people. The relationship is couched in terms of equality and reciprocity. As he talks it becomes clear that the 'team' approach is interwoven with others. Richard wants control. He admits he does not like sharing a secretary:

> Five years ago in my position I would have had my own secretary whom I would have shared with nobody. Right? Because of economies of scale, because of the nature of our business, because it's becoming tougher and tougher to make money, that situation no longer exists. Status-wise, I guess yes, I'd love to have my own secretary...But the nature of our structure dictates that she must work for a number of other people as well.

His numerous strategies for control operate not through coercion but rather out of his 'caring' for her. This is possible because of the emphasis placed on friendship, the joking and socialising, and the breaking down of the division between home and work. He is able to define what gives her pleasure and self-esteem and insist' that he knows what is 'best' for her. Sometimes she accepts his definitions and at other times she does not. When asked what makes a good secretary he stressed loyalty: 'Not just individual personal loyalty but loyalty to the organisation, loyalty to the ideals we hold dear. Loyalty to me. And that encompasses things like a willingness to work early, work late, work weekends...and to do that without any additional reward apart from perhaps the occasional thanks...Stephanie will never know what time she's getting home any night, you know.' She confirms that:

> I usually cancel what I'm going to do because I'm working. I do a lot of overtime but my friends are sort of used to me ringing up and saying, I'm

really sorry I can't make it...They're usually pretty good. Like on weekends you often have to work both days...and if you've got something on they let you disappear for a couple of hours and come back...There was a period of last year...when we were just constantly at work, seven days a week. I was whacking up about eighty hours a week...I'd be rich if they paid overtime!

The extent of the demand that is placed on her is both acknowledged and denied. Richard claims that it works on a 'swings and roundabouts' basis, and if there is nothing happening she can take time off. She agrees that it's 'give and take'. But 'give and take' hardly seems to fit the situation described. Not only does Stephanie put in as much as 70—80 hours a week, working overtime at short notice and with no additional pay, she is placed in a position where it is virtually impossible to have a social life, let alone a domestic life. In exchange she is allowed the occasional day off or a long lunch. This is constructed, by both Richard and Stephanie, as pleasurable. She is, he says, the kind of person that gets a 'buzz' out of it, the 'certain type of rare creature that is attracted to those sorts of challenges'. He concedes that a person who did not get this 'buzz' would have to be paid twice as much to be enticed into the position. Fortunately for him, the industry attracts the type of person who gets pleasure from working in this way: there is no need to pay them for it.

Stephanie has a lot vested in finding pleasure in what she does. Having failed to get into teaching, she is grateful to have a found a job that gives her mental stimulation, variety and self-respect. Stephanie is expected to pre-guess what is coming up next, be flexible and be able to deal with a multitude of personalities '*not* just on the work side but also on the client side...You've just got to think before you speak and just be prepared for whatever's going to come your way because they can throw you some real spinners...' She likes her job because 'they don't treat you as a typist...they ask your opinion'. Why should they not ask her opinion if they are really working as a team? Why is it regarded as a privilege to have one's opinion sought? She likes to be busy, finds even a steady flow of work boring and feels best under pressure. She is positioned as loyal, committed, able to rise to a challenge. The irregular hours actually give her status with her friends: they show that she is not a boring '9 to 5' person concerned only with catching the 5.30 train, but someone with an interesting and responsible job. As if this is not enough she takes work home: 'I'll go to bed and I'll have a notepad and pencil there because I'll wake up in the middle of the night and think, I should have done that and jot it down.'

Richard defines and controls her pleasure, even outside the office. Thus he forces her to take time off: 'I'll discover that she's out at lunch and having a good time and feeling under pressure to come back. I've rung her up a couple of times and said, for God's sake, if you come back here, I'll throw you out again. It works both ways.' Clothes are an important area of pleasure and control. Richard stresses that they all have to maintain appearances but that Stephanie does not have to dress in the old image of a secretary. She can wear jeans and riding boots if she wants to, as long as the boots are polished and have not actually been used for riding: 'We're an advertising agency. We are involved in creative endeavours. We are seen as being more modern, more upbeat perhaps, than a lot of other industries, so the girls should reflect that.' Stephanie says she wears what she wants. 'I get out of bed in the morning and I say, oh this will do.' But she does manage to reflect exactly what is required, looking casual but expensive and stylish. 'There seems to be at least one day a week when all the girls turn up in black...Like our receptionist, at the moment she's got all black on and she's got a bright red overcoat...People walk past and say, oh, very corporate today dear, aren't we'

As Richard moves on to talk about what is 'good' for her, he becomes more authoritarian and she appears as more resistant. He complains there is a 'degree of laziness' and a lack of the work ethic. When Stephanie gives him work with spelling mistakes he worries about how to instill a greater sense of pride. He is keen for her to get more involved in other areas of the business. What is actually being offered is additional responsibilities without any pay or promotion, but he represents himself as offering her a super job and the opportunity to do more interesting things. He is patronising about her declining the offer. 'There seems to be sometimes a lack of willingness or a want on her part to do that...I don't think that's ultimately the best thing for Stephanie but I respect her opinion and her decision. She basically likes what she does and to my mind doesn't seem to aspire to change that job function or improve it'. Stephanie says that so far no opportunities have come up that have interested her and that she does not want to be stuck in the accounts service side.

They are able to enjoy a joke with each other, which relieves day-to-day tensions and restores a sense of intimacy and equality: 'We call each other some of the most dreadful names...Like yesterday he said, you cheeky tart and I whacked him on the backside and said it's your fault you silly old fool...carry on like that. So there's no real problems.' This kind of reciprocity is important to Stephanie. She claims that Richard makes her coffee...but 'only when he knows I'm really busy. Like I'm always in here before him in the morning so there's a cup of coffee waiting on his desk. On the rare occasions he's in here first, I walk in and say, well, where's *my* coffee?'

Although he talks the language of reciprocity, Richard sees her as there primarily to meet *his* needs: to anticipate, protect and provide emotional support. It is a very gentle version of master—slave: she recognises him without any reciprocal right of recognition. Her pleasure is evidence that she does these things voluntarily and because she cares, not merely obeying because she is paid to do so. This obscures from both of them the underlying dynamic. This kind of misrecognition is very common among secretaries who have a lot vested in believing that they have a reciprocal relationship. Their self-worth is based on believing that there is an underlying equality, despite differences in function. That there is 'give and take' is an indication that they are respected as autonomous beings. To maintain this belief they have to deny the extent to which bosses withhold that recognition and treat secretaries as extensions of themselves.

Richard is able to get away with this because the relationship has been constructed in intimate, almost familial terms. Stephanie knows the wives and children of all the men she works for; the families have meals together and meet on social occasions. Because she is a close friend, he can intrude into all aspects of her life without it being seen as an intrusion, and ask things of her that he could not of someone more distant. If the untidy desk and constantly rotating chair are any indication, Richard lives in a high degree of chaos. He concedes that she is a 'total minder' for him: 'I mean anything that is needed in order to keep the thing running, Stephanie will do. She gets a cup of coffee or she'll book a flight or she'll, as it was yesterday, cancel it because I missed the bloody plane.' Stephanie's 'minding' activities stretch further than he is prepared to admit. She reveals, for example, how she gets together with his wife to organise basic everyday tasks: 'His wife writes him notes so I check through his briefcase to make sure he does everything that Jan's asked him to do...She will ring up and say, listen, make sure he does this...Between us we plot and plan his dentists and doctors because he doesn't want to know about it...'

For Richard to disclose this would be to admit a degree of dependence that could threaten his autonomy and take away his sense of mastery. What enters here is another discourse in which he is object rather than subject. To call this the mother—son discourse suggests that Stephanie exercises more power than she does. She is positioned as more servile than 'mother' or 'wife' suggests. 'Nanny' is the better term, if a trifle archaic, for it conveys a servant who is being paid to carry out this task. Notice that she covers for Richard if, as he puts it, 'I am out doing something I shouldn't be doing'. She often experiences her job as waiting on anxious children:

I know a lot of them get really nervous before a big meeting and so they want someone to mother them and sort of hold them by the hand and say it'll be all right. You know, little quirks...You know they like a certain type of coffee, a certain type of biscuit, or your client likes it, whatever. So you make sure it's there and you make sure the room's tidy...You wish them luck and all that kind of thing. Just sort of keep it light and breezy rather than 'are we going to get through this' type of thing.

Another part of her 'minding activities' is to screen visitors and telephone calls:

There's days when he's got wall-to-wall meetings. Like five minutes in between to have a cup of coffee and there's always something else going on in the background. So I try to shield him and if I can't handle it then pass it on to one of the guys. And if Richard is the only one who can answer the query... then I sort through the files to get out the information he might need...And just sort of sit down with him...lock him in his room and say, this and this happened, remember this relates to...stuff like that.

In most places this would be unexceptional. The 'gatekeeper' role is acknowledged as an important secretarial task. In the advertising industry it is different. Richard prides himself on the way he deals with clients direct. He cannot afford to think he is shielded: 'I would rarely say to a client, contact my secretary. It's almost...it's not that it's an insult, it's just not the way we do business. We operate in a service industry where we're expected to perform for our clients.' He spoke contemptuously of a client who hides behind his secretary. 'In fact it's a bloody moat with a portcullis.' In other industries there is a lot of mileage in being able to say 'contact my secretary', but not this one.

On the face of it Richard has the power in this relationship. What does Stephanie get out of it? In the first place, the sheer pleasure of being needed, of feeling useful, of identifying with the enterprise. Second, the pleasure of being needed as a woman. The sexual attraction between her and Richard is obvious, and it was an open question whether they were or had been lovers. He says the relationship is 'therapeutic' because she is a woman. He seeks her advice on personal matters, has lunch with her at least once a week and 'it's not unusual for us to have a drink after work'. He would not like a male secretary: 'I'd miss the softness...He would have to be more efficient than any female secretary before he could get a job...So, yes, I'd be totally discriminating!' Having grown up with four brothers she feels she is most used to being surrounded by males and relates better to them. 'That I guess has helped form my personality.'

There is another level too. Richard's power in the firm is on the wane. His emphasis on loyalty, pride, the work ethic and so on are partly a projection of what he considers important for himself. In his own eyes he has failed to the extent that he withdrew from the stresses of 'new business' and was unable to sustain working fourteen or fifteen hours a day. He concedes that two of his erstwhile equals have been promoted to deputy managing director and general manager, and is quick to say that all still do basically similar work. Moreover, Stephanie has been with the company for longer than he has. She has worked for the managing director, has a good relationship with his secretary and often learns 'vital information' that she would never tell Richard. Her personal power comes from being centrally connected to the boss's boss and having privileged access to knowledge. It enables her to deny as 'trivial' the power that Richard has and reassert that they are equals.

Tom Anderson and Carol Johnson

Tom administers the retailing division of a company based in Sydney's western suburbs. He is in his early fifties and a bachelor. Carol, his secretary, is 21 and also single. Tom is regarded in the office as something of a character, always laughing and joking and fooling around. He does not explicitly like to exercise power and is uncomfortable with his own power; nevertheless he has his strategies of control. These are based on his knowledge of people's family backgrounds and personal lives. This breaking down of public/private barriers legitimates a detailed surveillance of their lives.

Carol did not initially start out as Tom's secretary. She has no secretarial training and the job was mainly clerical. It included being relief switch operator, helping with the mail and coding. Over time she has come to see herself as his secretary: 'What makes it a secretarial job? I don't know. People just say all the time, could I speak to Mr Anderson's secretary...so I suppose it gets drummed into me.' What has happened is that Tom has taken her over and constructed a new role for her. Far from relieving him of trivia, Carol 'can do virtually all the things I can do and *she is going to be taught*'. He thinks that she can already do most of his job but lacks the confidence. 'I could see her in four years' time ready to sit straight in my chair.' Carol describes herself as a 'shitkeeper', which rather contradicts this image. As part of his attempt to control, Tom has not only introduced household chores but had her go to his home to perform them. He has no reason for doing this except to assert his mastery in a ritual way. Carol felt highly embarrassed at this overstepping of her boundaries: 'Just being there I suppose. And everyone knowing that I have gone up to take his washing off the line...Like he was with me because he showed me how to get into the house. And then coming back to work and everybody saying, where have you been, what have you two been up to, silly jokes. But I like picking him up when he goes and does his shopping in his lunch hour...I just drop him home and he puts the things in the fridge or whatever...' As she is unable on this occasion to resist, she rationalises: 'I see other ladies in the office who are secretaries and they don't do it and I think, oh, special treatment in a way.'

Tom believes you should 'never control anything that you can't do yourself'. Unlike most bosses he prides himself on being able to do every office task, for this is basic to his autonomy and power. He can sack anyone on the spot and do the job himself. Not only can he can operate the switchboard, the telex and the fax, but he does most of his own typing: 'Let me see, it would have to be close on 35 years ago, I had a lady friend who was doing shorthand and typing at tech. I was doing construction stages one and two which I hated...so one night a week I used to wag it and go to shorthand and typing with her...The reason I stayed at tech and did it was because the police in those days used to go to tech to learn their shorthand and typing so I wasn't the only man there... He is well pleased with Carol's progress: 'Not only that, she is a great sport. I can joke with her and she jokes with me, but she also draws the line. I know just how far to go with her. I am a bit notorious here. I do say some outrageous things but it is usually just to stir the place along.' Carol is still uncertain how to protect her boundaries: 'If you just joke with him and laugh back he is fine...So I just play along with it and...carry the joke on and he is fine.' Now that she is used to him, Carol thinks he is the best of bosses: 'He makes a joke out of everything that you do, even if you make a mistake. He gets cranky if it is bad, but he will work out with you what went wrong. Like, a lot of bosses won't. You have to work it out yourself. And he is always there and if you have got a problem then you can always walk into him...'

Because they have this relationship he can ask her to do just about anything. She keeps his coffee cup permanently filled up and looks after his lunches: 'If I have a tin of salmon for lunch and I want some onions, then she will go and chop the onion up and put in the salmon for me...She will go down to David Jones and do my shopping for me. She has been home and taken the washing off the line for me. I can honestly say there is nothing that I have asked that girl to do that she hasn't done and done willingly.' He attributes this to the fact that she comes from a large family where she had to learn discipline and she had to help. He thinks discipline is extremely important and he looks for it in school and family background: 'From the first interview you can

usually pick whether they have been brought up or dragged up.'
He finds it hard to discipline women: 'My switch girl, Susie, is so
highly strung that she is like a violin...I have shots across the
bow...but if I haul her in here then in two seconds flat she is
in tears. I have to listen to fifteen minutes of what she was
doing...then I have to wait another 25 minutes while she is out in
the loo telling all the girls what I said to her...and then you
have to wait a quarter of an hour while she has a cup of coffee to
compose herself.' Though it is cast as a joke he has Carol following
his every whim. He is very controlling and needs to know exactly
where she is and what she is doing: knowledge is power. Carol
comments that 'if I say I am going to be late back from lunch it is
fine. But if you don't tell him and you are late back then he gets
very cranky. And if you leave, it might only be a couple of
minutes early then there would be a joke about it but in his tone
of voice...there is a warning'. Tom likes to be in charge even of
taking breaks. 'If there has been a tremendous amount of private
ledgers to go through, and I know that that is laborious and
tedious because I have done it, I might say, Carol, duck out to
David Jones and buy me a chicken. I don't really want a chicken, I
just take it home and put it in the freezer...but it gives her a
quarter of an hour just to walk out. I always allow her the use of
my car. She can have the car if she wants it, but she likes to walk.
He is unable to allow her simply to take a break and to do with it
as she will. Even on Secretaries' Day, having taken her out to
lunch, they stop on the way back to do his shopping and he shows
her where to find particular items he likes. This is 'good for her
too' because it gives her a little break. He cannot give her anything
without being repaid many times over.

Tom controls her work, her break and even her private life. It
has the elements of a father–daughter relationship:

Does he see you as a daughter?
I think so. He's the spitting image of my father, in his ways and
everything. And I get on great with my father so that is probably why I
get on so well with him.

Was that obvious when you first met him?
No. I thought he was a cranky old bastard...But gradually I got to know
him.

Tom knows all about Carol's family. Her sister-in-law had worked
for him previously and he knows the brother. He thinks the sister-
in-law was a 'deceitful kind of girl' and a bad influence. She rules
the brother 'with a rod of iron, poor old Bob...but since she has
gone this one has changed, which pleases me, which is great'. He
teases her about her boyfriend and what she does on the weekends. They even went on a diet together. 'She worked it out that

if I could do it then so could she, and then suddenly a boyfriend appeared on the scene and she has slimmed down, which his great.' She says, 'He is trying to get me married...I just think that he wants everyone to get married'.

Tom exercises his male prerogative to comment on her clothes and appearance. He hates her wearing drab uniforms and prefers her in skirt and blouse or a dress. She is not prepared to get good clothes covered in ink or liquid paper. The result is a compromise: 'I have a few really old uniforms and if I haven't got anything to wear then I will just put those on...But there is a couple of uniforms I have got that I can dress up with a belt and different shoes and that.' The images of home and family, performance of household chores, constant trips to David Jones or home to deal with the washing, construct this workplace as unmistakeably suburban. The form that personal services take here is quite distinct, and the detailed knowledge of family situations could only take place in a suburban or country location.

That Tom is working in this job says something about his own career choices. At 40 he retired and then made a series of comebacks because he was bored. He stresses that he does not need to work, he owns everything he requires, and he can be independent of the company power structures, free to speak his mind. Nevertheless he *is* concerned to have his contribution recognised and he needs to be liked. At times he exaggerates his own importance, as in 'I am the minister for communications'. Lots of other managers, he says, come to him for advice rather than go to their regional managers. But he also 'gets into a bit of a stew' about changes that are going on around him. He is decidedly ambivalent about power. Part of him wants to be right in there while the other part would be happy to drop out. The constant joking both masks the exercise of power and hides his insecurity. In some sense he undermines himself, and Carol is able to see this and detach from him. His ritual with the coffee amounts to a complete send up of the master—slave routine: 'He has his own little percolator but he will say, I haven't had any coffee today. You have been in here ten times and you haven't poured me any coffee, and so I go in and pour his coffee...He likes to be waited on hand and foot...Half the time it is a joke because everybody in the office hears it. They laugh and carry on but it doesn't bother me at all.' Carol sees no reason to resist. She is fond of him, finds him entertaining and enjoys her job. She knows that he is attached to her and takes some pride in the fact that she, unlike many other people in the office, is able to manage him and is unaffected by his grumpiness. Performing personal services for Tom has been converted into 'special treatment'. To some extent she turns it round, invoking the 'nanny' discourse. He is like a kid and she is employed as his minder. Anyway she has no intention of staying any length of time. She sees herself getting married, having kids, leaving the workforce. In this she will be following in her mother's footsteps: she acts as secretary to her husband, Carol's father, who is a milkman.

Jane Morrison and Mr Howard

From a regional office in suburbia we move to the head office of a large corporation. Gone is the intimacy of the previous two relationships, the use of Christian names, the interweaving of work with family, personal and social life. There is a cool professionalism about these two; their relationship is not only impersonal but quite formal. Mr Howard is a divisional chief, in his late forties with a wife and children. I never did discover his Christian name. His secretary always referred to him as 'Mr'. Jane is in her early thirties and single. Though she has worked for him for more than two years he never referred to her by name, only indirectly as 'the girl who is doing the job at the moment'. There is little warmth in their relationship; as Jane says, it is humour that saves the day, that enables the relationship to flow. 'He has a very good sense of humour. If he didn't then I don't think there would be any job actually.' Howard certainly brought a great deal of humour to the interview. He had thought about what he wanted to say and he left me with some memorable lines.

Like Tom he does not like 'disciplining' women. 'I was brought up to believe that women were sugar and spice and all things nice...and I don't like to be too harsh with them...I find it very difficult to reprimand a woman.' He depends on the selection process to find the 'right' person who will already 'know' how to behave. He talks about secretaries with detachment, denying any emotional or work dependence on a specific person. He makes no demands at all for personal services and would not even expect a cup of tea unless he had visitors. He gives the secretary no access to his diary and has no desire to be mothered or nannied. He prefers women no older than 40 or 45: 'Because they do tend to become a bit domesticated at that age...Well their thoughts are around their husband and the home and the grandchildren or their children...and they really seem to lose interest in business matters when they get to about 45.'

Howard wants to desexualise the boss—secretary relationship and argues that sex has no rightful place in the office. Sexual attraction would undermine his authority. He believes you have to be wary of women using their sexual wiles to gain advantages, and places himself above those men who need to seek sexual solace in the workplace: 'If there was ever a waste of time in life it was shorthand. ...I think that shorthand is a device invented by managers who feel lonely and want to sit with a lady and talk to her a little bit and give them a cup of tea...It is a sort of sexual fantasy I think, shorthand...and I think it should be banned. I don't think anybody should be allowed to learn shorthand.' He would be wary of even paying his secretary a compliment: 'If it is a genuine compliment, say if you are looking very smart, yes. But if she has got a low cut dress on then...it becomes a form of harassment and I don't think that is a good thing. It can be too familiar.' He recalls two cases of sexual harassment: 'One of them I think was a mammary mauler and the other was a posterior pincher. Obviously the mammary glands have got more import-ance than the posterior because he was transferred and the other guy just became an office joke.'

Despite his refusal to interact personally in the office, he stresses the importance of their family situations in making his initial choice. He avoids secretaries with young children, believing that women should stay at home and look after them. He talked at length and amusingly about the selection process, turning the joke onto himself:

> Two secretaries back the specification, which was that she must be a non-smoker, must live within four miles of the office and not be divorced...Well, I thought that if she was divorced then she is probably neurotic and I don't want her taking it out on me...But it is actually difficult to know which are the better secretaries...the single girls, the married ladies or the divorced ones...This particular one fulfilled everything... Then she took up smoking, then she moved out to Manly and then she got a divorce.
>
> The next time I gave a one-word specification. I said I want somebody who is aloof. This ensures that they are a little bit of a cut above the average and don't mix with all the other girls around the building too much and...don't spend all day talking and holding...what I call their stopwork meetings.
>
> I got the perfect girl...and she was the best secretary you could have and she only lasted three days. I think the problem is that they don't like me, so perhaps we should ask them to supply specifications.
>
> For the present girl my specification was that she should be belligerent and in fact she is and that enables her to deal with solicitors and professionals. She doesn't take any nonsense from them.

There is a disjuncture in how the two of them see the secretary's job. What he describes as 'backup' covers a lot:

> She deals with solicitors on various aspects of property activities. She must know what is happening...and foresee some of the things that might happen. If we are selling property for instance...she knows what

stage it is at and when we have to sign contracts and when and how much deposit we are going to receive. And then she has to inform our cash flow money market people of the money coming in. Similarly when the sale is settled, the money coming in has to be credited to Sydney, Brisbane or some other state or even internationally.

Jane feels simultaneously undervalued for what she does and resentful that he will not delegate more to her. 'They like to keep it all to themselves you see, so it is very hard to be an assistant when you don't know all the facts.' The only way she can find out is to listen through the door to his phone calls. While this knowledge might give her some power it cannot be said to be very effective as an act of resistance. Howard seems oblivious to her frustrations. When he describes her job as interesting, it is by comparison with other secretarial or typing jobs, *not* with management or administration.

Jane's main line of resistance is to refuse to think of herself as a secretary: 'I didn't go to university and I didn't want to be a nurse...and then you seemed to do one of those three things...I don't think I see myself as a secretary very seriously.' She claims she had had a promising career as a money market operator before some hinted-at personal tragedy. She plays down the secretarial component of her work, by which she means typing, filing and 'everything to do with what he wants'. She enjoys the fact that she is kept busy. She composes most letters herself and carries out a lot of negotiations with solicitors, 'but I would like to do it a lot more'. The tasks she likes best are ones that have nothing to do with Howard (and which he neglects to mention). These include taking bookings on the London flat, and looking after the building, which involves organising cleaners and tradesmen. Both give her a measure of authority and a kind of class power. She presents herself as an upper middle-class woman managing the family estate.

Jane does not think she is badly treated but believes that there is an inherent inequality as long as secretarial work is seen as women's work. She recognises that this has something to do with the public/private division: 'Let's face it. We all want equal opportunities and I think that some people do just go overboard about it. Obviously somebody has to, like the home situation, somebody has to do the washing up and somebody has to go to work haven't they and I suppose that you could change roles if you want to.' As for male secretaries: 'Men don't usually type do they? And get cups of tea? And I must say I was a bit annoyed the other day, some chap was in there seeing Mr Howard and he said, you are the chief bottlewasher, or whatever the expression is. And I thought, blow you. I don't think of myself as that and I don't think he does either actually.' So she concludes: 'If you want to be treated equally don't learn to type and don't do shorthand and do do things that men can do...You are better off going and doing an accounting course or something and then you can work side by side with boys...if you want to stick being a secretary it is up to you then isn't it?' She is at present completing such a course. It will eventually get her out of secretarial work entirely; and in the meantime it enables her to restrict her working day and resist demands to work long hours. Howard would like his secretary to stay back with him till 6 or later. But, 'the girl who is doing the job at the moment is studying three nights a week so she has to get away about 10 to 5 and this is not a good thing. I knew when I took her on that she was studying but it was only one night a week and it has now progressed to three.'

Jane expresses her alienation from the workplace in a variety of ways. She denies that she is or will be secretary and treats it as a 9 to 5 job. She declined to talk at all personally and it was clear that she would not give any of herself that was not strictly necessary to the job. This was encapsulated in her attitude to clothes. In contrast to Stephanie she says: 'Work clothes are so boring I wish we had a uniform sometimes and you didn't have to think what to wear. The clothes that you like to buy are night clothes or evening clothes or your sports clothes. Not a lot of thought goes into what I wear to work I must say. Just being reasonably neat...I just like to have five things and not think about it and put one on each day.' Nonetheless she looked sufficiently corporate for head office dressed in a navy suit and cream blouse, jacket over the back of the chair. It would be unthinkable to see her in a uniform like the one Carol was wearing. Her aura is entirely upper middle-class whereas Carol is clearly from the working class.

How does one summarise the ebb and flow of power between them? He has chosen. her because she is 'belligerent'. This seems to mean stylish and assertive: a balanced match for him. It enables him safely to delegate a lot of work that involves dealings with professionals. But because he refuses to teach her more about the work she maintains a wall around herself. She declines to get much pleasure from her work or to express any liking for him. Her detachment limits the power he is able to exercise over her. Humour makes the day bearable but does not have the capacity to provoke loyalty or personal commitment. She does not feel part of the company and he is not able to make her feel part of it. While he enjoys talking about his strategies with secretaries in general, he gets little pleasure from talking about Jane. It is as if the interaction finishes, with the selection process. He, of all the bosses discussed here, is the embodiment of 'abstract rationality'. But as a master—slave relation it does not work because neither is sufficiently involved. Each denies the need for the other. While they complement each other they are hardly a 'team'.

Paul Fiola and Suzanne Bellesi

Paul is divisional manager of a subsidiary company located in Sydney's western suburbs. He is in his late forties married with two school-age children. Suzanne is in her mid-twenties, has no children and has recently remarried. She refers to him throughout the interview as 'Mr Fiola', but this is for my benefit. Their relationship is otherwise quite informal.

Paul is committed to an open management style. Whereas his predecessor was remote, he likes to pick up the phone and to walk around the factory. He wants his secretary to assist him to be seen as popular and accessible. He thinks the previous secretary became too dominant, for she had to do some of the things that really should have been her boss's responsibility. Unlike Tom he draws a very clear division between the secretary's job and his own. It is undesirable that she do parts of his job and inconceivable that she could take over from him. He is quite clear about what he wants in a secretary: to be there when he needs her, and to handle 'trivia', including correcting his grammar. Where some bosses would feel threatened by the implicit inferiority of needing their grammar corrected, Paul casually includes it with 'trivia'. Suzanne tells us that the 'trivia' also include personal chores such as taking his car to be fixed, shopping, collecting his drycleaning. She is unhappy about doing this but has been forced to accept it on the grounds that he does not have time.

Unlike Richard, he is cynical about loyalty. In these days of takeovers it is a limited concept. Despite this, his ideal is a master−slave relationship. When he says the most important thing is that she always be there when he needs her, he means it. He would like his secretary to be at his call at weekends; to be able to ring on a Saturday morning and ask her to come in and do a few letters or a telex. If he is overseas he finds it convenient to ring his secretary at home at any hour of the day or night. Not only has Suzanne refused this but she has made it clear that she does not want to rung at home unless it is a matter of life and death. This is a big disappointment to him—he looks back nostalgically to a 'girl' who was willing to be permanently at his beck and call.

Though his style is very different from Tom's, Paul too is keen on establishing control by breaking down the boundaries between home and work which represent resistances. They battle it out day by day. Suzanne says: 'I am a morning person...Unfortunately Paul is an afternoon person. So at 5 o'clock when I am all sparked up to go home, he wants to send a telex. So we try and work it out...It means I work back.' That is, she submits. She is obliged to perform personal chores and to work some unpaid overtime, but she has so far largely managed to resist his intrusion into her private life. It seems unlikely though that he will give up.

Paul readily concedes that he likes to have a 'sexy' secretary. 'It is like in South America, if you have a male secretary, particularly a European male secretary, then you have made it...It is a status thing over there, the same as here if you have a very attractive secretary, then you are doing well'. She is there, not as an object of desire, but to help him establish a compelling masculine presence:

> I get the most kick when people say to me, she is a good looking woman or gee, Suzanne looks nice...A guy came in the other day...and she came in offering us coffee or tea, and Jim said, Suzanne, since you got married you look luscious. And she went all red and tingly as she walked out...And it gives me a kick...I would hate it...if my secretary brought us some coffee, and one of the guys said, Jesus, Paul, why don't you pay Jane to get her bloody hair done and buy a new skirt. Now that would upset me. So if that upsets me, then the reverse would make me feel good.

Like Howard, he believes a sexual involvement gives the secretary the upper hand. He has trained himself 'not to really establish any personal or romantic feelings...' He does not confide in his secretary, either about work or private life: 'Some guys tell their secretary what they had for breakfast, how many times they have sex with their wives, whether it is good or bad.'

Paul is a good example of 'machismo'. As far as he is concerned women are there to enhance his masculinity and authority; they belong to another world. He is willing to depend on Suzanne and he recognises her skills. He insists that he would not trade skills for looks, but the skills he seeks are the traditional ones. In any case, he argues, Suzanne is better as a hostess than she is as a typist. These are the two feminine skills and he thinks there is always some kind of trade-off between them. His assumptions about secretaries become clear when he talks about the possibility of male secretaries. While they may be status symbols in other parts of the world he thinks that in Australia the occupation is so thoroughly feminine that 'a male secretary...would not be called my secretary but my assistant...I think I would get a male secretary to do additional work because he was male...and don't accuse me of being a racist [*sic*]...It is the expectation. Simply because other males here that are helping me, the marketing manager, the accountant, the product manager...are doing work of a particular level...I would imagine this guy taking on more and more responsibility and then one day I would say, why don't we get a typist?' The balance of power is clearly with Paul. He is patronising towards Suzanne: she is sexually attractive but she is a woman and therefore there is a limit to what one can or should expect. He uses her gender and sexuality to boost his own masculine ego and to trivialise her. He denies her both the authority her predecessor had, and any power she might acquire as his confidante. He refuses to admit any dependency specifically on her.

There are limits on his power. He too is reluctant to discipline women: 'I tend to be a little bit disappointed rather than chastise...I doubt very much if I would improve the situation if I said, Geez Suzanne...If I was to adopt that then she wouldn't be here and I don't know if the next person would suit me better.' Like Mr Howard, he prefers his secretaries to be pre-disciplined. Married secretaries are the best: they are milder, more tolerant and 'there are little things that they learn after they have been married about males and their comfort'. He likes them to be 'domesticated' but not to the extent that home overshadows work. Home and work connect again here. In this case Paul looks to benefit from the ways husbands have trained their wives to look after themselves and others.

Suzanne has her own quiet means of resistance. As well as protecting her private life and limiting her overtime, she deliberately plays down her sexuality: 'I think it is important to come to work looking presentable...but you don't have to go overboard. Sometimes women wear clothes that are better for the evening... because that implies something about yourself too that is perhaps really not what you want to imply.' When she talks about her job she stresses that she works on her own initiative following things through down to the last detail. Paul has neglected to say that Suzanne also works for two assistant managers, who are in fact women. No one in the company gets to have a full-time secretary any more, she says. She quietly reduces him to scale by commenting that she worked for someone equally senior in her previous job. She also makes it clear that she can take much of the credit for Paul's success: 'I feel that if you have got a good secretary, even an average sort of manager can look great and also that people want to visit that person too. If they feel that...there is that dragon at the desk I have got to go through, it is no good, it is not what a secretary should be there for.'

By implication, Paul is only 'an average sort of manager'. He is moody and unpredictable and never offers even an occasional pat on the back. Paul admits he is not much good at giving compliments: 'I would rather pay her a compliment unconsciously...If she said to me, Paul look, on Friday I would like to take the afternoon off, and I felt she has been doing a lot of work,

I would have no hesitation. But...I wouldn't dream of saying, Suzanne because you have been working well, yes, all right.' What he is unaware of is the extent to which his failure to give compliments or open up emotionally, limits his power. It enables Suzanne to close off and resist his intrusions on her time and sexuality.

Jim Porter and Kate Griffin

Jim is a man of about 60, a lawyer who has risen to be deputy general manager. He is fatherly in appearance, courteous in an old-world way. This is exactly why Kate has chosen to work for him. She has had some unfortunate sexual encounters in previous jobs, first a broken engagement with a man at work and then a bad experience of sexual harassment. Now in her late twenties, Kate deliberately looked for an office where the risk of sexual interactions would be minimal. She wanted an older man and Mr P, as she calls him, is ideal. He treats you like a lady, she says, because that is the way he has been brought up.

None of the secretaries claimed to be sexually harassed by their current bosses. But many had experienced it in previous positions and had usually left and found other jobs. The experience continued to affect both their choice of jobs and the stances they took up. In her previous job Kate had done a lot of telephone work and had got to know a number of people quite well through this medium. One day her boss took several of these people out for what turned into a long lunch. On their return she came to the doorway so that she could meet them in person:

> I was standing a bit of a distance away and he yelled out at the top of his voice, 'This is Kate. She will suck your cock and have sexual intercourse with you. . .' I stood there as you can imagine I was shaking, and I thought, what could you do. . .? Do you turn round to a man who you have spoken to on the phone for nine months and say, 'Please step into my office and allow me to service you?' . . . And in that split second, I stood there and just said to him, 'Don't you ever speak to me like that again'.
>
> And then at 5 o'clock he came into my office and told me that he wanted to see me on Monday morning at 9 o'clock on the dot. . .and I said, 'Well that makes two of us'. He said, 'Why do you want to see me?' and I said, 'How dare you speak to me like that, who do you think you are?' and he said, 'Well, that was the terms and conditions of your employment'. I said, 'Well, okay then, are you sacking me?' But he didn't have the guts to sack me because he knew I was in the right.

She accepted a transfer but resigned six weeks later following her broken engagement. Her father wanted her to take the case to court but she felt that wouldn't stop anything. She claimed though that from that point on the other secretaries had jacked up. They were fed up with the constant snide jokes and innuendos and attempts at flirtation. They just got sick of this man in the middle of the room yelling out, 'I want a cup of tea right now'. Though she had not won a legal victory, and indeed had left, her resistance shifted the power relations in that office.

Kate would like sex to be banned entirely from work, but it seems unlikely. Hard though it is to see Mr P in sexual terms, even he expresses a certain kind of sexuality. He says: 'The hidden element in the success or otherwise of a secretary is still chemistry. I don't know what it is...You either get on well together, you rub along, or you don't...I think a chemical thing is very important...and that's a growth thing.' For him, this is 'just the normal attraction of male and female', which is present in some form wherever you work. Public relations people go for smart upmarket secretaries, while banking and retailing are more conservative: 'My wife, I think, dresses very well and...I still see her as a most attractive woman. So I have a standard. I like somebody who is respectful and not at all familiar...I don't want to have to discipline a secretary all the time. I don't like disciplining women, you know. That's just the way I'm made. I like them to be able to initiate work themselves and not have to be policing them all the time...I'm conscious of manners.' Once again we have a boss looking to a family model to help him choose the kind of secretary he wants.

Kate feels quite powerful in her current position. In fact she sees Mr P as a bit of a geriatric—'he thinks better in the morning'. She is ambitious and has also chosen this job to get experience in industrial relations. She already has a personnel management certificate and is studying industrial relations at tech. Whether she will actually be able to move up is doubtful. Mr P makes all sorts of bland comments about how secretaries should be able to move into management. Yet he admits:

> Once a secretary starts a secretarial career then she seems to stay in that mode...People don't see secretaries as career jobs and I think they should...When a secretary gets to when she is just reporting to two managers, they become so dependent on so much information that she carries at her fingertips it is unbelievable...We do reward them...there is a really good career in it as a personal assistant...Our senior secretaries are on...our managerial pay structure and when we look at pay rises for our managers, our senior secretaries are considered automatically.

He moves in a few sentences from acknowledgement of a problem, through restating the issues, to an apparent resolution. One cannot have a career as a secretary but one can, apparently, have one as a personal assistant.

Mr P's expectations of a secretary are traditional. He likes someone who can take shorthand though he accepts the argument that it's wasteful and is perfectly capable of using a dictaphone. He could easily fall into Howard's category of managers who like to 'sit with a lady and talk to her a little bit and have cups of tea'. He expects her to do his banking and to run errands. She says 'it gets me out of the office, I love it', but it runs completely counter to her professional expectations. Still, there are no expectations here that she work longer than 9 to 5, so she has control over her time. He treats her with respect, and she is able to some extent to place herself in the 'nanny' discourse, on this occasion looking after a geriatric old father. Yet he gets what he wants and she does not. Despite her qualifications she looks like being locked into a secretarial role.

Family games

What is striking about most of these pairs is the centrality of sexuality and family relations in strategies of power at work. It takes a number of forms. In some cases sexual or family relations are symbolically constructed. Tom and Carol and to some extent Jim and Kate have a father—daughter relationship. Stephanie is Richard's wife-cum-mistress. And Paul attempts to construct Suzanne in the mistress mould though she resists it. Bosses frequently try to break down divisions between home and work, either by asking their secretaries to do 'non-work' tasks or by intruding on their non-work lives. Tom is an extreme case of the first—he gets his secretary to do his grocery shopping and take his washing off the line.

Bosses often control their secretaries through a detailed knowledge of their personal lives. Tom knows all about Carol's family, her boyfriend, her future plans. This knowledge can be very one-way. On the basis of an hour with him I actually know more about some aspects of his life than Carol does, for he told me 'secrets' which he claimed never to have revealed to anyone in the office. Richard and Stephanie know a great deal about each others' lives. They spend a lot of social time together, talk about their personal problems over a drink, and she knows his wife and children. As a result he can ask her to work incredibly long hours and organise her whole life around the job.

Bosses try to stretch the limits of the working day, demanding long overtime for no additional pay. This is presented as pleasurable, a sign that the job is interesting and challenging, evidence that the secretary is part of management rather than a mere worker, a superior sort of person to the nine-to-fivers. Paul likes his secretary to be available to him 24 hours a day. He has not been able to achieve this perhaps because Suzanne has clammed up tightly about her personal life and made it very clear where the boundary is to be drawn. If he wants to treat her as a bit of a sex symbol, she does not acknowledge it.

Male bosses can decide for themselves the extent to which they will keep home and work, their public and private lives separate. Secretaries do not have this luxury. Male bosses go into their secretaries' offices unannounced, assume the right to pronounce on their clothes and appearance, have them doing housework and personal chores, expect overtime at short notice and assume the right to ring them at home. Men regularly 'invade' women's private space and women have to defend it. The sexual metaphor is apt. Women have the responsibility to decide what is going 'too far'. Their resistance is thus crucial to the exercise of power. While secretaries may have access to much of the boss's private life, it is entirely on his terms and thus hardly an 'invasion'. Their task as gatekeepers is to protect that privacy. And they are often angered or embarrassed by having to do personal chores.

Bosses are embarrassed by any signs of overt conflict with their secretaries and like them to be able to work largely unsupervised. Hence they worry a lot about how to get the 'right' person. Howard dreams up a new specification each time in the hope of achieving this. Even where the boss knows nothing about his secretary's life outside work, family situation is frequently used in the selection process. While Howard avoids women with young children or divorcees, Paul likes young married women who have been taught by their husbands how to please men. Tom goes for women from large families because they have learnt 'discipline' and Jim favours women who dress like his wife.

Relationships run most smoothly where each accepts the 'natural' authority of the man over the woman. This is seen as so natural that a power relation is barely perceived to exist—which minimises overt conflict. This is not to say that women are power-less. But when they do claim authority it is in family terms, as mothers, for example, rather than as women. Their authority has a limited domain. While men may be perceived as husbands or fathers, their authority at work rarely depends on this. Though they are necessarily engaged in power relations with their secretaries, the outcome will only marginally affect their power within the organisation.

Power and pleasure

We often think of power as involving one person making another do something she would not otherwise do. This would suggest that it is quite easy to specify when and how power is operating.

We would know when power was being exercised over us and we would experience it as highly unpleasant. Power operates more subtly than this. A person may 'voluntarily' do what another wants, without any sense of coercion, or she may take pleasure in her situation. If coercion is experienced as pleasurable can it any longer be called coercion? If people seek out the erotic pleasure of actually being dominated, what does this say about power relations?

There is now quite a large literature on the master—slave relation as a fantasy or erotic domination which, it can be argued, underlies much of our everyday interactions. This is not to say that the fantasy is a conscious one. On the contrary, I am drawing attention to what is unconscious or, at most, semiconscious, in our interactions. Debates about sadomasochism have been a central theme of the sexual politics of the 1980s. This may sound crazy to anyone who associates sadomasochism purely with pornographic images of chains and leather and torture chambers, of teachers spanking schoolgirls or punishing naughty boys. But what is at stake is the pattern of emotions, fantasies, desires that might underlie 'normal' interactions. While only a tiny minority of people self-consciously practice sadomasochistic rituals, the issue has been a lively one because it raises fundamental questions about exchanges of power. It involves a recognition that power may inhere in sexuality rather than simply withering away in egalitarian relationships. In pointing to the importance of fantasy it places on the agenda questions about subjectivity and identity. This suggests a highly complex picture of the interplay of power, pleasure and desire. 'Master—slave' is, of course, the archetypal model of the boss—secretary relationship and we have already seen the kind of fantasising that goes on around it. The nanny—naughty little boy who needs punishment also fits comfortably into the S/M theme. In talking about secretaries we are forced to confront the extent to which power relations at work are organised around a particular form of heterosexuality based on sadomasochistic fantasy.

Jessica Benjamin (1983) engages directly with the relationship between rationality, gender and sexuality. She argues that violent erotic fantasy can be understood as a response to the increasingly 'rational' character of our culture and the deprivation of nurturance. As the burden of rationality becomes intolerable, erotic fantasy appears as a response to a crisis of male rationality. Eroticism itself is rationalised and coded through the discourses and practices within which it is reproduced. Thus the rational and the irrational permeate each other. Instrumental rationality, while it presents itself as autonomous and indeed the opposite of the private, is actually embedded in a (masculine) discourse of sadomasochism which structures all our emotional relationships.

Benjamin looks at the development of individual identity in terms of the relation between the need for autonomy and the need for recognition. Rather than finding a balance, in the reciprocal giving of self, the genders are polarised into subject and object. Men gain autonomy at the price of denying the other's subjectivity and thus being denied recognition. Violence is a central part of maintaining their boundaries and denying their need for the other. It is also a way of searching for recognition through attempting to find the other person as an intact being who will set limits. Benjamin suggests that male individuality dovetails with what Western culture has defined as 'rationality'. We have been taken over by impersonal forms of social relation and an urge to control and objectify every living thing. Thus, she suggests, it is hard for any of us, male or female, to satisfy our desires for recognition, transcendence or continuity. These desires were once satisfied by religion and its rituals and by a sense of community. They are now catered for by sexuality and its associated rituals. She looks at the pleasure involved in fantasies and rituals of erotic domination and subordination. While her case study is from pornography (*The Story of O*) she makes it clear that the same tantalising issues of control and submission flow beneath the surface of *all* sexual relations. Through his mastery the man can remain in rational control, maintaining his separateness, denying his dependence and enjoying a sense of omnipotence. For the woman, the man's masterful control is a turn-on: it means she can safely lose control and experience a merging. In each case, the pleasure is at the price of denying one side of the self. Violence, whether actual, ritualised or fantasised, is an attempt to break out of the numbing barriers of self, to experience intensity and to come up against the boundaries of the other. Thus, says Benjamin, 'the fantasy, as well as the playing out of rational violence, does offer a controlled form of transcendence, the promise of the real thing'. The 'real thing' she believes is a balance between the opposing impulses for recognition and autonomy. Since we live in a system in which this is very difficult to achieve, we are locked into a permanent set of games, fantasies, rituals of domination and submission from which we derive a great deal of erotic pleasure.

This abstract masculine subjectivity may in practice be highly vulnerable, for it 'exists only by constituting everything with which it comes into contact as other, and thus separating itself from everything which could give it content' (Poole, 1987). Obsessive consumption and a quest for power are among the strategies for reducing this threat. In fantasies of erotic domination the man confirms his identity through the exercise of power over the other. What is important is that the submission be voluntary and that the annihilation of the object be indefinitely deferred. This prolongs the moment of recognition and thus, at least in fantasy, provides partial resolution.

The archetypal form of S/M is male domination/female submission but there is nothing absolute about the gender positions. Gendered subjectivity is produced in a number of contradictory discourses which make available different positions and different powers for men and women. While masculine and feminine identities are to some extent 'fixed' in early childhood they also have to be constantly reproduced. They are never fully or permanently constituted and are always, in some sense, in a state of flux. Most discourses are gender-differentiated so that subject positions are not equally available to men and women. But since the meanings have to be reproduced in specific situations there is room for negotiation and change. There is space for games to be played and roles to be reversed. Master—slave games need not always be between men and women: they may be played out between men or between women. Women may take up the position of master and men of slave, but we cannot assume that such role reversals involve a reversal of power. The ultimate power trip may be for a man to play the masochist. It is men rather than women who seek out masochistic pornography and go to brothels seeking various forms of 'punishment' from the likes of Madame Lash. We cannot always assume that it is the sadist who holds power. The masochist may control the whole situation by determining how much violence (symbolic or otherwise) is permissible and by making her (masochistic) pleasure the centre of attention.

The master—slave framework clearly sets up the boss as subject and secretary as object. The latter may take a number of forms including subordinate wife, devoted spinster, attractive mistress. Difficulties arise when women take up the subject or men the object position. Male bosses fear that if they have a male secretary they will have to give him recognition—and he may then not be a secretary. Secretaries fear that a female boss is not powerful or prestigious enough to give them the recognition they seek. Even if she is they may not feel the safety in merging with the powerful that they feel with men, because they cannot trust her to set the boundaries. Even in the 'master—slave' situation, women have possibilities of resistance and reversal.

Alongside master—slave is mother—son. Here it is the secretary who is in the subject position as mother, dragon or dominating wife, while the man is the object. This does not simply parallel or reverse the master—slave theme. It does not necessarily disempower men to play the 'naughty little boy' when it suits them; and they can resist 'mothering' by denying their dependency or trivialising it. A man may concede he is dependent in a limited way but insist that she is replaceable. Often in the interview, men would agree that 'office wife' was an appropriate way to describe their secretaries, while the secretary would insist that 'mother' was more accurate. The secretary may exercise a lot of power through setting up as 'second in command' and insisting that everything go through her. Difficulties can arise where the boss is a woman: the two may be rivals for the position of mother and the secretary is in danger of losing out and becoming the daughter. Secretaries are ambivalent about mothering women. The difference between mothering sons and daughters is reproduced here. They tend to think the latter should learn to do things for themselves and hence are reluctant to do as much for women bosses who should do their own secretarial work.

Finally there is the theme of reciprocity/equality. This is supposedly gender-neutral with no fixed subject and object positions. Boss and secretary work as a team. The secretary works *with* rather than *for* the boss. This is the 'modern' form, often accentuated by the fact that the secretaries work for a number of people and not just one. Even in this situation some remnants of the one-to-one relation seem to be preserved and are sought by both sides. Thus 'the boss' is differentiated from the others she 'works for' and is the only one to receive personal services. In turn she expects his protection and support. Secretaries can increasingly call on the language of 'team' to insist on certain rights and reciprocities. It is also in the boss's interests to talk the language of 'teams' and disguise the actual workings of power. To the extent that bosses and secretaries are already positioned by the other two frameworks it is hard not to take up gendered positions in this one too. Secretaries talk a lot about reciprocity but in most cases the 'team' dimension is subordinate to the other two. Where it does appear to predominate the relationship is barely recognisable as a boss—secretary one at all.

The assumption of an institutionalised heterosexuality, a basic liking and complementarity between men and women means that overt conflict can be minimised. Jim calls it 'chemistry'. Women are constructed and construct themselves as soft and feminine. Even where they believe in equal opportunity, secretaries constantly reiterated how much they like men's company, appreciate men's jokes, enjoy working with men rather than in all-female groups and, have a distinct preference for male bosses. The question then arises, what happens when the boss is a woman? When this natural flow, this chemistry, is presumed not to exist? Where to acknowledge its existence would be an admission of deviance? I have argued that several discourses structure the boss—secretary relation and that each has gendered subject and object positions. What happens when the gender of the person occupying some or all of these positions is changed? Are power relations between secretaries and women bosses constituted on a different basis? Do they challenge existing discourses or get incorporated into them? These questions will be taken up in the following chapter.

·3· Office relations: female bosses

I *would* expect more of a female boss. I would expect
more consideration, more understanding...Yes. I
probably would cop things from a man I wouldn't
cop from a woman. It seems likely doesn't it?

Secretaries are remarkably unenthusiastic about working for
women. Women bosses are stereotyped as dragons who make you
work harder; as women who have had to struggle so hard to get
where they are that they become hard; as moody, picky, erratic.
They put you down. They are 'snooty and bitchy'. They take
advantage of the fact you are both women to get you to do more.
Women are either 'all-powerful' and they chew you up—or they
are not powerful enough to look after you! Or they are just plain
boring. Where active hostility was not expressed, the most common
response to working for a woman was 'I wouldn't mind' or 'it makes
no difference'. Those who had worked closely with women were
more positive, describing the ways in which their horizons were
broadened or how they broke out of the boss—secretary strait-
jacket. Only a minority had worked more than fleetingly for
women. Others were willing to generalise on the basis of one
or two negative experiences or the hearsay of friends. Rachel
acknowledged she would not similarly generalise from one
bad experience with a man. Men are perceived as a universal
category, hence unstereotypable, whereas women are treated as a
minority group about which generalisations can be made.

These attitudes indicate the kinds of difficulties that women
have in establishing their authority. Women bosses have to assert,
continually, that they are powerful. Men do not, unless they are
still in relatively junior positions, or they come from working-class
backgrounds or otherwise lack the qualifications or experience to
feel secure. How women project themselves, and particularly what
they wear, takes on a distinct importance, as is attested by the
'Dress for Success' literature. It was impossible not to be aware of
what the women wore, whereas that was seldom the case with the
men. Where men's authority is taken for granted women have to
go on proving themselves. Often they will be seen to be harder, to
be going by the book, to be more rigid.

I did not manage to get detailed information from women bosses and secretaries who actively hated each other. It is an inevitable part of a research process that depends on a high level of voluntary cooperation that such people will either decline to be interviewed or will be extremely taciturn in their responses. Sometimes information would come from other people in the office or from gossip networks. On one occasion three-quarters of the office declined to talk, apparently because they did not want to be questioned about their attitudes and behaviour towards the woman in charge. They resented her because she went by the book, whereas her male deputy could be more laid back. They regularly brought in his favourite chocolate cake for morning tea, whereas she was left out in the cold. Even her secretary kept a distance. While remaining discreet in her answers, she said she would prefer to work for a man, that women are harder on each other and less tolerant. The boss said: 'I think some of the women have problems that they might not even acknowledge to themselves in working for a woman. They are quite young women from a very protective traditional environment...and middle-aged women in much the same mould. They feel that they have a nice strong place at home as a woman and a comfortable place at work as a woman...A woman boss just doesn't fit into that.' This woman was rather brittle and obviously hurt by having to deal daily with such hostility. An intensely private person, she hinted at personal disappointments in her life but put on a very formal, protective exterior. Had she been able to show her warmth or vulnerability she may have been able to evoke the protective or mothering impulses of the older women in the section. She rejected this as an acceptable strategy.

For the women I interviewed, the most effective strategies of exercising power required non-coercive methods, charming people into acting voluntarily, 'asking' rather than 'telling' them to do things. This meant evoking the 'team' discourse of equality and reciprocity. Pleasure, in this relation, is organised around reciprocity rather than coercion. Women do not like other women exercising authority directly over them, perhaps because it evokes their earliest fears of being merged or suffocated by the mother. They experience women's authority as 'unnatural', whereas men's authority is taken for granted. If reciprocal relations between the women are expected or promised, there may be bitter disappointment if things do not work out that way. Bosses are disappointed if the secretary treats it as just a job, while secretaries may feel they are being taken advantage of:

> I think a woman in the hierarchy... tends to feel she can ask more of
> you because after all we are the same sex and we must stick together etc.,

whereas with a man you tend to think, well, it is unreasonable that he should even ask that of me...With a man I found that I used to remind him that after all I had a family and they were waiting at home and dinner was meant to be cooked...Whereas the woman would say, I know... but... can you just do this, and put this guilt trip onto you.

Some felt that women worked them harder but often respected their bosses for what they achieved: 'If I was working for someone who didn't work hard and expected me to work hard, then I might be resentful. But because I see her working so hard I don't.' Another said: 'I think women work harder than men. They have to. The reason that men get 50 per cent of where they get to is because they are men...My basic objection is that the woman, because she was a woman, wouldn't be sufficiently senior. And I have been down there and I am up here now and I don't want to go down again.' For many women bosses secretarial work represents everything they do not want to be. They may feel guilty about asking someone else to do it for them: 'She would use flowery words for me to do something for her because she is a woman and she probably thinks that she could do it just the same, but she would rather that I did it...because I have got more time and I am supposed to do it...A man would say, two copies of that please, straight away and then the girl would get up and do it straight away...I think a man is more demanding...I don't mind. I am not very worried about it.' Though fond of her boss this secretary is not impressed with such indirectness. Since the work is there to be done, it makes little difference to her to be asked in a 'flowery' way: she would prefer to get on with it.

In most cases women bosses have a male boss as their more senior manager. To this extent they have experienced both sides of the divide and this is likely to make them sympathetic to the secretary's predicament. Those who have been secretaries themselves are likely to exercise particular care in negotiating the relationship. One such woman says: 'I don't believe that people like to be told...I am not very good at telling. I would prefer to ask them to do something...I am different from male managers because I have been there...I like to be treated well and I like to be asked to do something.' Her style is indeed different from those of men. For a start she is in direct touch with the network of secretaries working for member organisations. For a man this would always be mediated through his own secretary: 'I make it may business to know the secretaries for the executive members that we are dealing with here...Some years ago I introduced a system whereby we invite all those secretaries to our annual luncheon at Christmas time and we make a definite point of welcoming them and making them aware of how important it is for them to assist us and I find that that has worked wonders.' Nevertheless there is an, at times uncomfortable, gap between those women who have 'escaped' from aspects of the female predicament as represented in secretarial work, and those who remain 'trapped.'

Mothers and daughters?

'Family' is important in constructing women's relationships but in a different way from men's. Here it is the mother−daughter relation that is powerfully evoked. The secretary is rarely able to exercise the limited power she is able to construct with a man as wife/mother/nanny. With a woman boss she is herself in danger of being reduced to daughter, symbolically the most powerless position of all. Though the notion of equality was frequently evoked as a counter, 'sister' imagery was never used in this context.

Psychoanalysts tell us that the girl retains more frightening dimensions of the mother image than does the boy. The boy, because he has had to give up his early identification with the mother, is able to be more detached. In identifying with the father he is promised that, in time, he will be powerful in relation to women. For the girl the spectre of the all-powerful 'phallic' mother of her earliest childhood remains strong, and creates the psychological basis for her turning to her father. She enters the triangular oedipal situation later than the boy and never completely gives up the pre-oedipal relationship with her mother. Elements of this early relationship with the mother continue to be found in adult relationships between women. Since the mother−daughter relationship is characterised by intensity and ambivalence it is not surprising that women can feel comfortable and cosy with each other at one moment and anger, envy or betrayal at another.

Patricia was quite explicit about some of these tensions:

> I didn't feel as second rate with a man as I did with her. I felt that I never came up to her expectations and I didn't know where I fell short. . . She had wanted to bring her old secretary with her. . . She made me move my desk forward on the floor so she could see me from her office and the relationship got worse. She used to make me feel bad about having half a day's study leave. . . and she used to report me a lot for little niggly things. . . I was really angry that she put me down because I didn't think that she had that much more ability than I had. She just had more experience and had developed confidence, poise and personality.

She felt humiliated, as she had in the past been humiliated by her own mother. She had previously said she was angry with herself for not having been able to stand up to her mother, a bossy woman who pushed her into secretarial work against her will. Her relationship with the boss evoked memories of her own mother, and she interpreted all kinds of things as slights that may not have been so intended. The fact that someone wanted to keep their secretary will not automatically mean hostility to the newcomer. And it is quite common for bosses and secretaries to arrange their desks so that they have eye contact with each other. Another secretary described rather gleefully how she had fought to keep it that way when they were renovating the office. When her boss claimed she was being ridiculous she found a solution: 'We now have double sliding doors and it is very grand and he loves *that*.'

Some women evoke the good, caring mother and incorporate this into their strategies of control. Dedication and loyalty are won by looking after staff properly. One small businesswoman described herself in these terms: 'Without their dedication I wouldn't be anywhere. I'm like a right-wing shop steward and I try to look after them. It's important that they feel secure in their jobs and to make them part of the team, and I rely on them. At the moment I want to kick one over the head but I'm a softie. I'm not over-indulgent but I make them feel secure and appreciated...Insecurity is what leads to bitchiness.' Her staff, all female, experience her as a generous and flexible boss. She is considerate, she is not a slave driver and they are able to take time off when they need to. In addition she brings lunch for them every day and pays for their train tickets. It is almost impossible to imagine a man operating in this way. Yet it makes for good working relations and is achieved at no cost to herself. All her staff are paid on an hourly basis, while the perks provide her with a convenient tax deduction.

Two examples will detail the ways in which authority relations are organised around mother—daughter relations. Susan Ashton and Clare Thomas are a stylish pair who could have walked straight out of the fashion pages of Vogue. Both are tall and blonde with model-like figures. Susan was wearing a gold shirt that matched her hair, slung loosely over a white skirt. Clare had on a red skirt, white shirt with loosely knotted red tie and a long string of pearls. Both wore carefully understated make-up and had immaculate hair and fingernails. Susan, in her late forties, is the sales manager of a fashion company. She is married with four children. Clare, her secretary, is just 22 and lives at home with her parents. There is not much doubt that they represent mother and daughter: the physical resemblance, the style of dress and the narcissistic investment in each other are quite striking. It was obvious that they liked each other enormously. The narcissistic pleasure was not reliant on men but there was a powerful voyeuristic attraction both to men and to other women, myself included. Women are encouraged to see themselves as men see them and to enjoy their sexuality through the eyes of men. While not explicitly exhibitionist there was a certain power and confidence in this invitation to voyeurism.

Susan had chosen Clare over a woman with much more experience so that she could train her and mould her:

> She was well-presented; she wasn't flashy; she didn't overdo it; she was quite and dignified, which I liked and, in a young girl it was quite unique, I felt. I thought that here was somebody that had a lot of potential and she deserves a go... She is about my own daughter's age and she reminds me a bit of my daughter...perhaps it was that...I thought she really deserves it more than maybe the older woman who would have the confidence to go and get another job.

She can see that she is drawn to Clare as a daughter:

> If she is a bit sick, I say to her, don't do this or that. Sometimes when we are working, it is like two friends, and she will say, oh mum was this, that and the other, and I say to her, now don't be like that. You think of your mother...Sometimes the reps will crack a smutty joke or twist things around and I often think, I don't want them to say that in front of her...Then I think, that is not fair, because that isn't my role to protect her...and she is all right. She gives a bit of a grin and a bit of a laugh and she can cope with that quite well.

Much of Susan's authority comes from her status as a mother. It is clear that she has the reps and the warehouse boys under control and will not take any nonsense from them. The narcissistic attraction between Susan and Clare makes it easy to extract loyalty and commitment. These are not enforced as a mother's right, but rather on the basis that she is a contemporary, liberal mother—more of a 'best friend'. Susan says 'I am not the traditional mummy'. She claims that because she works she has been more easily able to treat her children as separate individuals rather than extensions of herself: 'I am able to sit back and look at my relationship with them and think, I have to let go...I need to let them develop in their own way. So I have been very conscious that that doesn't happen with Clare here.'

Clare had started off with reservations about working for a woman—which came from a girlfriend's experience and one woman at the previous job with the law firm who had terrified her. She is not consciously aware of Susan as a mother figure—if she were the relationship probably would not work. It is not unusual for teenage girls, in achieving individuation and independence, to transfer their affections from their own to someone else's mother. They are thus able to separate while still expressing their feelings of dependence and identification (Chodorow, 1978: 133–38). Clare thinks Susan is terrific not because she is like her own mother but because she is 'very different' from her. Susan is able to incorporate this into her exercise of power.

In choosing a 'daughter' Susan also chose someone of a suitable class background, though she was reluctant to put it in these terms. 'There are certainly the ones I have had in the past I would never have taken to any function...It is from no snob point of view it is just simply business...They wouldn't know how to talk to people, they wouldn't have known how to cope with the situation. I don't know, what is working-class background? I mean we are all working-class aren't we, when it comes down to it, in Australia?' Like the male bosses Susan is very concerned with home and family background when she chooses a secretary. Women's skills and personal characteristics, unlike men's, are assumed to be developed in the home, rather than developed through outside 'training'. This is partly why they are undervalued. Yet the male and female bosses had different emphases. The men saw the home as creating desirably feminine characteristics, for example, submissivenes or amenability to discipline. Women, perhaps taking these for granted, often stressed the class aspects. Thus Susan comments: 'I think the home environment does have a lot to do with it and I was interested in her home environment. I felt that it was a good steady home environment...Girls we have had in the past have come from migrant backgrounds and their parents... have worked very hard to achieve what they have...but they haven't really thrown off that environment.' She concedes that in the fashion industry the way someone dresses is extremely important and with Clare it comes naturally.

Clare did not want to become a secretary. She wanted to follow her father into the rag trade and become a fashion designer. But she 'realised this was not practical...since there are very few openings for fashion designers in Australia' and instead enrolled at a prestigious private business college in the hope of finding another way into the fashion world. A few weeks after she came to work for the company she developed RSI quite suddenly. This was most likely the result of a lot dictaphone work in her previous job at a law firm, but 'it could have been pressure here'. When she first started the present job, she was working for several people. After developing the RSI she came to work almost exclusively for Susan.

She expressed indebtedness to Susan for being 'understanding' about the RSI and putting her on light duties. Yet in some ways it worked to Susan's advantage, since she acquired her protege's services full-time: 'We looked after her all through that. We just employed temporaries until she could come back. She was terrific. She did all the right exercises and she kept saying she wanted to come back. This was actually very good in a way because it was proof that I had chosen the right personality.' Despite this concern Clare was still expected to get the job done. This is very typical of the way RSI is treated. Lip-service is paid to the importance of instigating correct procedures but little or nothing is done to ensure that they are in operation. Susan had surprisingly little idea of the proportion of time her secretary spent typing:

> I don't really know. We do actually have a lot of typing.
> *Is it a half? A third?*
> Perhaps a third. She would probably give you a better answer on that.
> I... just dash off letters and I really have only just got to the stage now where I can say to her this is a 'no' letter or this is a 'yes' letter...

Susan trusts her gut feelings in choosing a secretary. Where a man might put this down to 'chemistry', she is adamant that it is to do with experience. She believes that if you employ the right people they can be given responsibility and left to do the job without close supervision:

> I tend to look for somebody who is not just a secretary but a sort of personal assistant... I do a lot of work out in the field, on the road and what have you and, because it is a very one-to-one sort of business you need somebody who is back in the office... as a troubleshooter really... I like her to come out and be with me and get to know people in the trade... It has got to the stage where she can meet some of the buyers or ring the stores for me. She is getting to know some of the people very well.

And she is very proud of her: 'In fact, the little secretary I have now is the best I have ever had. She is terrific. She has got a little bit of initiative and she will go ahead and do something. She doesn't work to the clock.'

There are similarities here with Tom's exercise of power as a father as well as significant gender and class differences. Coming from a working-class background, Tom deliberately merges home and work and delights in having his secretary, Carol, off doing his shopping. He plays down the division of labour between them and insists he is going to teach her everything. Susan, on the other hand, is careful *not* to load Clare up with personal chores. While men can ask for domestic support, women are often proud of having their domestic lives under control and are much more sensitive about asking for help with 'housework'. Susan's requests are more in the area of 'male' chores such as dealing with car repairs. Anything else she claims to be voluntary. Clare will ask if there is anything she can get, if she is going to the shop. She will often get tea and coffee or lunch but 'I would never expect her to do that all the time. Of course I love it when she does it'. Women are aware of the awkwardness around this issue: 'If she is really flat out and busy I wouldn't sit here and wait for her to bring it in. If I wanted one I would go and make it. I think it is very important that you don't expect somebody to be your slave.' Getting the coffee so often represents a master–slave ritual which women bosses cannot afford to become involved in. Chances are they have been on the other side of it and may still, in certain contexts be expected to perform such tasks themselves.

While Susan presents the job as leading to exciting possibilities in the fashion industry, Clare is more cynical. She does not see any great opportunities for advancement without finding ways of getting a wider grip on the business. And she denied that she had been taken to any business gatherings. Susan's claims about this were reduced to one vague promise. Where she stresses that it is an exciting job, Clare feels that she is underpaid. Nevertheless she stays because 'I get heaps of job satisfaction. I love my boss. I like the cosmetics. The cosmetics has got me in. I am very interested in it so I enjoy doing it.'

Susan and Clare could easily be mistaken for mother and daughter. They look and dress alike and the age gap between them is right. These elements do not have to be present, however, for the mother–daughter script to be evoked. It may even be the younger woman who sets herself up as mother as it was in the following case.

Barbara and Joan work in an almost entirely female section of a department. Apart from the director, the only men present are in relatively junior positions. Barbara heads the division and Joan is her secretary, though, in public service style, she is classified and paid as a stenographer. She made it clear that she felt undervalued and, if she chose to work in the city, could earn considerably more. Barbara is in her early forties and Joan close to retirement age. Both are married with children—in Joan's case they have long grown up, but are still in regular contact. While *both* women are acknowledged as mothers it is the boss's mothering which is central.

Barbara thinks that women bosses have got a bad press. She is intent on restoring the balance; demonstrating that groups of women *can* work happily together. It is, she says, precisely *because* men are absent and no one is in direct competition with them that the office is such a happy, friendly place to work. Yet it is the women's shared *family* situation that binds them together. She distinguishes sharply between 'career' women, obsessed about work to the detriment of everything else, and the 'balanced' family women who work in this office:

> 'Office wife' doesn't apply here at all. . . It's not only that we are
> predominantly female. Many of us are married with children so we are
> not single-minded about careers. . . While our work's important, it's not
> necessarily the most important thing in our lives and our identities aren't
> defined by it. . . A lot of tension that happens in the work situation isn't
> here because we have all these other roles. . . If I've had a crappy day

here I go home and forget about it. There are my beautiful children, or there's my husband to get cross with...or the garden.

She contrasts this with a colleague who lives alone: 'I mean one of my staff goes home to an empty house. She doesn't live with anybody and she of course is one of the most super uptight people...' A 'balance' between home and work is an important employment criterion: 'I try and make sure that the people I appoint are reasonably well-balanced or if they're not, that they can sustain a balance at work, even if they're not at home... They've got to be able to sustain normal working relationships with other people...' Barbara is faced with the challenge of motivating a predominantly female clerical staff to do a lot of the routine work. She encourages interest in each other's families to create a 'family' experience at work. What makes the office work as a 'team' is

> the fact that people do know and are interested in each other outside the work relationship. So they know about their family set-up. For most of us that is our main activity outside. But we will also know if people have hobbies or are very keen and doing something else...We just sit and talk at tea. People care about each other. There is always people having birthdays when everyone brings them cakes...There's a lot of social activity goes on. We have a very cooperative family feeling...

Actually it is part of Joan's responsibility to 'play mother', that is, to know exactly when everyone's birthday is, to instigate lunches and morning teas and 'coerce everyone into going'. The atmosphere of this office would be suffocating for anyone who is not in a nuclear family or does not enjoy family 'carry-on'. There is evidence of some passive resistance, for 'there's a hard core of participators and an equally hard smaller core that does not'. Barbara is dismissive of 'one particular person who doesn't enter into this'. She is defined as 'less flexible and adaptable and just doesn't find social interaction easy'. Others are accepted as long as they concur with her estimation of them. Thus: 'Two of the main guys in my department...as blokes who don't fit the normal successful male mode...Well, one is gay for a start and the other one is just miserable...And both of those will come and talk to me...'

Barbara's relationship with her secretary is also cast in family terms: 'I know all the dealings of her children and she knows all the dealings of my children...We certainly know all the family notes and who's doing what and where the children live and what the grandchildren are up to.' She suggests that they share the mother role: 'Sometimes she is mother but sometimes I'm mother. It sort of fluctuates depending on what's going on.' Though she talks the language of equality and 'teamwork' Barbara is a dominant and controlling personality. Like the male bosses, she uses humour effectively to keep control: 'I can't tell jokes, right. I am not a person who stands there and declaims jokes. But I think you can quite often take the steam out of a situation by cracking a funny...and I think it's very important for people to laugh during the day.' The contrast between them is striking. Where Barbara is loud, assertive, confident, Joan is quiet and cautious, making her points indirectly rather than head-on. She was at first reluctant to have the tape recorder on at all, worried about confidentiality, it was part of a secretary's job!

Though Joan is old enough to be her mother, it is Barbara who hogs the mother role and defines it for both of them. She allows Joan a role as social secretary and pays her some token respect on account of her age. She acknowledges that Joan is the boss of the filing system and would not change it without discussing it with her. And she protects her from having to 'crank up' her 'rusty' shorthand: the adult daughter 'looking after' the ageing mother: 'I've been motherly to her instead of the other way round!' Joan, in her quiet way describes how she taught Barbara when she arrived in the job. 'She was a fast learner' she says, with a hint of maternal pride. She went on to speak about her own growth. In the early days when the boss called her in she was petrified. But with a lot of work experience, and seventeen years of bringing up children, she gained a more confidence. She is quite happy to say so if she thinks Barbara is making a mistake and she sets clear limits on what can be asked of her. Her comment that 'Barbara's no trouble' must be a classic remark that mothers make about their daughters. They are warmer about their sons.

While Joan's status as mother is acknowledged it does not gain her much power. She is relegated to grandmother; the 'daughter', in the prime of life, takes over the mother position in a big way. She does this not only in relation to her secretary but as central to her strategy for managing the office as a whole:

> One of my nicknames in this place is 'mother'. One of the people in another place rings up and asks to speak to mother and he means me. I mean he's older than my mum or dad and got four kids of his own...A lot of people...come and tell me their problems...I'm known as strong and cheerful...My door is never closed.
>
> It's because I'm an out-and-out family woman...and therefore no sexual threat to anybody that the men and the women will come...I'm more the mother earth type than the glamorous female sexual thing...If I was that other sort of woman they wouldn't come near me.

Barbara thinks she's different from a male boss in that:

> I'm very attuned to what people are thinking and feeling...and I regard that as super-important for the way I do things...If somebody is not

> ready to hear something, for instance, I can judge that. . .My deputy can
> be sitting next to me and won't have the faintest idea. . .You might be
> trying to turn somebody round. . .We have to develop systems that
> everybody can use so the nature of the place is bureaucratic and some
> people, particularly young ones, hate it and will always want to change
> everything. . .The person who comes to you with their idea hasn't quite
> given up on their idea yet and that's not the time to say. . .I've decided
> how we're going to do it.

Feminine intuition is a common theme with women bosses. They
pride themselves on being directly in touch with what is going on,
where men might rely on their secretaries for this information or
use more formal means of control. It may also be that because
women's authority is relatively shaky they must give more attention
to the nuances where a man can afford to ride roughshod over
them. 'You spend a lot of time in meetings picking up vibes,
rather than listening to what's going on. . .I'm a vibes person and
I think that contributes to why I do things. . .whether that's because I'm female. . .or whether it's because I'm like that, I don't
know. . .In my experience most of the people who do that successfully have been women.'

If anyone is the 'office wife' in this organisation it is Barbara,
not Joan. She describes her relationship with her own boss as
being very similar to that with her husband. Both men are cautious,
intelligent, conscientious, and careful. 'They need somebody that
will be there as support but equally will push them when they
need to be pushed.' In working as his de facto deputy she expands
her authority beyond the section for which she is responsible.

Joan will not be drawn on the question of whether she prefers
male or female bosses. She stresses that a good secretary must be
discreet and her view of the power relationship between herself
and Barbara is expressed ultra-discreetly via a discussion of
whether men could be secretaries:

> I don't think they could be condescending enough. . .especially with a
> woman boss. Yes, I don't think they could come down to that. . .I've got
> very big macho sons and I can't imagine them doing it. . .I don't think
> they would have the patience for a start. . .They don't have the flowers in
> the vocabulary. . .they're not diplomatic enough. . .Be all right in
> Parliament or something like that. . .Would be good for the likes of the
> Prime Minister or the Opposition. . .but I can't imagine Barbara having a
> male secretary for a start. . .

It is not unreasonable to infer that she experiences Barbara, and
perhaps many of the people she deals with on the telephone, as
condescending, that she needs a lot of patience and a lot of
'flowers in her vocabulary' to achieve the easy understanding that
Barbara describes.

It is women bosses who monopolise the role of mother—whatever the ages and actual mothering experiences of themselves and their secretaries. Since 'mother' is the most powerful symbolic figure available to women, it is central in their strategies for control, both over secretaries and over other staff. Old secretaries, the ones who could set up as mother, seem to find it difficult to do so. There are, of course, exceptions. Penny, who has been a union secretary for nearly 30 years, knows more about its workings than anybody else. She does not have children of her own and sees her involvement with the union as a substitute. All its officers are in some sense her 'children'. The woman president volunteered that Penny had been like a mother in teaching her the job. She felt that all the secretaries had been more protective and caring because she is a woman in a difficult position.

There is a certain tokenism about this acknowledgement of secretary as mother. Whether working for a man or a woman, she is as much nanny, nursemaid or paid servant as she is mother. It is rather different from the powerful, threatening mother figure that the women bosses evoke. Given what has been said about the reluctance of secretaries to mother women, it may be a sign of the woman boss's power to extract mothering from a secretary! Penny's boss projects a certain 'vulnerability' which makes people want to give support and is no doubt part of her negotiating skills. To see it merely as 'vulnerability' would be a big mistake for behind it there is enormous strength.

Mirror games

Much has been written about men's homo-sociability, their preference for male company and their tendency to appoint men in their own image (Kanter, 1977). It has been suggested that patriarchal culture is founded on homosexual relations between men (Irigaray, 1985). If women are regarded as objects of exchange between men, their narcissistic attraction to their own sex is overlooked. One does not have to go far beneath the surface to realise that the 'boredom' that is so often expressed about working for women involves a denial of even the possibility of a sexual attraction. Relations with women are represented as colourless because they lack 'the phallus', the element of flirtation/excitement/danger. (They will at times be preferred for exactly this reason.) Men may use bribery or flattery to keep their secretaries on side, taking them out to lunch or giving them presents: 'A compliment from a man is totally different from a compliment from a woman. Isn't it really?...When Bob comes into work he says, the Secretary of the Year.' Where women refuse to work in this way, the secretary may not feel she is liked or appreciated to the same extent.

One woman boss said pointedly, 'girls aren't lesbian-intended...A
secretary gets the role of work wife and she can't have that,
relation with another woman unless she is that way intended'.
Working for a woman is seen, in a sense, as going against the
grain, denying heterosexual pleasure and getting nothing in its
place. Heterosexual relations are expected to flow more smoothly;
women will make more allowances for men and be much tolerant
of their moods and demands, more accepting of male authority.

Despite the disavowals, sexuality is important in relations between
women bosses and their secretaries. Where heterosexual attractions
are based on an interest in the other, same-sex relations depend
on a process of mutual identification, a liking for what is similar.
Sexuality is organized around a narcissism of shared taste, clothes
and style. The kinds of pleasure in exercising direct coercion that
are present with male bosses are notably absent. Power rests not in
the obvious domination of one by the other but in a subtler kind
of mutual identification. A boss may choose a secretary who reminds
her of what she once was or who is a junior version of herself; and
a secretary may strive to be 'like' her boss. Where a relationship
works well it is often because the heterosexual expectations are
not there. Women can be more open with each other, not needing
to put up the barriers that they do when men are present. They
relax and enjoy joking and gossiping and the sense of flowing in
and out of each other's personalities. But because the barriers are
down they risk losing their autonomy: it is not always clear where
one begins and the other ends. Where men may treat their secretaries 'narcissistically' as an extension of themselves, it is in the
sense of an appendage; with women it is more like holding up a
mirror to each other.

While there is a strong element of narcissism in mother—
daughter relationships, it can exist separately from them. This
was the case with Gillian Vandenberg and her secretary, Naomi
Russell. Gillian followed her father into the advertising industry
soon after she left school. Now in her late thirties, she is a senior
executive with twenty years of experience. A forceful personality,
she concedes that she is often the one that cuts through the
nonsense and bulldozes people when things have to to get done.
She was certainly a challenge to interview, for she was constantly
throwing back the questions and forcing the interviewer to reveal
parts of herself. Married, but with no children, she describes her
work as her *passion*. What is *your* passion, she asks?

Several frameworks jostle with each other here to construct the
power relations. Gillian is certainly dominant but her style is a
feminine one. She is decidedly not maternal—she even avoids
socialising with her colleagues at the weekend because she is
'frankly, not interested in mixing with kids'. But her relationship

with Naomi, her secretary, partakes of a the mother—daughter narcissism. Naomi is perceived not only as a useful appendage but as a mirror image, a junior version of herself. She is about ten years younger and lives with her boyfriend. She too has no children and has expressed a degree of ambition. Though Gillian does not lay strong claim to the subject position in the mother-child discourse, Naomi is left in the object position of the child. She invokes the 'team' discourse to protect herself from being treated as a slave, stressing instead the importance of friendship and reciprocity.

Gillian believes that to be successful in the advertising industry one must be able to be able to read people at a glance. She describes herself as a 'visible achiever', by which she means 'somebody that enjoys wearing good clothes well, looking as successful as I am at that point in time...I think I say in the way I dress...and the car I drive, and the home I live in, that I'm a successful professional'.

Gillian goes to some lengths to remind us that she has made it as a 'successful professional'—men rarely need to point out their success in these terms. She derives a sense of power from the way she dresses and takes pleasure in this power. Where Susan and Clare are fashionable in an elegantly casual sense, Gillian and Naomi cultivate a stylish well-groomed professionalism. They share many jokes about dressing like executives. Gillian favours the 'beautiful female equivalent of a man's suit', a style so far seen more frequently in New York than in Sydney and one that looks set to replace the 'beige suit syndrome' at the top. She was wearing a black suit with an expensive, camel-coloured shirt, a string of pearls and large pearl earrings. She comments:

> I wear a lot of suits because it's convenient. You can look very smart, very elegant and very individual without terribly much trouble...Accessories in my opinion are the key. Yes, I've seen the beige suit scene. It usually doesn't work because unfortunately the suit...has got to be very expensive to look good. It's got to be beautifully cut otherwise you're much better off wearing something more casual. The rumpled suit more often than not looks crummy. It's got to be great fabric, beautifully cut and if you can't wear a suit, then don't bother.

Naomi was not wearing a suit but she was elegantly dressed in a grey skirt and rolled-neck woollen jumper. Gillian had surmised from her clothes that she had the kind of personality she wanted: 'The fact that she came into the interview elegantly dressed in more or less the same style of clothes that I might choose, obviously that's in her favour!' Gillian could infer from this that Naomi would share her own good qualities. She, like Susan, was looking for a professional, competent person, young enough to mould, but mature enough to stand in for her and to work unsupervised. Naomi provided exactly the right combination. She got the job because of 'her personality, her drive, her enthusiasm and her maturity. She's fairly young but very together and mature...'. Gillian delights in having her own secretary—recalling her early days as an account executive when she had to share with three men and was always left till last. (It's the same as flying first-class on JAL, the woman gets served last, she says. In this way she establishes her current 'first-class' status in a casual throwaway line which seems to be saying the opposite.) She still thinks of a secretary as a glorified typist and telephone answerer and filer, who works for as many as four or five people. So she uses the term personal assistant to distinguish Naomi from the secretaries and to 'place' her as part of management. This is undercut, however, by the connotations of personal service—Naomi is there to do her bidding and to anticipate her wishes.

Though Naomi has expressed a desire to get further training and become a junior executive, her progress into management will not be easy. There are shades of the controlling mother who knows what's best, in the way Gillian has put her foot down: 'It wasn't what I read in her at all. I mean she's a fantastic PA. She loves it and I think she'd be very frustrated being an executive...there's a lot more control running our lives internally than she would have in running her client's business as a junior executive.' For the moment Naomi seems to have accepted this. In compensation she distinguishes herself from the other secretaries in the way she dresses, in declining to gossip with them in the tea room and in presenting herself as an 'arm of management'. She feels much more important in this job than she has in previous ones. She likes the colour, the informality, and opportunity to know what is going on in the business as a whole. For her, 'it was like moving from four walls to an open space'. She enjoys the power of managing the office and the freedom she is given to make decisions.

Gillian's authority rests on developing a feminine management style: 'I can't rush off to the pub with one of the guys and rip his ears off and then buy him a drink...So the way I handle a reprimand has to be totally different. It has to be just as clear but buying the drinks and all that has to happen some other way...It might just be the way I have to handle subsequent meetings...the subsequent ego boosting.' With women she relies on a more directly personal and emotional understanding: 'Maybe walking up to the shops with them when we're looking at clothes and discussing something on a personal level that says, look personally we can relate but there's that business problem...With guys the personal relating is a little more difficult...You can't take them up to the shops and say, don't you think this new range of jewellery is stunning, wouldn't it just suit you—it just doesn't work!' She rejects flirting as a method of dealing with senior men. 'It irritates every single woman within coo-ee and it irritates the less senior men...' She plays down both sexuality and gender while at the same time admitting they are important: 'I don't use my sex as a battering ram, which is the feminist way, or as a sweet doe-eyed, "if you fulfill this maybe some way in the future there could be a promise of sex". I don't think either is right... I love being a woman but I don't like women's issues.' Feminists represent for her both an assertion and denial of sexuality; they are obsessed with gender issues while at the same time she thinks they do not enjoy being women.

While Gillian places a lot of emphasis on good human relations she is a dominant personality who likes to get her own way and who knows how to charm, seduce and manipulate people. How does Naomi deal with this? She concedes that some people feel threatened about having a woman boss and that there are difficulties precisely because the element of 'natural flirting' between men and women is not present. So she makes a special effort to get on, by 'becoming friends with them first' and 'working as a team'. She has many disagreements with Gillian, and it is important to her that Gillian acknowledge when she is in the wrong.

Behind this decidedly unequal friendship, and making it pleasurable on both sides is the mutual narcissism. This replaces the heterosexual attraction that is assumed to be present at some level in the relationship with a male boss. While it is not perceived as 'sexual' it is actually more intensely so than many a heterosexual relationship. Susie Orbach and Luise Eichenbaum (1987) discuss the sexual elements in close female friendship and even talk about shopping expeditions as a way of giving expression to suppressed sexual desire. This seems to be exactly the sort of thing that Gillian is talking about. Though she declines to flirt with men, she understands (subliminally?) how to use her sexuality with women. The narcissism creates a basis for friendship while making acceptable the inequalities that otherwise grate.

Where neither narcissism nor mother-daughter symbolism are present in any obvious way, the relationship almost loses its 'boss—secretary' dimensions. This was the case with Nancy Grey and her boss, Janet Scott. Janet is the personnel manager of a suburban subsidiary company. She was somewhat reserved, though friendly and helpful, sympathetic to the research and more than willing to help organise interviews, both in her building and in other parts of the organisation. As it turned out she had worked her way up through clerical work and had been used to doing much of her own 'secretarial' work in previous personnel jobs. She conceded that she was inexperienced at working with a secretary and often unsure what to pass on and what to do herself. Gaining experience has meant learning to delegate, being less concerned with details. A small, neat woman in her late thirties, Janet has remained single: 'I don't think I could stay home and look after a family. And I think I'd find it difficult to work and then come home and look after a family. Either way would be difficult for me personally. So I just decided that I'd much rather work.' Not dramatically ambitious, she expects to stay with the organisation and eventually take personnel responsibility for a larger and probably more diverse group of companies. Her secretary, Nancy, is some seven or eight years older, divorced, with teenage children. The styles of the two women are very different. Janet was dressed in a navy tailored skirt and a ruffled cream blouse, high heels and careful make-up. She is smart and feminine, without being obsessively fashion-conscious. Nancy, a large, big-boned woman with wispy hair, was dressed in 'sensible' clothes—a simple summer sleeveless frock, flat shoes and no make-up. On the subject of feminism she jokes, 'I won't burn my bra because my boobs are too big'.

The interviews took place shortly after a management shake-up, which had sent the general manager packing and inaugurated a major restructuring. As a result, the flow of work has been much reduced. Janet says there is not enough to occupy Nancy and she is concerned to find things for her to do. This is in striking contrast to the masculine style that would create service work with no trouble at all. Tom, from the previous chapter, would no doubt have his secretary mending his socks or shopping for his favourite foods! Janet still feels uncomfortable even about being brought a cup of coffee.

Janet and Nancy have worked together for little more than a year and the relationship is still being established. The age reversal seems to make for a rather low-key relation without the pleasures or the tensions that are generated by playing out familial and narcissistic themes. Janet does not attempt to impose anything of the 'master'; Nancy might, in other circumstances, play a maternal role but this is not usually deemed appropriate where the boss is a woman. There is an absence here of the personal and family discussion that has characterised so many of the other pairs and seems to construct a relationship as 'boss—secretary'. Here it is the 'team' discourse that most structures their relationship and it begins to look simply like two people who work together. In short, Janet does not treat Nancy as a 'secretary'.

Because the relationship does not have the 'normal' structures it appears a little lukewarm. They seemed very detached from each other, and this was reinforced by spatial separation: a corridor came between their two offices. Nancy said she was 'unconcerned' that her 'boss' is a woman: 'Oh the two that I've worked for I've got on very well with. It doesn't worry me that my boss is a woman. I'd give them the same respect I would a man. No, it doesn't worry me. I suppose I've been lucky.' Nancy is a sociable person who enjoys a joke, and has on occasions had the whole office back to her place for a shared meal. Her relationship with Janet lacks the 'chemistry' that she is used to in working for men, and she has had some trouble adjusting. Her uncertainty in how to categorise the relationship is interesting. After some initial confusion about 'what she is', Nancy is beginning to enjoy the situation and to get a different kind of pleasure from it: 'I love coming to work because you never know what's going to happen...She really likes me to follow things through. She doesn't believe in just giving me piecework...I really like that. It scared me at first...' Because of the detachment she can move some distance from being a secretary and think of herself in more autonomous terms. In other companies she might be called a personnel officer. As well as typing, she organises the office, follows up memos, updates survey materials, arranges advertisements and does some interviewing for junior positions. Though Janet is struggling to find things for her to do, Nancy claims to be so busy she never even has time to have tea with the other secretarial staff. She is beginning to move away from them.

Janet tries to give Nancy research and administration but has no particular concern for her promotion. She declines the role of mother or patron and merely says, 'I'm sure she would have the potential...I couldn't answer whether she would be interested'. This may seem surprising since this was her own route up and she has expressed mildly feminist sympathies. She is critical of the company's conservative approach to women, concerned to see more women in management, and part of a network of like-minded women across the organisation. She and Nancy both see themselves as victims of misogyny. Nancy has experienced male managers as rude, if not hostile, to women like herself.

> We do have a few men in this company who don't like women to have too much education...They feel that women should know their place—a secretary's a secretary. I do have to go to them to collect information and I find this resentment coming through...I've often come back and said to Janet, this individual's so rude. And she said, oh don't worry about it...She's got more control of the situation...I probably sort of boil over. It does get to me.

She is not able to get any assistance from Janet in changing this situation. Yet they are not equally victims of it. While Janet is able to extract much better treatment for herself she does not have the authority to improve conditions for her staff. Does Nancy resent it that

Janet is not powerful enough to look after her properly or to give her recognition? While the relationship 'works' in some sense, neither derives much pleasure from it. Their pleasure derives from a wider network of interactions and from the nature of the work itself.

'Not lesbian intended'

Though sexuality and mother—daughter symbolism are central to the flow of power between women bosses and secretaries, the subject of lesbianism is taboo. The fear of lesbianism undoubtedly places limits on the expression of intimacy and affection between women. Ironically, where one or other of the women is openly lesbian, the intimacy may be less threatening because a formal barrier has been set up. Where the lesbianism is acknowledged, the possible sexual meanings behind one adult woman 'mothering' another do not have to be suppressed. A lesbian boss could be mothered without the heterosexuality of the secretary being in any way threatened. The secretary could indulge in role plays and flirtations with the 'deviant' boss. It is not that she treated her 'like a man' but that she could joke about how she *would* treat a man. Tina compares her boss with her husband—they share the same star sign. But this is a reciprocal relationship based on some two-way mothering:

> Fran is the only person...that I have really talked to about my personal life...Other bosses...don't want to know your personal life. You are there, you sit at that typewriter, you do your job, but they want to talk about their personal life, you are the sounding board...I always said I would never work for a woman...and now I think I would find it very hard not to...I have never had a person who would feed me so much.

A degree of reciprocity has also been achieved by Pat, a lesbian secretary who works for a media boss who is known to be 'difficult'. She says: 'I find it a little bit challenging to be working with a difficult woman...to manage to cope with her and learn to get on with her...you know, I wouldn't bother with a man...' They had a major row one day when Pat criticised the program:

> All hell broke out. She told me...this obviously proves one thing I've always known, you don't have any sense of humour and that I wasn't to have an opinion about anything...This was the end. I couldn't handle this. So I said, 'Now listen here...Either we sort this out or or something else has to be done...because I'm not willing to work under these circumstances'...What about me taking a stand after I'd adopted a low profile! That seemed to break the ice a bit...but...I'd thought very carefully about what I'd buy her for Christmas...she is the sort of woman who has everything...And I bought her little girl a tiny little

tutu. . .as cute as could be. And I think that was the final blow that put us on a really good basis. I put it on her desk at Christmas and she burst into tears. She was really overcome by it you know. I think the kid was her little Achilles heel. . .she said later on, you put so much thought into buying that. . .From then on we got on fine. . .

They have reached a point where it is possible to joke about each other's sexuality. The boss is curious about lesbian social life and can be teased to 'try it out'. In this way they construct a difference which in a sense marks out territory. A relationship that would have been destructively one-sided has been transformed into something much more equal by the secretary's lesbian sexuality. Far from being a handicap, lesbianism has on this occasion been empowering for her.

Carole works for a travel company and shares a secretary with her immediate boss and one or two others. She writes her letters out in longhand and, if necessary, types them herself. A bright working-class girl who has moved up through the ranks of clerical work, she is bouncy, confident and exuberant. She thinks it is 'a bit bloody pretentious' to say 'I have a secretary'. She stresses that 'we're all equals. And Julie to me is not my secretary, she's one of us'. She was one of the few women to 'come out' in the interviews. Her sexuality is part of a larrikin self-definition:

> We're not just not workmates we're all friends. . .And we talk a lot about our personal lives. . .I send up my sexuality sure. . .We have a screech and a hoot and say a few sort of gay remarks. . .I've always been able to laugh at myself. . .It breaks the ice sometimes too. If someone comes in and gives you a kiss. . .you say, it's all right, you're not going to get AIDS or anything and we laugh about it. . .I don't want them to look at me and say, oh, that one over there! Know what I'm getting at?

Carole's loudness is a way of protecting herself. She will get in ahead of other people's ridicule. The team discourse suits her both as an ex-secretary and as a means of asserting that she is accepted as a lesbian. Yet her relationship with the secretary seems to be minimal. We could hardly get a word out of Julie about any of them, certainly an indication that she did not feel 'one of us'. What was striking was the way in which Carole almost completely displaced Julie from the interview and concentrated the attention on herself. While the mother–daughter bond was absent so was any indication of friendship. She admits that Julie does not really handle her carry-on and opens up more easily to the others. The team discourse seems to have given her more sway with her colleagues and superiors than it has with the secretary.

The male secretary's power

The focus so far has been on female secretaries. What happens when the gender positions are reversed and the secretary is a man? To what extent does gender modify the kind of power that a female boss is able to exercise? Geraldine Milner is a senior manager with a large merchant bank for whom she has worked for the last fifteen years. Her main responsibilities are with advisory services and public relations. She is 41 and single. Beyond that she told us virtually nothing about her private life. Obviously she has had to struggle to get to the top, and to assert her authority in a very masculine environment: 'Maybe I'm ageing into the role. A few years ago when I used to look a lot younger, they'd say oh no, we want to speak to the senior gentleman. But that's only in the public's perception...I mean, initially when I turned up at the first few Rotary Clubs or something, they weren't too sure...but, I mean, it only lasts five minutes...as long as you know your job.' She thinks her predecessors patronised people and that, as a woman, she has made a range of financial services more accessible to people who, though otherwise well educated, have no background in the industry. 'It's probably not as big a trap when you come into the position as a young woman because you're not very convincing if you try to pull it off, so there's not much point in trying to do it. Whereas if you come in as a very well established gentleman in his 50s with greying hair, it's very easy to play the paternalistic, patronising role.' She does not attempt to become one of the boys and would seldom go to Friday night drinks. Like many women in management she is aware of the importance of her personal appearance in establishing her authority. She was wearing a pleated frock, with a high neckline, and pearls. She acknowledges she has to dress in a certain way but, unlike some of the other women, does not derive any particular pleasure from it—'I'd love to come to work the way you do'.

> When I first came to this department the senior assistant was also a girl...and we had discussions, as we were both trying to re-finance our whole image department, on whether we had to go the full American way of the standard woman in business. We both decided that no, we didn't...Things were still free enough that women weren't in moulds...and we felt we shouldn't start putting ourselves into moulds when we had the opportunity not to.

Though very aware of the problems of being a woman in a male-dominated industry, she does not think it is any big deal to have a male secretary and plays down its significance. We asked her what she thought about the common view that it would be hard for men to be in those sorts of support positions:

Rubbish! What a load...! Have they ever tried it? I mean this is it! It's crazy! I've always had men working for me and I haven't noticed any difference...I've never really expected my secretaries to get my cups of coffee or cups of tea or anything like that...if that's what they term support...I suppose some men expect their secretaries to go out and buy thir wives' birthday presents and all that sort of nonsense...I would never consider asking them to do anything other than what was required in a professional capacity

Her secretary, Raoul Wicks, is 26 and single. He was dressed in a rather crumpled looking suit. Though it fulfilled the formal dress requirements it thumbed its nose at the style we have come to associate with merchant banks. Having dropped out of a bachelor of business degree halfway through, he has had a rather chequered career as an actor and odd-jobs person. He is in this position and this industry rather accidentally, having originally contacted the bank about another clerical job. Though that had not been appropriate he had got on well at the interview and the personnel manager offered him this one which they claimed to have difficulty filling.

Geraldine stressed there was no difference between what Raoul did and what previous female secretaries had done:

I want someone who can do the basic school lectures for us. Someone who can handle the phones and preferably who knows the industry at least enough to answer a lot of the basic queries. I don't really have sufficient typing and normal things like that to warrant a full-time secretary. Raoul's here because he's studied and wants to work in the industry so it's a very good training position for someone in the long term. Another former secretary has not gone into a broker's office and is doing extremely well.

Raoul, on the other hand, is not happy about being called a secretary and goes out of his way to explain why the term is inappropriate. He says that when the job was first discussed the term secretary was never mentioned. They just said: 'I would need to do a little bit of typing...It looked like an attractive job. There's a certain amount of prestige in working for this organisation...At that point in time I couldn't type but I rapidly learned...I went and did one of those bloody student receptionist centre courses...' He stressed the ways in which his job is different from that of a secretary—and went on to give what is a very typical job description:

My job involves doing all the administration in the Department...I answer all the mail...and discern where it should go and who should answer it. If I can answer it, I answer it. I handle all the bookings for schools for our educational talks...for community organisations...and for companies. . .I also take lectures for school and community groups. I handle all the merchandising for the department. I sell all the sweatshirts. I am in charge of the accounts. . .I do the banking. . .I also take phone enquiries.

'Lecturing' to school and community groups may be a little unusual for a secretary but it is the only task that stands out. Nevertheless there had been some concern to find him an alternative title, befitting his status as a male. Geraldine, his boss, would not be a party to this. Where his strategy of power was to emphasise his difference from secretaries, hers was to assert his similarity with his female predecessors. On this occasion she won. As he describes it:

The personnel officer rang me. . .She was updating the telephone directory. . .and she said to me, oh Raoul what are we going to call you? You're not really a 'secretary' are you, you do more than that. . .how about we call you 'Information Officer'? I said that's fine, that sounds good. And she said, I'll talk to Gerry and get back to you. . .No more was said. . .and when the telephone list came out, there I was, a secretary and that was that. . .I didn't say anything to Gerry about it. I didn't feel I could.

He goes to some lengths to enlist our sympathy for his 'predicament': 'If one wants to belong to a club, particularly a men's club, there are certain do's and don'ts. There are certain mores and it therefore doesn't augur well to be a secretary. Maybe 30 years ago. . .if you had been a private secretary. . .that may have been different. . .Now if you're doing a woman's job, the implication is that you are somehow feminine. And femininity has no place in a men's club.' He gets a lot of flack from young girls who think he is not a proper man. And if that is not bad enough,

An old retired bloke comes in regularly to relive the old days. . .The other morning he came in. He stopped and he looked at me and I was typing. And I was aware that he was looking at me. . .and he said, what's your name Miss? And I looked at him and said, it's Jacqueline actually! He didn't get it. He just sort of grunted and walked off.

I don't object to having overtones of femininity. I mean, everyone's got their yin and their yang. But the implication in a male-dominated society, and particularly in the last bastion of male domination. . .is that femininity is associated with homosexuality which is a taboo. . .which conjures up all sorts of nasty images. So that's what I cope with every day.

Yet what comes across is the power that this man is able to exercise. Frequently when I interviewed pairs, the boss was loquacious and open, the secretary more guarded. On this occasion, the boss restricts her range of comments, while the secretary talks freely, explicitly and quite personally about her. I did not meet a single female secretary who talked in quite this way about a boss, male or female. On this occasion gender quite clearly over-rides formal position in determining what can be said. Thus he comments:

> I think she's perceived as a hard arse. But I think she's had to be a hard arse to get where she's got to. I also think she's perceived as pretty neurotic and I do know that she has a nickname around here.
>
> She gets bad-mouthed a lot behind her back. I have to be careful as there may be times when I agree with what people are saying. I have found myself slip on a couple of occasions and say, yes, you're right...or reinforce their prejudices rather than just taking a neutral stance.
>
> Yes she's perceived as being hard and tough, particularly with women. She's tougher on women than she is on men...So I think...you know, jobs for the boys doesn't necessarily operate with jobs for the girls.

He talks at length about the way in which Gerry exercises power over him. As he talks it becomes clear that the flow of power between them fluctuates very much more than is the case with female secretaries and either male or female bosses. He thinks she's got 'very definite limits and very definite boundaries that cannot be overstepped', but seems to delight in playing games with them. On one occasion she asserts her authority because he has forgotten to leave her a message. His comeback is, first, that only a woman would be concerned with such 'trivia'—dismissing the possibility that it may have been important to make every effort to return the call. Second, he implies, it is because he is a man that she has to bother asserting herself in this way at all: 'I think she expects that she doesn't have to exert any authority with women. I mean someone who has authority doesn't feel the need to display it...With women I don't think she feels the need to display it. But with men she does have a need to display it.' Raoul continues in this vein, ostensibly describing her power and his subordination, but actually imposing his own power in the situation and reducing hers through stereotyping her—first as a dragon and then as typical neurotic woman. 'The male bosses I have had are more even. They're less prone to ups and downs. With my boss at the moment...I leave her alone for at least a good hour. I've learned that now. Leave her alone till half past ten and probably it'll be OK. But as soon as she walks in the door, the first thing I have to do is sum her up...and see what kind of mood she's in.'

It is hardly unusual for secretaries to suss out their bosses' moods and adjust their behaviour accordingly. But he turns this into a kind of reverse power base. He concedes that men's moods fluctuate too: '...but I don't think it's as visible...That's kind of more dangerous because they're actually prone to exploding on you without any warning whereas with Gerry I've got a pretty fair idea in advance.' He claims the power to read her accurately, literally placing her via a detailed description of her clothes. " female secretary would *never* say this of her boss:

> I can tell a lot from the way she's dressed...There was one dress that has a very high collar...it's quite rigid...and it's pleated all the way down...I know that she's in a very no-nonsense mood when I see that dress...Like today we've got work to do...She has a little crimson suit and that's another no-nonsense outfit. But it says...I'm more available today. I'm more open. I will probably be meeting executives or important VIPs...There is another dress that has a split up the centre and that has its own connotations. And that's usually when she's far more relaxed. The perfume she wears tells me how she feels that day too. So I try to sum those things up.

While Geraldine denies that the gender of her secretary makes any difference, Raoul thinks she's very aware of having a male secretary. Unlike female secretaries, he is quite happy to talk about sexual fantasies and interactions, assuming that he has control. 'I can imagine having an affair with Gerry. But I can't imagine having an affair with Gerry and working here because I just think it would just alter the relationship entirely and it would become untenable for her and for me.' He thinks in the first few weeks in the job there *was* a kind of sexual attraction going on. Whether the attraction was mutual or his fantasy we do not known, but *he* curtailed it. As if to have the last word he says: 'I've never told her when I'm pissed off, never. I think that would be to take advantage of the relationship between the sexes, so I don't. Because I couldn't do it with a man. I couldn't go to a man and say, look, what you have just done really annoys me, or the way you've spoken to me really annoys me.'

In other words, he believes he *could* take advantage of male power, but claims he does not. The implication is that she depends on his gallantry and cooperation. Remembering his unease at being called a secretary, he has had to turn the situation round in fantasy, and to some extent in practice, to make it acceptable to his masculine ego. Geraldine's counter-strategy is to deny that his masculinity has any relevance to the situation and to try to ensure that it brings him no extra privileges. The louder the denial, the clearer it is that gender does matter.

Continuums and boundaries

The normative boss—secretary relationship involves a male boss and a female secretary. When the gender of either is changed the relationship is very considerably transformed. A male secretary is, on the basis of his gender, frequently able to take the subject position in relation to a female boss. While women exercise power as bosses, the strategies open to them are both different from those open to the men and more fragile.

They have to differentiate themselves from secretaries to establish their credibility as managers. It used to be thought they had but two choices. Either they can desexualise themselves and become 'honorary men' (the 'beige suit syndrome') or they can stay within femininity and be disempowered. Women are beginning to cultivate a number of distinctively feminine styles based on a celebration of their difference from men and often depending on class images for their authority. Gillian and Susan are good examples. And yet their power over secretaries is based on what they have in common as women. While this works to the advantage of boss rather than secretary, it may also provide the basis for the transformation of the boss—secretary relationship. Women bosses are likely to be more sensitive in the demands they make of secretaries, less likely to demand personal services. The very fact that they cannot offer the protection and patronage of a male boss may be an impetus towards independence and assertiveness on the part of the secretary. Moreover, the secretary may be able to adopt the same strategies of power as her boss. She too can adopt mother—daughter relations, and mirror games, to her advantage; she too can construct more assertive models of femininity. The relationship may be oppressive but it also affords the possibility of mutual recognition that is so difficult to achieve in our polarised gender relations. In their relationships with each other women may be able to find a balance between autonomy and connectedness. Where the boss is a woman, both the master—slave and mother—child discourses may give way to the team discourse and to a much more equal relationship.

•4• Sexuality at work

Sex is like paperclips in the office: commonplace,
useful, underestimated, ubiquitous. Hardly
appreciated until it goes wrong, it is the cement in
every working relationship. It has little to do with
sweating bosses cuddling their secretaries behind
closed doors—though lots of that goes on. It is more
adult, more complicated, more of a weapon.

BRENDA JONES, NT, DECEMBER 1972

. . . women are constantly and inescapably
constructed *as women*. . . Men are sustained at the
centre of the stage precisely because they can be
'people' and do not have to represent their
masculinity to themselves. They. . . can never be
displaced from the centre until they can be forced to
recognise themselves as men and to take
responsibility for this.

BLACK AND COWARD, 1981: 85

If the boss—secretary relation is organised around sexuality and
family imagery this seems to place it outside the modern bureaucratic structures that are a feature of all large organisations. The
relationship is often conceptualised either as archaic or as marginal to the workings of bureaucracy 'proper'. It is argued here
that, on the contrary, the boss—secretary relationship is the most
visible aspect of a pattern of domination based on desire and
sexuality. Far from being an exception, it vividly illustrates the
workings of modern bureaucracies. Gender and sexuality are
central not only in the boss—secretary relation but in *all* workplace
power relations.

Two bodies of theory are important to the development of this
argument. A variety of feminist analyses, particularly of sexual
harassment, indicate the ubiquity of *coercive* sexual encounters in
the workplace; and theorists such as Marcuse and Foucault have
indicated, in their different ways, the connections between sexual
pleasure and the operations of power. By contrast, most organisation theory continues to treat sexuality and gender as marginal
or incidental to the workplace. In doing so, however, it expresses
a widely held view that while gender was central to 'traditional'

social relations it has become outmoded in 'modern' society which is more concerned with 'personhood'. Since degendering is implicit in the modernist emphasis on rationality and in the development of liberal democratic institutions, it is important to start by considering the ways in which gender is suppressed in the main texts.

For Weber bureaucracy is progressive in that it breaks down the old patriarchal structures and removes the arbitrary power held by fathers and masters in traditional society. He distinguishes between traditionalism, which is patriarchal, and the rational-legal order of the modern world which promises the end of tyranny and despotism and the development of liberal democracy. All attempts to theorise bureaucracy have been carried out in the shadow of Weber's classical account. He still sets the terms of the dominant frameworks for studies of power and organisations. Although the limits of his theory have been clearly shown in more than half a century of organisation studies, Weber's version retains a powerful ideological hold. People's views of how organisations actually do work and how they 'ought' to work are still filtered through Weber and the theory becomes, in some sense, a self-fulfilling prophecy.

Weber has been given a favourable reading by liberal feminists because he does appear to provide a basis for understanding the breakdown of patriarchal relations. Equal Employment Opportunity and Affirmative Action plans, for example, emphasise the importance of excluding 'private' considerations and insist on the impersonal application of rules. Secretaries, it is thought, should ignore or reject the sexual and familial images and focus on skills and career ladders. The implication here is that secretarial work should be 'rationalised', made to fit the bureaucratic pattern. In her broadly liberal feminist analysis, *Men and Women of the Corporation*, Rosabeth Moss Kanter denies that gender or sexuality have much explanatory potential. She observes that 'what look like sex differences may really be power differences' and that 'power wipes out sex' (1977: 201–12). In this framework the problem for secretaries is that they lack power; they are caught up in an old-fashioned patriarchal relationship that is out of kilter with 'modern' business practices. The question then becomes how can individual secretaries remove themselves from these backwaters and place themselves on the management ladder? Kanter's very lucid analysis of the power structure is designed to help individuals articulate their positions and thereby improve their own manoeuvring for power.

It is not surprising that Weber should have had such influence for he is one of the great spokespersons of 'modernity'. Thinkers of his stature are not easily 'overturned'. Even theorists who take a critical stance, or who self-consciously define themselves as 'post-modern', find themselves returning to at least some of the 'mod-ernist' assumptions. Kanter herself was explicitly rejecting the Weberian emphasis on the rationality and goal-directedness of bureaucracies, yet by playing down gender and sexuality she eventually returned to that which she had criticised. Whatever modifications or even radical revisions are made to the theory it retains a core of 'truth' which makes it difficult to move outside it. This 'core' needs to be deconstructed if gender and sexuality are to be made central to the analysis of the workplace. While 'mod-ernist' analyses and bureaucratic structures offer certain gains for women they are not, in fact, gender-neutral and may in fact represent a subtler and hence more stable version of male domi-nation than the earlier models. Feminist and 'post-modern' criti-ques are therefore very important in informing political and workplace strategies.

According to Weber the overriding concerns of bureaucratic organisations are efficiency and consistency in the application of rules. Authority established by rules stands in contrast to the 'regulation of relationships through individual privilege and be-stowals of favour' which characterises patrimonialism. Traditional forms of domination are based on the household unit and are patriarchal in the direct sense that the father, as head of the family, possesses authority. In larger forms of traditional organis-ation authority is patrimonial, that is, it takes the form of personal allegiance to the master. In bureaucracy, by contrast, loyalty is to an office not to a particular person. Impersonality and the separ-ation of the public and private spheres distinguish bureaucracy from traditionalism. As theorised by Weber, bureaucracy 'has a "rational" character: rules, means, ends, and matter-of-factness dominate its bearing...The march of bureaucracy has destroyed structures of domination which had no rational character, in the special sense of the term' (Gerth & Mills, 1958: 244).

According to Weber's 'ideal type', bureaucracies are based on impersonality, functional specialisation, a hierarchy of authority and the impartial application of rules. There are well-defined duties for each specialised position and recruitment takes place on criteria of demonstrated knowledge and competence. Authority is held in the context of strict rules and regulations and graded hierarchically with the supervision of lower offices by higher ones. Authority established by rules stands in contrast to the 'regulation of relationships through individual privileges and bestowals of favour' which characterised traditional structures. Above all there is a separation of the public world of rationality and efficiency from the private sphere of emotional and personal life.

The boss—secretary relationship runs against every one of these criteria. By having direct access to the powerful, secretaries are outside the hierarchy of authority. Far from being specialised, they can be called upon to do just about anything, and their work may overlap with that of their bosses. The relationship is based on personal rapport, involves a degree of intimacy, day-to-day familiarity and shared secrets unusual for any but lovers or close friends, and is capable of generating intense feelings of loyalty, dependency and personal commitment. How are we to explain this least 'bureaucratic' of relationships? Is it merely an exception or does its existence suggest problems with the way bureaucracy itself has been theorised?

Organisation theorists argue that Weber's 'ideal type' was never intended to have any empirical existence and that other kinds of relationship can coexist within bureaucracies. The boss—secretary relationship may thus be explained as a kind of pre-bureaucratic relic. Kanter portrays it as 'the most striking instance of the retention of patrimony within the bureaucracy' (1977: 73). It is patrimonial in that 'bosses make demands at their own discretion and arbitrarily; choose secretaries on grounds that enhance their own personal status rather than meeting organisational efficiency tests; expect personal services with limits negotiated privately; exact loyalty and make the secretary a part of their private retinue, moving when they move...' This begs the question of why bureaucracy would retain a relationship that appears to be 'irrational' and 'inefficient'. Theorists of bureaucracy have long recognised that the personal intrudes into the workplace all the time; even that it is necessary to have an informal arrangement alongside the formal structure to motivate people and to make things actually work. It is acknowledged that, far from being a limitation on bureaucracy, informal relations and unofficial practices actually contribute to efficient operations (Blau & Myer, 1958: 25). The 'human relations' theorists of the 1920s and 30s showed that people want more from their work than just pay and that the existence of cohesive bonds between co-workers is a prerequisite for high morale and optimum performance (Rose, 1975, Part 3).

In these accounts the existence of 'the personal' in the workplace is seen as consistent with bureaucratic organisation and even as supportive of it. While the human-relations theorists added an informal dimension, they did not challenge the theorising of the formal bureaucratic structures. In some ways they reinforced the idea of managerial rationality: while *workers* might be controlled by sentiment and emotion, *managers* were supposed to be rational, logical and able to control their emotions. The division between reason and emotion was tightened in a way that marked off managers from the rest. Where the secretary might have been

seen as a source of order in the office, she too came to be positioned as the bearer of sexuality and emotion, while the boss was
represented as cool and rational. The successful manager was the
'man' who could control his emotions, and women were perceived
as 'temperamentally unfit' for management because they were too
emotional (Kanter, 1975: 46–47). In making these assumptions
explicit, Kanter opened up the potential for making sexuality and
gender central to the analysis. Instead she veered away. She
concentrated her critique on the 'rational bias' itself rather than
on the ways in which the 'discourse' on rationality has operated to
maintain male domination and exclude women. While rejecting
much of Weber she was committed to the degendering strategies
of liberal feminism and sought to explain differences between
men and women in terms other than sex or gender. While drawing
attention to the existence of separate organisational classes and
internal labour markets, she overlooked the appearance of *new*
forms of power and control based around the construction of
sexuality.

Kanter, and other critics of Weber, argue that instead of thinking of one 'ideal type' of organisation as characteristically modern
it is useful to consider a range of different types. Part of the
problem is the attribution of goals or purposes to the organisation.
This avoids the issue of the specific and possibly conflicting interests of the individuals or groups who are the actors in organisational settings. Silverman (1970) suggests that the 'structures' of
organisations are a good deal less solid and permanent than is
often suggested; that they should be seen as the transient outcomes
of the actions and interactions of individuals and groups pursuing
their own ends with whatever resources are available to them.
This shifts the analysis away from the relation between formal
and informal structures and opens up new ways of understanding
power relations in organisations.

It remains important to analyse the discourse of 'bureaucratic
rationality' as it affects men and women. This involves not so
much a rejection of Weber as a rereading designed to bring out
the underlying assumptions. It can be argued that while the
rational–legal or bureaucratic form presents itself as gender-
neutral, it actually constitutes a new kind of patriarchal structure.
The apparent neutrality of rules and goals disguises the class and
gender interests served by them. Weber's account of 'rationality'
can be interpreted as a commentary on the construction of a
particular kind of masculinity based on the exclusion of the personal, the sexual and the feminine from any definition of 'rationality'. The values of instrumental rationality are strongly associated
with the masculine individual, while the feminine is associated
with that 'other' world of chaos and disorder. This does not mean

that men are in fact 'rational' or that women are 'emotional' but rather that they learn to recognise themselves in these conceptions.

Erotic bureaucracies

It may be argued that 'rationality' requires as a condition of its existence the simultaneous creation of a realm of the Other, be it personal, emotional, sexual or 'irrational'. Masculine rationality attempts to drive out the feminine but does not exist without it. 'Work' and 'sex' are implicitly treated as the domains of the 'conscious' and the 'unconscious'. But far from being separate spheres the two are thoroughly intertwined. Despite the illusion of ordered rationality, workplaces do not actually manage to exclude the personal or sexual. Rather than seeing the presence of sexuality and familial relations in the workplace as an aspect of traditional, patriarchal authority, it makes more sense to treat them as part of modern organisational forms. I am concerned here not with 'actual' families but with the family symbolism that structures work as well as personal relationships. The media, advertising and popular culture are saturated in such imagery, which provides a dominant set of social meanings in contemporary capitalist society.

The gist of structuralist and post-structuralist work is that there is no unitary human consciousness and that 'identity' itself is a precarious achievement, constantly undermined by the repressed wishes which constitute the unconscious. It is the claim of psychoanalysis that conscious intentions are only a tiny part of our being and that the unconscious and its investments have to be investigated. A theory of the subject thus requires a theory of the unconscious. 'Subjectivity is formed as individuals become aware of their alienation from themselves, in the pre-oedipal imaginary realm which always remains with them; and then as through the oedipal process, individuals become aware of the structures of human sexuality which they acquire through the acquisition of language' (Weeks, 1985: 171). The 'I' comes about only through the 'discourse of the other', that is to say, through practices of signification. We are all subject to the laws of language and our task in childhood is to insert ourselves into that order so that we may secure a place from which to speak. Since the symbolic order is patriarchal, girls and boys, it is argued, enter it differently. In particular, they have to become aware of the presence or absence of the phallus, the signifier, in our culture, of sexual difference and of power.

Different schools of psychoanalysis have different ways of conceptualising gender identity. The object relations school, as represented by Nancy Chodorow (1978) stresses the identification with real people in the formation of different types of self, masculine and feminine, the one autonomous and the other relational. The structuralists, represented by Juliet Mitchell (1975) place less emphasis on the ego but also stress the formation of a core gender identity. In this approach women are constructed as 'non-men', making a 'negative entry into culture'. Recent post-structuralist readings of Lacan have a more fluid conception of sexual difference and gendered subjectivity. Jacqueline Rose, for example, argues that 'if psychoanalysis can give an account of how women experience the path to femininity, it also insists, through the concept of the unconscious, that femininity is neither simply rational—legal or bureaucratic form presents itself as gender-unified but diverse, fragmented and contradictory.

If we accept that a series of discourses on sexuality underpin bureaucratic control it is possible to see secretaries not as marginal but as paradigmatic of how that power operates. Thus the boss—secretary relation, need not be seen as an anomalous piece of traditionalism or of an incursion of the private sphere, but rather a site of strategies of power in which sexuality is an important though by no means the only dimension. Far from being marginal to the workplace, sexuality is everywhere. It is alluded to in dress and self-presentation, in jokes and gossip, looks and flirtations, secret affairs and dalliances, in fantasy, and in the range of coercive behaviours that we now call sexual harassment. Rather than being exceptional in its sexualisation, the boss—secretary relation is an important nodal point for the organisation of sexuality and pleasure. This is no less true when the boss happens to be a woman.

Sex at work is very much on display. It is undoubtedly true that for both men and women sexual fantasies and interactions are a way of killing time, of giving a sense of adventure, of livening up an otherwise boring day. As Michael Korda put it, 'the amount of sexual energy circulating in any office is awe-inspiring, and given the slightest sanction and opportunity it bursts out' (1972: 108). Marcuse was one of the first to recognise the pervasiveness of sexuality in the workplace and to try to theorise it. He recognised that it was not just an instance of incomplete repression but was encouraged as a means of gratification in otherwise boring jobs. If open-plan offices are about surveillance they are also, he suggests, about controlled sex.

Marcuse introduced the concept of 'repressive desublimation' to explain how people were being integrated into a system which in its sweeping rationality, which propels efficiency and growth, is itself irrational (1968: 12). He pointed to the ways in which,

> without ceasing to be an instrument of labour, the body is allowed to exhibit its sexual features in the everyday work world and in work

relations...The sexy office and sales girls, the handsome, virile junior executive and floor worker are highly marketable commodities, and the possession of suitable mistresses...facilitates the career of even the less exalted ranks in the business community...Sex is integrated into work and public relations and is thus made susceptible to (controlled) satisfaction...But no matter how controlled...it is also gratifying to the managed individuals...Pleasure, thus adjusted, generates submission (1968: 70−71).

In Foucault's account, sexuality in the workplace is not simply repressed or sublimated or subjected to controlled expression. It is actively produced in a multiplicity of discourses and interactions. Modern Western societies have accumulated a vast network of discourses on sex and pleasure. We expect to find pleasure in self-improvement in both our work and non-work activities. Purposive activity operates not through the denial of pleasure but its promise: we will become desirable.

Foucault is concerned with the processes by which individuals come to think of themselves as 'sexual subjects'. Sex has become not merely another object of knowledge but the basis of 'identity'. The greater the valorisation of the individual as the ideal subject, the greater the demand for techniques of individual training and retraining. The emphasis on individual choice is consonant with the maximising of disciplinary controls. 'Controls' operate not to repress but to prolong, intensify and refine the possibilities of pleasure: 'Pleasure and power do not cancel or turn back against one another; they seek out, overlap, reinforce one another. They are linked together by complex mechanisms and devices of excitation and incitement (Foucault, 1980: 48).' This may not be as far from Weber as it at first seems. Where Weber treated sex as 'irrational' Foucault looks at the ways in which sex came under the control of 'sexuality' operating through techniques of power. For Foucault power relations are always rational in the sense that they are 'imbued, through and through, with calculation' (1980: 95) and they follow a series of aims and objectives. Both see rational-isation as characteristic of modern life; but whereas Weber (and Marcuse) see it as a global historical process, and one based on a distinction between public and private, Foucault is concerned with specific rationalities that cut across the public/private division. For Weber and Marcuse the dominance of instrumental reason was a general process to which the whole society was assumed to be uniformly and inexorably subject. Where they are pessimistic about the future Foucault finds some grounds for optimism in the fact that resistance is ever present. While this may mean that resistance is merely an inherent part of the exercise of power it must also create the possibility of displacing that power. People are never just victims but free subjects faced with choices and real alternatives.

The dual possibilities of 'resistance' make it appealing for considering the situation of secretaries. Secretaries have been represented as sellouts, as victims, stooges of management, or alternatively as the potential bearers of a proletarian consciousness based on their deskilling and reduction in status. Rather than simply placing them on one side or the other, Foucault's analysis suggests a more fluid and confused situation:

> Instead there is a plurality of resistances, each of them a special case: resistances that are possible, necessary, improbable; others that are spontaneous, savage, solitary, concerted, rampant, or violent; still others that are quick to compromise, interested, or sacrificial...the points, knots, or focuses of resistance are spread over time and space at varying densities, at times mobilizing groups or individuals in a definitive way, inflaming certain points of the body, certain moments in life, certain types of behaviour...(1980: 96)

Far from being victims secretaries necessarily engage in resistance. This does not mean that they constitute a revolutionary group but neither are they totally inscribed within existing power relations.

The difficulty with both Marcuse and Foucault is that they are gender-blind. While they establish the centrality of sexuality in the workplace they pay very little attention to gender. Marcuse presumes that men and women are equally and similarly oppressed, ignoring the ways that women are required to market sexual attractiveness to men. Foucault acknowledges gender struggles but does not afford them any priority or permanence. Central to his work is the idea that there is no constant human subject or any rational course to history. If there is no human subject then for Foucault there is no gendered subject. Feminist struggles are, like any others, merely immediate responses to local and specific situations. Foucault's account of power is counterposed to any binary opposition between rulers and ruled. Though he underplays the significance of gender he does provide the basis for developing a more dynamic and fluid conception of power relations between men and women. 'Male power' is not simply and unilaterally imposed on women—gender relations are a process involving strategies and counter-strategies of power.

Harassing sex?

Where organisation theorists have maintained a division between sex and work, women are left in little doubt that the two go together. Women are constantly aware of sexual power structures and the need to put up barriers against men. Though they might enjoy male company and male jokes they are careful to limit their participation and to make it clear to men 'how far they can go'. Many secretaries have chosen their current jobs on the basis of minimising any further experiences of sexual harassment. One head office, nicknamed the 'twenty five year club' because of the length of time most of the managers had been there, was regarded as something of refuge. If there was no sexual excitement on the sixteenth floor, at least there was no danger.

The term 'sexual harassment' came into the language around 1976 and was quickly taken up as a dimension of gender inequality at work. Mackinnon argued that 'intimate violation of women by men is sufficiently pervasive...as to be nearly invisible. Contained by internalized and structural forms of power, it has been nearly inaudible...Tacitly, it has been both acceptable and taboo; acceptable for men to do, taboo for women to confront, even to themselves' (1979: 1). In the 1980s it became possible in Australia to bring sexual harassment cases under anti-discrimination legislation.

Sexual harassment has often been dismissed either as trivial and isolated or as referring to universal 'natural' behaviours. Secretaries who discussed it in the interviews tended to feel that they are responsible for controlling men's behaviour, that women should be able to deal with unwanted advances and preferably avoid getting into the situation in the first place. Yet a number of them had experienced sexual harassment and had even left jobs because of it. Feminists have insisted that sexual harassment is not only an individual problem but part of an organised expression of male power. Sexual harassment functions particularly to keep women out of non-traditional occupations and to reinforce their secondary status in the workplace.

The most claustrophobic example of control through sexuality (no one had yet labelled it 'harassment') concerns a legal practice which was, for a country town, quite large. The atmosphere was one of compulsory jocularity: solicitors and secretaries gaily exchanged insults and sexual banter with each other all day, and there was a great deal of friendly fondling and patting of bottoms. They also intermarried and had a shared social life of parties and barbeques. Ex-secretaries with their babies were regular visitors, and often came back to work on a part-time or temporary basis. Beneath the enforced egalitarianism and informality there was a rigidly enforced sexual division of labour. The partners could not imagine taking on a woman lawyer or the possibility that any of the 'girls' might have the capacity to do law—even though one of them boasted that he had got through the Leaving Certificate with five Bs and depended heavily on his more literate secretary to conduct his correspondence. The women were clear that their role was to service men and were willing to put up with what was constant sexual innuendo. The overall feel of the place was not dissimilar to a brothel. While the secretaries made continuous use of mockery and parody, it seemed only to reaffirm them in 'traditional' boss—secretary relationships.

Gutek and Dunwoody (1987) cite a lot of evidence that even non-harassing sexual behaviour has negative consequences for women. The office affair, particularly if it is with a supervisor, can have detrimental effects on a woman's credibility as well as her career. Many women report that they are not flattered by sexual overtures at work and experience even complimentary remarks as insulting. They would prefer to avoid all sexual interactions at work. Men, on the other hand, report virtually no work-related consequences of sexual behaviour and, if anything, are flattered by sexual overtures from women. While it is generally assumed that men are more sexually active than women, the cluster of characteristics usually associated with the male personality do not include a sexual component! Men can behave in a blatantly sexual way without it being identified. Playboys and harassers go largely unnoticed because 'organisational man', goal-oriented, rational, competitive, is not perceived in explicitly sexual terms. It is ironic that women are perceived as using sex to their advantage. They are much less likely to initiate sexual encounters and more likely to be hurt by sex at work.

Hearn and Parkin have pointed to the ways in which male managers use sexuality, harassment, joking and abuse as routine means of maintaining authority. This may be embedded in the taken-for-granted culture of the organisation (1987: 93). They also suggest that harassment can be interpreted as men's attempt to create some human contact as part of, or in reaction to, alienated working conditions. It may then be seen as 'a form of labour in which women become commodities for men, as a "reserve of sexual labour" ' (1987: 85).

The sexual division of labour is mediated by gender constructions that in numerous aspects bear on sexuality. Rich's notion of 'compulsory heterosexuality' (1983) can be applied here, for the sexual 'normality' of daily life in the office is relentlessly heterosexual. The norm is reproduced in concrete social practices ranging from managerial policies through to everyday informal conversations (Hearn and Parkin, 1987: 94—95). It involves the domination of men's heterosexuality over women's heterosexuality and the subordination of all other forms of sexuality. It was striking how few homosexuals, either bosses or secretaries, we turned up via our workplace visits, though we attempted to give cues that it was 'safe' to talk about the subject. Those who identified as homosexual were nearly all volunteers who had been contacted via 'non-work' channels. Few of them were 'out' at work in any more than a limited way. Those who were tended to be in 'creative' areas where it was acceptable, or they were treated by the rest of the office as the tame pervert. The only secretary who was completely open about her lesbianism was a woman who had been married and had children and could thus claim to have paid her dues to 'normality'. She said, 'I think I'm good PR for lesbians...because I'm so bloody ordinary. You know, I've been married, I've had children, I own a house, I own a car. I'm Ms Middleclass Suburbia!' Another secretary told me that she deliberately chose temporary work so that she could move on before having to face the chit-chat over morning tea about private life.

In naming and theorising sexual harassment feminists have drawn attention to the centrality of sexuality in workplace organisation. However, they have largely restricted sexuality to its coercive or unpleasurable dimensions. Radical feminists have emphasised sexual aggression and violence as the basis of men's power. If women experience pleasure it is treated as 'coerced caring' (Mackinnon, 1979: 54−55). In these accounts either virtually all heterosexual activity may be labelled as sexual harassment or a line has to be drawn between what is harassment and what is 'acceptable'. The identification of some activities as 'sexual harassment' may legitimate and obscure other forms of male power. But men control women not only through rape or through forcing them to do what they do not want to do, but through definitions of pleasure and selfhood. Control through pleasure may be more effective in that it is much less likely to provoke resistance than control through coercion.

At this point the argument becomes complicated for it is not clear where 'male power' begins and ends, whether women are in all cases 'victims' or whether they too can exercise sexual power. It is by no means certain that women are yanked screaming into 'compulsory heterosexuality'. Most actively seek it out and find pleasure in it. It is hard to know what a 'free' choice would be. Rich seems to assume some underlying bond with the mother that would be free to develop, flowing into 'lesbian continuum'. But women may choose heterosexuality precisely to get away from the constraints of the mother−daughter relationship and because it does give them access to masculine power. If mothers were not held uniquely responsible for childcare the intensity and ambivalence of the mother−daughter bond may actually lessen. It is less likely that we would experience pressure to 'choose' between heterosexuality and homosexuality or that 'lesbian continuum' would be set up in contrast to 'compulsory heterosexuality'. We may see a construction of sexuality that did not favour men over women, heterosexuality over homosexuality, intercourse over other sexual acts.

While it has opened up discussion of sexuality and power in the workplace, sexual harassment is not an adequate way of conceptualising the issues. It is not sufficient merely to assert that secretaries are workers (as much feminist literature has done) and that sexuality and femininity have no place at work. There is an important additional step of deconstructing the boss—secretary relationship and analysing the place of gender and sexuality in workplace organisation. Opposition to sexual harassment is only one component of a sexual politics in the workplace. It needs to be supplemented with analyses of the ways in which sexual pleasure might be used to disrupt male rationality and to empower women. Merely to attempt to drive sexuality from the workplace leaves the ideology of separate spheres effectively unchallenged.

Strategic dilemmas

Foucauldian analyses situate 'bureaucratic rationality' in a larger context of discursive strategies in which sexuality and pleasure become central to the operations of power. In doing so they challenge the liberal and modernising assumptions behind organisation theory as it has developed since Weber. However, they have little to say specifically about gender and tend to deny any fundamental antagonisms between men and women. Feminist analyses, on the other hand, emphasise the existence of gendered sexuality in the workplace. Whether sexual interactions in the workplace are coercive or voluntary, pleasurable or unpleasurable, they are seen as disadvantageous to women. Feminists thus appear to throw in their lot with neo-Weberian approaches in which sex is seen as an unwelcome invader which should be pushed out of the workplace. Feminist and Foucauldian approaches sit uneasily together and at many points contradict each other. They have different priorities and different understandings of power. Yet both offer important insights about the situation of secretaries and, by implication, all women in the workplace. While it would be premature, and perhaps undesirable, to try and integrate the two frameworks, it is necessary to keep them in some kind of tension.

What I have alluded to as 'modernism' covers a range of approaches that either deny the centrality of class, gender or sexuality or displace them. It includes technocratic, liberal or 'progressive' tendencies within capitalism as well as Marxist, feminist and other radical strands which are committed to the completion of the 'modernist' project through the transformation of the capitalist system. Most political conflict takes place within these parameters and it may seem surprising to have bracketed together movements and ideologies that are usually counterposed. When it comes to bosses and secretaries, they share some blind spots.

New technology is often represented as marking the end of the special relation between boss and secretary. Management consultants, employers, journalists and particularly computer retailers argue that in the new paperless office secretaries will either be redundant or transformed into all-round communications workers with sophisticated computer skills. Automation will break down 'traditional' relationships, removing the 'drudgery', and offering secretaries new opportunities. Marxist accounts are less sanguine but they too predict the end of the 'traditional' secretary. They concede that a small proportion of the workforce is becoming 'hyperskilled' but consider the vast majority are headed for proletarianisation or unemployment. The 'sexy secretary' with her 'bourgeois' pretensions is here overtaken by the *proletarian* figure experiencing similar conditions to those of factory workers. Her gender is subordinated to her changing class position. She loses control of her own work processes and becomes subject to time and motion studies. As the work becomes deskilled and routinised, health problems emerge that were once more typical of the factory than the office. In this account, secretaries disappear into the broader category of office workers, part of a new working class.

Feminists have taken up and extended both the liberal and marxist analyses. Liberal feminists are optimistic about the possibilities for secretaries to move into the management hierarchy and point out that far from being unemployed, secretaries are in short supply (Porat and Will, 1983). Marxist feminists find themselves in a dilemma. Capitalist relations are seen to break down the old 'feudal' elements of the boss–secretary relationship while increasing exploitation. In their accounts 'secretary' disappears into that amorphous category of 'woman office worker'. What is most specific to her definition in other discourses, her sexuality and femininity, is deliberately ignored. It is easier to deal with the tangibles of health hazards, wage rates and unemployment.

Though the above approaches differ in significant ways all represent the boss–secretary relation as an archaic remnant of 'traditional' society that will be swept away by the extension of the bureaucratic model to all aspects of workplace organisation. They view sex in the workplace as at best frivolous and time-wasting and potentially at least a form of harassment. 'Modernisation' involves the application of a single, rational and objective standard to everyone. Sex discrimination legislation, equal employment opportunity and affirmative action programs may be seen as a logical extension and application of 'modernist' principles. Feminists of all kinds have supported such programs. Whatever their limits, their presence signals a whole new climate. 'Modernism' has become the official, though not necessarily the dominant discourse.

Most Australian states have had sex discrimination legislation since the late 1970s. New South Wales and some other states have also had equal employment opportunity (EEO) programs since 1980. These applied to government departments and public corporations, requiring them to draw up a management plan of action to overcome 'systemic' discrimination. Some private companies voluntarily set up similar programs. The Hawke Labor government passed a national Sex Discrimination Act in 1984. It had intended to include affirmative action with this legislation but this policy was sufficiently controversial for the government to decide to delay. Instead it set up a 'pilot' program involving some 25 companies and tertiary institutions. Each was to conduct research into patterns of discrimination in their workplace and come up with proposals for ending it. Most of the interviews were conducted during the period of this scheme (1985–87) and a number of companies visited were participating in the pilot. National affirmative action legislation finally became operational in March 1987 and applies to all companies with a staff or more than 100 (Ronalds, 1987). The legislation avoids any notion of 'positive discrimination', or the imposition of 'quotas' of women or minority groups. Instead it involves setting broad targets and establishing guidelines. Unlike the United States, the penalties for non-compliance are fairly nominal and implementation depends largely on the willingness of organisations to cooperate. Being 'named in parliament' is assumed to function as a deterrent.

Liberals hope that such programs will remove the last vestiges of inequality and discrimination and open up the career hierarchy to ability regardless of gender. For socialist and radical feminists they are but one starting point, and not necessarily the most important one, for addressing the structural inequalities at the heart of 'capitalist patriarchy'. They point out that the benefits are so far restricted to business and professional women who are already competing, albeit at some disadvantage, with men. These programs do not as yet direct much attention to the secretarial and clerical, sales and service jobs in which most women work. In the face of such criticisms, the attitude of organisations to secretaries has become something of a litmus test of their sincerity with regard to affirmative action. Some companies have begun to explore ways in which career opportunities might be opened up to secretaries and in a few cases set up senior secretaries' groups. Publicly at least they are obliged to treat secretaries with greater respect than they have done in the past. It remains to be seen whether these moves are any more than token.

By the time affirmative action legislation was passed and machinery set up to implement it nationally, many feminists had become disillusioned with it. At the 1987 socialist feminist conference in Sydney, women argued that it is token, that it sidetracks feminists from other demands and threatens to bury feminist politics under a mound of paperwork. Affirmative action operates in the public sphere and is not easily adapted to working on the public−private relation. Domestic problems, particularly lack of adequate childcare, have been largely excluded from liberal discourse even though they probably provide the greatest stumbling block to secretaries who wish to take up extra training or move into management. It remains to be seen whether the framework can be used as as a basis from which to push for further change. While some feminists (e.g. Eisenstein, 1986) argue that it can be used to challenge the 'embeddedness' of male power, others have become more cynical. They claim that by trivialising gender differences and treating sexuality as the 'other' to be driven from the workplace, affirmative action actually preserves a form of patriarchal domination in the gender-neutral guise of 'bureaucratic rationality' (Game, 1984). It allows women to make it as 'honorary men'. Critiques of affirmative action merge here with broader critiques of the phallocentricity of Western thought (e.g. Lloyd, 1984) and the ways in which rationality and objectivity embody masculine values under the guise of gender-neutrality.

For many feminists secretaries are part of a disappearing act, either on the way to becoming part of management or in the process of being proletarianised. They have rejected the 'office wife' and 'sexy secretary' definitions, insisting that sexuality *should* have no place at work and analysing the particular vulnerability of secretaries to 'sexual harassment'. Only rarely have they considered why the discourses are there or the kinds of resistances that are open to secretaries within them. Perhaps because of a certain embarrassment about what secretaries represent, they have preferred to avoid sexuality and instead to talk briskly about the recognition of skills. Secretaries, along with nurses, were seen as suitable candidates for 'comparable worth' cases involving comparisons with appropriate groups of male workers. The fact that secretaries may not *like* being compared with groups like male truck drivers is left unanalysed. Many secretaries who work in companies and industries where the Federated Clerks' Union have 'closed-shop' agreements, are proud to have reached the point where membership of the union is no longer mandatory. 'Clause 31' exemptions are given on the basis of their closeness to management and the confidential nature of their work. To the Federated Clerks' Union, the rule-of-thumb definition of a secretary is, then, any clerical worker who can claim a 'clause 31' exemption.

Feminists have been wary of the 'servility' of secretaries, their femininity, their tendency to align themselves with management, their loyalty to their bosses and reluctance to insist on decent working conditions—their willingness, for example, to work long hours for no overtime. At best secretaries appear in feminist debates as 'victims', whether of technology, bosses, sexual harassment or of their own lack of assertiveness. This has created something of a gulf between feminists in general and those activist secretaries who have struggled for change. If feminists as a whole have embraced 'degendering' strategies it has not been so easy for secretaries to do so.

Secretaries cannot simply withdraw from the stereotypes and insert themselves into a 'degendering' approach, nor do they necessarily want to. While most share the feminist concerns for equal pay and equality of opportunity, they perceive feminists as either wanting to be 'like men' or hating men. Feminists are seen as both strident and joyless, obsessed with 'finding a rapist behind every filing cabinet'. In seeking to remove sexuality and femininity from the workplace they threaten to remove not only dangers but also pleasures. Secretaries do not necessarily want to take on 'masculine' work profiles and career goals, develop new skills, or perpetually be off on training courses in order to become part of management.

What the secretaries express is dissatisfaction and scepticism about an approach that attempts to set up one path for all workers. Though their militancy is limited they want a range of options based on recognition of skills, better pay, and working conditions that give them (rather than the employers) flexibility and security. Though they often prefer the predictability of bureaucracies over the more idiosyncratic decision-making of small organisations, they do not want sexuality or gender difference to be driven from the workplace. While feminists cannot be held entirely responsible for their unflattering media representations, all of this suggests the importance of reviewing our assumptions and priorities. Arguments about the relationship between 'equality' and 'difference' have been central to feminist theory for more than a decade but have had surprisingly little impact on practical politics or workplace struggles. Despite the emphasis placed on sexuality, the sexual investments that secretaries and other groups of women have in the existing system have not been understood or acknowledged.

Sexuality cannot be 'banished' from the workplace. Attempts to treat it as an 'intruder' are basic to the negative representation of women/sexuality/secretaries. It is by insisting on its presence, making it visible, asserting women's rights to be subjects rather than objects of sexual discourses, that bureaucracy can be challenged. This does not mean organising orgies in the office, encouraging sexual harassment or sitting on the boss's knee! All of these things things would imply that women's pleasure is first and foremost in pleasing men. It is actually quite difficult to imagine a secretary sitting on the boss's knee in a way that was purely for her own pleasure and not pandering to his desire.

Making sexuality visible will involve an exploration of what it means to be sexual *subjects* rather than objects. Our culture has such a fear of female sexuality that its autonomous expression is viewed as horrendous: Salome demanding the head of John the Baptist. Given such images it is hard even to begin to imagine what subjectivity can mean for women. But there is a growing body of feminist work on female sexuality that is relevant. While some feminists have concentrated on the coercive aspects of sexuality: rape, incest, domestic violence, paedophilia, sexual harassment and so on, others have claimed that the priority given to danger and coercion has led to a marginalisation of female pleasure (Vance, 1984). Lynne Segal (1987) and Gayle Rubin (1984) argue instead for a libertarian position. Segal simply wants a return to the early 1970s concern with sexual pleasure, claiming that sexuality has been overemphasised and that men's sexual domination is based on their social and economic power and not the reverse. Rubin, drawing on Foucault, points to the tendency in our culture to treat sex with suspicion, to sanction certain kinds of sexual activity and to create a hierarchy of sexual values. She wants to challenge this by siding with the 'outlawed' sexual minorities, destroying the notion of a single universal ideal sexuality by developing a pluralistic sexual ethics. The difficulty with both these writers is that they risk falling into an essentialism that takes any sexual desire as somehow authentic. They avoid any critical examination of the material basis of consent and historical shifts in sexual power.

On another tack, difference theorists celebrate the multiplicity of identities and pleasures based on the female body which they contrast with the one-dimensional, instrumental and abstract culture of the male. This enables them to develop a rhetoric of pleasure which completely bypasses current realities. Silverman (1984) argues that female sexuality has been constructed by the interaction of (male) discourse with the female body. She uses the *Story of O* to show the ways in which discourse quite literally maps meaning onto bodies. Women will not challenge the symbolic order from 'outside', she argues, but by altering their relation to discourse.

Given the difficulties involved in establishing women's subjectivity, it is important to be accepting of female sexuality as it is currently constituted. Rather than assuming, for example, that secretaries are always the pathetic victims of sexual harassment, it might be possible to consider the power and pleasure they currently get in their interactions with people and raise the question of how they can get what they want on their own terms. As Barbara Creed (1984) pointed out in her analysis of Mills and Boon novels, even here, in what is regarded as romantic trash, there are opportunities for subversion. While hardly feminist, these novels do cater for women's sexual pleasure and to some extent acknowledge their active sexuality, for example by presenting the male body as the object of their gaze. The acknowledgement of such pleasure may do something to bridge the negative representations that feminists and secretaries currently have of each other.

Establishing female subjectivity is only part of what is involved in making sexuality visible in the workplace. Just as important is exposing the masculinity that lurks behind gender-neutrality and forcing men to be responsible for their own sexual behaviour. If the current stereotype of men is 'the perfect picture of asexuality' (Gutek and Dunwoody, 1987: 261), then it is masculinity, not femininity, that needs to be made visible, and it is men's 'refusal to recognise the effects of masculinity which constitutes the problem for women' (Black and Coward, 1981: 85).

In this context the insights of post-structuralism and/or post-modernism are of interest. While they do not replace modernism they do provide a critical stance and the possibility of deconstructing existing frameworks and thus opening up some blockages. Men's experience of themselves as unitary and autonomous is achieved through the repression of the 'feminine'. Given that 'identity' is at best a precarious achievement it may be that masculine identity is particularly vulnerable. While women have long been aware of the 'fragility' of the male ego, the implications for the larger structure of 'male' rationality are only just beginning to be explored. For women, the lesser likelihood of perceiving themselves as centre-stage, and their more decentred notions of self, may emerge as strengths rather than weaknesses. Should women struggle for autonomous identities or celebrate their fragmentation? The political consequences are complex.

While 'post-modernism' has as yet had little to say about the workplace it has been critical of the universalising tendencies of modern culture, the failure to acknowledge or celebrate difference and plurality. It is concerned with the politics of play and pleasure and its main strategies are exaggeration and parody. It delights in being 'over the top'. Oscar Wilde's version of *Salome* may be interpreted in this way, as parodying the puritanism and negative attitudes towards female sexuality of Jewish men. Among contemporary feminist theorists, Irigaray is most closely associated with mimicry and ridicule. In a similar way the 'Olympia' montage created by a community artist working with a group of Sydney secretaries in 1985 attempts to subvert existing definitions of secretaries. Instead of rejecting or moralising about these images she recreates them in loving detail and plays with them. Here the naked reclining figure of Olympia the prostitute is brought together with every imaginable image of secretary, as sex object, femme fatale, temptress, worker, wife, mother holding the boss in the palm of her hand and so on. The whole thing is lit up with flashing lights; it is flamboyant, garish, loud, and above all celebratory. It is constructed to create the possibility of multiple interpretations and indeed everyone who looks at it sees something different. Whether it subverts or reproduces the discourses it parodies is an open question. The author cannot guarantee meaning or ensure that her audience will not take the parody seriously!

In their office humour and sometimes in public expression secretaries use parody of themselves and their bosses to powerful effect. Much pleasure is derived from imitating, exaggerating and ridiculing the existing stereotypes. These interventions are necessarily localised, sporadic, spontaneous and may amount to little more than a letting off of steam. To dispense with other political strategies in favour of parody would be a regressive move. Yet it is not unduly romanticising to suggest that parody has a place in the critical assessment of what 'modernism' has to offer and in the creation of a larger-scale politics of change.

·5· Corporate cultures and the public sector

Secretaries work in all parts of the country and in all Australian industries. The heaviest concentration is in New South Wales, Victoria and the ACT where they comprise a higher proportion of the employed population than in any of the other states. Though all industries employ secretaries there are six which have consistently accounted for more than half of the secretarial and typing workforce (Sweet, 1983: 13−14). Three of these are in the private sector (property and business services, wholesale trade, finance and investment) and three are predominantly public (public administration, education and health). If anything secretaries have become more concentrated in these areas in recent years. Demand has been most reduced (or perhaps I should say, productivity increased) in industries which already employed fewer secretarial workers—industries such as transport, retailing, minerals and energy.

Offices feel very different from each other, depending on what industry they are associated with, whether they are located in city, suburbs or country, whether they are large or small, part of the public or private sector, a head office or a regional backwater. There are images and traditions to be maintained. Some organisations present themselves as public-spirited employers, while others do not care. Multinationals like IBM seek local acceptance through identification with Australian themes and landscapes: its head office is situated in a natural bushland setting to the north-west of Sydney. Styles of management (and masculinity) range from paternalism to ruthlessness or detachment. Some organisations are rigidly hierarchical or authoritarian while others are more egalitarian; some are hostile to unions while others make union membership compulsory. There are different workplace cultures, including formal rules and regulations, conventions about dress and behaviour, organisation of family and sexual symbolism.

The two main axes that were identified were whether the organisation was large or small and whether it was a part of the public or private sector. Secretaries often say they prefer to work for small organisations on the grounds that the work is more varied, they can gain an all-round knowledge of the job and there is more chance of moving into managerial or professional positions. Others perceive small employers as offering little more than 'Girl Friday' positions with less chance of specialisation or promotion, fewer opportunities to meet people, and greater danger of sexual harassment. Secretaries working for professionals have a high status but face difficulties in career advancement. Whatever professional knowledge they pick up, they cannot become doctors, lawyers or architects without going through the necessary training. Secretaries in personnel departments, advertising and travel agencies, insurance companies and even estate agents and accounts, stand a better chance of moving into the business, even if they still need the relevant certificates and diplomas.

It is often assumed that small organisations work differently from large ones: 'family' is contrasted here with 'bureaucracy'. If, as I have argued, sexuality is central to the workings of large bureaucracies, the differences are not as fundamental as this suggests. Large organisations differ from smaller ones in their greater complexity, but invariably they too break down into a series of smaller structures. It is to the second axis that I now turn, comparing a range of 'corporate cultures' with the conditions in public and semi-public organisations.

Secretaries frequently contrast conditions and opportunities in the public and private sectors. For many, 'secretaries', with all their cultural and sexual meanings, belong only in private enterprise. Government stands for bureaucratic red tape, narrow job definitions and minute rules right down to questions like how many lines to leave between headings. Bureaucrats are not perceived as 'bosses' in the same sense as their private enterprise equivalents. The private sector is regarded as demanding, pressurised and more heavily sexualised but also more exciting and, at the top at least, offering greater financial rewards. Takeovers and restructurings involve a fairly constant movement of managerial staff with all sorts of repercussions for secretaries. Only a minority of secretaries had worked for one boss for more than five years.

Secretaries in the private sector are mostly non-unionised. The Federated Clerks' Union has closed-shop agreements with some sectors such as oil companies and breweries and encourages individual membership by workers in other organisations. Trade union secretaries tend to belong although they hate the FCU's right-wing policies. Some of the larger companies run their own in-house unions. Secretaries working for the federal government belong to the Australian Public Service Association (APSA), New South Wales employees are covered by the Public Service Association (PSA). It is likely that APSA will combine with the Administrative and Clerical Officers Association (ACOA) following the government's proposed merger of the third and fourth divisions. Secretaries in tertiary institutions are covered by the amorphous Health and Research Employees Association (H&REA).

It will be argued that there are significant differences between the public and the private sectors but that they are not as sharp as the stereotypes suggest. The high-flying corporate raiders and the bumbling government offices undoubtedly exist, but in between these extremes there are a lot of similarities between public and private organisations, and they share the same boss—secretary discourses. But these discourses operate in highly specific contexts and the ways in which secretaries experience themselves and their work vary considerably from one workplace to another. The differences may be subtle and they operate between and within workplaces, not simply across the board. I shall illustrate this by describing a range of offices visited in the course of the research.

Manufacturing macho

Malvern is a predominantly manufacturing company with a strongly macho image, which has been involved in ruthless take-over struggles in recent years. It has survived and expanded in an industry that has had to cope with international competition and rapid technological change. To achieve this it has been quite ruthless about shutting down plant that is inefficient and in laying off production workers. Since it is so fiercely competitive it is perhaps surprising that it agreed to cooperate with us: the oil companies, which are equally paranoid about their competition, all refused on the grounds that we would steal their secrets and eat into their profit margins! They seemed in little doubt that their secretaries had access to the 'secrets' we were thought to be seeking.

Malvern's main strategy involves ruthless cost-cutting. This is evident in the pared-down nature of its office structure. Compared with many other companies it is unconcerned about its public image. Its head office is shabby and cramped, located in an unsalubrious inner-city suburb where space is cheap. The building is divided into a series of extremely drab offices marked out by high wooden partitions and opaque glass. The western suburbs division was described by one of the women as 'like a factory...the typewriter's really bad and there was an old telex machine which was so loud. There is no carpet, no airconditioning and you have to buy your own heater or you freeze. There are jagged edges on the stairs. And you have to have muscles to open the filing cabinet because it is really old'. She believed that secretaries 'at the front' (that is, head office) got better working conditions, carpet and higher wages 'because their bosses are higher'. The offices of manufacturing companies typically are minimal and 'feel' quite close to production.

This is not because they have advanced technology which has proletarianised the workforce. On the contrary. Though they had put word processors into head office, the regional sales office looked archaic, weighed under with what seemed (by comparison with the retailers) a lot of unnecessary paperwork. If it 'feels' like a factory it is because there is a crudeness and lack of sophistication in the workplace culture that derives from the shop floor. Attitudes to gender are rigid, to say the least. Though women comprise roughly half the factory workers, women are treated as incapable of understanding the appliances that this firm produces. Production is men's business. Manual work is invested with masculine qualities and manual workers have a contempt for office workers, who are deemed 'effemininate'. Secretaries are permitted only a marginal role and are treated with considerable contempt by most managers. They take it upon themselves to ensure that secretaries do not get 'above' the male factory workers. The secretaries summed it up by saying: 'There will never be women in senior positions here. It is very male-dominated. You are more stupid than stupid. Any woman at all. In this company there is no room for women, only secretaries.' All women come from working-class backgrounds and most are married to tradesmen or builders, who move between wage labour and working for themselves. It would be absurd to suggest that the wives, in working as secretaries, are of a higher social class than their husbands. Their jobs actually reinforce the working-class culture from which they come and the position of women in that culture. They are treated as little more than typists, though the women know they are capable of doing more: 'Women are just something to do the typing and the clerical work and that is it...When I am on the telephones taking service calls, well, you could say no or yes to a customer because in here I know the answers. But if I was to say yes, go ahead and do that, somebody would come back and say, what authority do you have?' Marlene, who made this comment, is married to a builder and does his books. She knows a bit about computers because she bought one for her kids. But she is not prepared to make that knowledge available because she knows they would just take it for granted. 'They are not going to use me and avoid sending someone else on a course...the boss should be more amenable to training girls.' So the company misses out on using its secretaries to full advantage; at the same time, it knows only too well which staff it wants to hang onto and which it will let go. Wherever it can it draws on past experience. Jan, who had previously worked as a demonstrator and a telephonist, was asked to come back as a secretary because the company found her product knowledge useful.

Most of the secretaries are in their thirties and forties. Malvern does not take on any responsibility for training office juniors and always recruits experienced staff. Many of these women are hanging on for long service leave or superannuation and nominate that as their main reason for staying. There is an air of hostility and discontent, particularly in the regional office. Despite the resentment against the macho nature of the company male approval is important to them and they establish their worth at least partly by their ability to ensure that their bosses look after them. Where there was bitching it was about women whose bosses let them get away with anything, or who had been able to use their feminine wiles to get pay increases or perks such as parking facilities. Their resentment is sometimes relieved by playing 'male chauvinist pig/militant feminist' games. Yet their attitudes to gender and to feminism are conventional. They claim to believe in equal opportunity but feminism is taking it too far. Few could visualise working for a woman and some stressed that they enjoyed working for men: 'they are excellent, they are funny and they make the day go faster.' Flirtation is one of the few pleasures of the working day: 'There is a fellow round here, I say to him, you are all talk John. But he's been here twenty years and...I think he keeps a lot of girls on the ball as far as looking nice...Jane, my friend here...her husband drinks a lot. Jane needs that. I don't need that—my husband pays enough attention to me.' They agree that flirtations could overlap with sexual harassment: 'I can think of one person at the moment who thinks he is flirting but I could class it as sexual harassment and get him into an awful lot of trouble...' But they consider women should be mature enough to handle this. Rather than being a demonstration of men's structural power, 'it could work either way. It could be a woman doing it to a man'.

The idea of male secretaries was treated with mirth. They nominated a young chap in the electronic data processing (EDP) centre as a likely candidate and the 'confirmation' of this was that he was rumoured to have RSI! This finally demonstrated that he was effeminate. The man in question declined the 'secretary' label and defined his work as 'trouble shooting'. His supervisor explained 'he naturally has to talk with the computer somehow and that is through the keyboard'.

The EDP coordinator was the only woman who could remotely be seen as part of management. She claims that the men treat her differently from the secretaries because she is not in any way subservient. Yet she seemed subservient to the secretaries! They certainly treat her differently from the men and exude a certain reluctance to do anything for her. There is an unarticulated feeling that women should be responsible for their own secretarial chores (just as they should their own housework). In turn, she feels guilty if she has to give them word-processing material and likes to be able to do it herself. Since she had started out as a secretary she may well fear that they resent her moving up and out of her place. Perhaps they do. Or perhaps she just projects this fear.

Personnel pay lip-service to the need to have more women in management but have done nothing to ensure that this happens. The personnel manager was actually married to a secretary who worked for an organisation that was part of the AA pilot scheme. He shared his wife's frustration that nothing had been done to open the career ladder to secretaries. But there was no way his company was going to get involved in such programs until it was absolutely forced to do so. Malvern will be a hard nut to crack. It represents in an extreme form that view of secretaries as merely low-level typists, lacking the interest or the capacity to take on more senior positions in the company. This is a long way from the reality.

Retailing paternalism

Colesworth Jones is a large retailer with branches throughout Australia. Unlike Malvern its head office is situated right in the centre of town. It was in the process of moving some sections to the north shore but it remains a more centralised outfit than Malvern and more bureaucratic. A security clearance was required to enter the building. Its offices are on a grander scale, with conference and reception rooms, a library and archives which indicates some pride in company history. Staff are spread over a number of floors, and status is represented spatially: it increases with each floor up. Senior management are on the top floor, protected from the public and the more routine enquiries; the buyers are lowest to the ground. Managers have the rooms with windows and views; secretaries generally occupy partitioned-off spaces in the centre known as 'horse-stalls'. The contrast between head and regional offices was extreme. In the stores not a foot could be spared from potential selling space: if sales work is classified as production, this was again quite close to the factory in atmosphere. In areas where the public seldom goes, these offices exist in cramped, dark windowless spaces often in basements. Head office was friendly and cooperative, the interviews were leisurely and mostly conducted in a corner of the conference room. In the stores it was different. Hard-pressed managers were reluctant to help and strict about time. Here the law of surplus value reigns supreme.

As a retailer, Colesworth Jones's staff are predominantly women, while management is almost entirely male. There are the occasional women store managers and a few women have moved into the lower ranks of personnel and buying. The company takes pride in needing only a relatively small number of secretaries and clerical staff to back up their sales and buying teams. It was able to take advantage of computerisation in the 1960s and 70s to reduce the proportion of low-level clerical staff. The secretaries are concentrated in head office. Yet the personnel people were unable to say quickly how many secretaries there were or where they were to be found. To them secretaries are invisible until they are forced to go looking for them. The EEO officer was a man approaching retirement. Secretaries were not seen as part of the company 'proper' and it had not entered their heads to include them in affirmative action proposals.

Eventually personnel came up with a list of women that they thought might fit the definition of 'secretary'. They covered a range from senior secretaries (none had the official title of personal assistant) through to typist clerks, as well as the archivist and several personnel assistants whose work was seen to overlap with that of secretaries. The typing pool was no longer in existence. Over the previous four years it had been reduced through natural wastage to a pond, and finally to a 'puddle' of one. Even quite senior managers were sharing secretaries or accepting that 'their' secretary would be doing additional work for other people. The technology available to secretaries was not very advanced. Golf ball typewriters were still very much in evidence. Personal computers were used mostly in the personnel section. Because they contained so much confidential information they were closed off in separate rooms. As a result personnel officers had offices while the secretaries typically worked in open-space areas, at most enclosed by glass partitions. Only the secretaries to the general manager and managing director had their own offices. Some sat in the unenclosed space outside the boss's office, guarding the inner sanctum.

If the ethos of Malvern is macho working-class the ethos of Colesworth Jones is paternalistic. The secretaries are used in very 'traditional' ways, doing shorthand and typing, answering the phone, organising the diary and so on. Even those at the top are given little executive responsibility. Though each is secretary 'to' someone they actually work as a team and depend on reciprocal helping arrangements. They function more as an elite typing pool for top management than as personal assistants. Anyone who does not 'fit in' does not last very long and those that stay manage to develop close working relationships with each other. Because of the 'team' arrangement the workflow is constant. This means that all of these secretaries are spending at least 50 per cent of their time typing and have only limited opportunity to do administrative work. Any attempt to turn the job into something more would be constrained by this need to cooperate with the other secretaries.

What is immediately noticeable at head office is the substantial age gap between managers and most of the secretaries. Sexual harassment on the senior managerial floors is unthinkable. If it happens anywhere it would happen on the buying floors, for the buyers have the reputation for flirting, making passes and telling dirty jokes. Their risque lifestyle, and the glamour attached to travel, plus the possibility that they will have some bargains to pass on, makes the buyers seem quite exciting: they add interest to an otherwise staid environment. Traditionally there have been marriages between buyers and secretaries though officially office romances are frowned upon. This is not formally stated, 'it is just an unspoken thing'. Unlike Malvern, where you can wear just about anything to work, even jeans, there is at CWJs a lot of concern with dress and general appearance. Slacks are discouraged and the emphasis is on clothes that play down sexuality: being 'neat and tidy' with functional blouses and skirts in 'sensible' colours. The senior secretaries are expected to 'speak to' the nonconformists where necessary.

The secretaries at head office are solidly middle-class in their backgrounds and many are married to business executives. Some welcomed the move to the north shore since it meant working closer to home. They are not resentful of the lack of career opportunities. They believe in 'equal pay and equal opportunity' for others but see their own 'careers' as bound up with being professional wives. This does not mean that they identified simply as housewives. They took pride in the fact that, as a result of their contribution to family income, their children could go to private schools and they and their husbands could entertain in the manner that they wanted. If they had complaints about the company it was mostly about the pay, which was little above award rates. Feminism was largely irrelevant to them since they felt they had what they wanted out of life.

Most were unaware that their employer was part of the affirmative action pilot study and did not see many openings for women in the management structure. The official ideology was that anyone can progress in the company regardless of gender if they have the ability and are willing to acquire the qualifications. But there was no attempt to encourage secretaries to get formal qualifications or to find ways of valuing their secretarial experience. The secretaries were stereotyped as women who were not interested in careers, whose main interests were with their husbands and children, and it became a self-fulfilling prophecy. Managers gave off a strong sense that this was how it 'should' be—hence the paternalism. Their reason for being part of the pilot scheme was to improve their self-image and appear to be public-spirited while minimising their commitment to change.

Conglomerates

Pacific Industries is a nineteenth-century company which has built on its original trading interests to become a large conglomerate. Through a series of takeovers it now has diverse interests in transport, travel, retailing and finance. These are organised into a series of divisions and agencies, some of which are located in Sydney and its western suburbs, while others are interstate or overseas. Since they retain considerable policy initiatives the regional offices are substantial. Less elaborate than head office, they are still luxurious compared with their equivalents at Malvern or CWJ. Head office is a stately late Victorian building which evokes its colonial origins: panelled meeting rooms, leather armchairs, chandeliers and glass cases filled with artifacts and memorabilia. A tour de force is the ladies' room, with its mirrors and stools, feminine colours and washbags for each woman. It is the kind of bathroom one might find in an upper middle-class home and as such provides an interesting sidelight on the public/private division and on how the secretaries are constructed. Pacific Industries is a great deal 'classier' than either of the corporations considered so far.

The patrician image and its associated conservatism are expressed in strict dress rules which apply to both men and women. Gerald Robbins, about to retire after more than 40 years with the company, is a stickler for detail and considers that even a neat sportscoat is inappropriate for the business world. He says: 'I'm a military-type person and I try to be fairly punctilious about these things...I think any man who is careless about his appearance and his dress is thoughtless to others and...lacking in one of the managerial attributes.' A recipient of Robbins' warnings complains: 'If my hair gets longer than normal, or what is regarded as longer than normal, they make comments about it...if I wear a tie that is a bit different or a shirt that is a little bit different then someone, particularly the chairman, makes a comment about it. So there is a strong push for wearing a white shirt and a dark suit...'

Not only must secretaries not wear slacks, they have even been admonished for wearing flat shoes. One had been in trouble for this piece of 'sloppiness' while recovering from an ankle injury! Secretaries must not only be neat and tidy but smartly turned out.

The rules are relaxed in the suburbs, where the divisional per-sonnel manager was wearing a sports coat (had he been warned?) and dismissed ties as 'bloody stupid'. It is a different story if he has to come into head office.

While the divisions have some independence, the group main-tains its old colonialist image. Its activities are concentrated in male-dominated fields, such as hardware, groceries and shipping. One division had 151 managers, not one of whom was a woman. The divisions present strongly masculine management styles though there is a difference between the gentlemanly and military approaches at head office and the more casual, boisterous and even larrikin images that may be found further west. Where the men at head office have a 'personal' secretary, suburban or re-gional managers often take pride in 'their' secretary being a gen-eralist who performs a variety of tasks and looks after the whole department. The occasional woman manager is to be found in areas associated with femininity, such as fashion and cosmetics—quite recent additions to the organisation. These women had no expectations of being moved up and out to other divisions.

Behind the paternalist old-world facade is a ruthless drive to rationalise as companies are acquired and stripped of elements that are unprofitable or which do not fit the overall plans of the corporation. Since the early 1980s there has been continuous reorganisation, management cuts and an end to the free nego-tiation of salaries. One such company had just had its head office reduced from 52 to 12 and its total staff reduced by about 15 per cent. Many had been transferred and some sacked, including the previous general manager. What then happens to his secretary? Such secretaries are not automatically allocated to the next general manager who may, as was the case here, want to bring his existing secretary into the job. It is clear that management would like to apply some ritual such as suttee. The secretary is in the same embarrassing position (from a management viewpoint) as a widow or divorcee who cannot easily be reallocated to another man of appropriate status. On some occasions, such as this one, they are moved sideways to positions where their expertise can be used. On others, the secretaries themselves solve the 'problem' by taking early retirement. Frequently, as in the current reorganisation of the newspaper world, the secretary is simply given notice. Not surprisingly, they speak of takeovers as creating the biggest dis-ruptions in their working relations.

Pacific Industries is a good example of an organisation that has replaced the old paternalistic model of authority with a more bureaucratic model. Staff who had been there for a long time recalled it as 'like one big happy family when everybody knew everybody else...' One secretary recalled, with some nostalgia, the days when there were dinners and balls, snooker tournaments and cricket days, when there was a sports room and when everyone played table-tennis or darts at lunchtime. The days of 'caring' have been replaced by ruthless staff cuts and, she believes, deliberate attempts to get rid of old staff who, 'as thinking people', do not fit into the new structure.

Roy Spalding the financial controller encapsulates this new era. A man now in his forties, he presents himself as a ruthless technocrat, his life so completely devoted to the pursuit of power that even his leisure activities are taken up with competititive squash and competitive sailing! He says: 'We have suddenly replaced old guys with young guys and computers so the ordinary office workers are frightened...They see that it has suddenly gone from being an old-fashioned establishment to a whizz-bang, computerised-type office with young guys working late at night.' Since his ambition is to reduce the office from 100 to about ten, it is hardly surprising that people are wary of him.

While secretarial positions have not been cut, clerical and typing positions certainly have. Secretaries have taken on responsibility for work that was once done by more junior staff. In this they are aided by the new technology: word processors are firmly in evidence here. Pacific Industries may be conservative politically but it has kept up with the times and secretaries typically have a word processor on their desks whether or not it takes up a large proportion of their working day. While the one-to-one relation is preserved in head office, in the regional offices they work for a number of people. There is concern, if not to abolish the 'traditional' boss—secretary relationship, then at least to 'modernise' it.

Modernisation had not included giving secretaries executive responsibility. Those who joined as secretaries with, say, personnel qualifications, in the hope of getting experience and promotion have found themselves contained in the old model, still obliged to type and make the tea. One woman who finds herself in this position is bitter. She had been promised the opportunity to move into administration: 'He said that he understood. That, in fact, there was only 10 per cent secretarial work in this job. But my worst fears came true and I would say about 50 or more per cent of the work is secretarial. By that I mean shorthand, typing, photocopying, tea-making and that sort of thing...The symbol of her slavery, which is joked about in the entire building, is his injunction to make tea at precisely allotted times during the day. He simply comments: 'I try not to have too much in the way of personal expectations but I've got a couple of foibles. I like a cup of tea, you know, a couple of times a day...'

Though a handful of women have reached senior positions in

the divisions there are none in head office and the company is implacably hostile to affirmative action. It mouths the ideology that 'anybody can make it without "special" treatment', but is not prepared to do anything more than appoint the occasional token woman. This combines with a generally reactionary political position. One manager said 'they see Labor as Reds and think you shouldn't deal with them because you are only encouraging them to stay in government'. The male EEO officer certainly took this position. The personnel department, like many others, was terrified of the likely paperwork. The requirement to do a detailed statistical report on their workforce seemed beyond their resources and they feared being put to the test. They retreated into completely unfounded cliches about how the government was going to impose quotas.

Other corporations have developed more progressive images, often by voluntarily supporting affirmative action. Darling and Universal are large conglomerates which include agriculture, mining, manufacturing and retailing among their activities. Neither is any less hierarchical than Pacific. Like the latter they regard unions as anathema and even the conservative Federated Clerks' Union, which has made numerous offers, has been quietly told to 'bugger off'. The support for AA arises from the same paternalism that opposes unions. Darling had involved itself in EEO from the mid-1970s, long before there was any danger of compulsion. Under this umbrella it included English language classes for migrant women, attempts to identify their work issues, efforts to alleviate resettlement problems of staff, and to monitor the effects of the company on wives and families—which concluded that 'wives really need an induction course on the company'. In one region, discussion groups were set up, first for wives and then for women employed both in the office and the factory. The awards and conditions at Darling are more generous than those of companies covered by the Federated Clerks and it likes to think that its workers do not 'need' a union. The company's philosophy is 'to be and be seen to be a good employer, just and responsible in its dealings with employees, concerned with their welfare and providing the opportunity for all to have satisfying work'. EEO is seen as being 'about good people management, a critical issue in the 80s because of escalating labour costs' (*EEO News* June 1985). The EEO Steering Committee argued that it would bring full utilisation of all human resources, greater productivity, better retention rates, increased sensitivity to consumer needs and financial benefits from an improved public image.

The support for AA is done partly to look good politically and partly, a research officer suggested, out of some naive belief on the part of the men that they should 'look after the ladies here'.

Only a handful of managers thought it would involve any more than token changes and fewer were aware that secretaries could be affected at all. Affirmative action translated into 'getting a few women into management', but not any reassessment of the value of particular jobs, the skills involved or the criteria for promotion. Some managers were opposed even to token changes, believing that 'equality' already existed and structural changes were unnecessary. However, both Darling and Universal appointed as their EEO officers women who consider themselves to be feminists. Compared with the responses of Pacific and Colesworth Jones this at least indicated some degree of seriousness. It enabled the issues to be raised and the arguments rehearsed and, in addition, created the space to insist on the inclusion of secretaries.

Both companies had set up senior secretaries' groups within their head offices (significantly, where most of the senior secretaries were located) and were promising to extend them to the regions when it became 'appropriate'. The ostensible aim was to expand opportunities for top secretaries, especially through job rotation, moving them from head office to sales administration and personnel positions in the regions. After attending some of these meetings at Universal I became aware how limited the prospects for change were. The meetings were tightly controlled through the EEO officer and several key secretaries, and anyone who was too assertive was quickly put in her place. There was no interest in integrating the secretarial grades into the career structure and arguments about improving conditions had to be put in terms of cost savings if they were to cut any ice at all. The more serious items such as pay increases, childcare and job opportunities were kept off the agenda. The meetings had become sessions where secretaries could let off steam about short-term problems such as delays in the ordering of stationery or a shortage of printers. It was claimed that younger secretaries were not interested in the group, assuming they will be out of the workforce in a few years anyway. Yet the group had little to offer such women except a glass of company sherry and the opportunity to stay back at work one night a month.

Stronger initiatives for change came from areas other than corporate headquarters. Outside the management structure, women staff formed their own group to participate in development of equal employment opportunity. The group called itself AUNTIE—Action for Unbiased and Neutral Treatment in Employment. Throughout the Australian women's movement the use of such acronyms, or of ordinary women's names (one thinks of newspapers like *MeJane* and *Mabel*, refuges like Elsie) has always generated a lot of enthusiasm, and AUNTIE was no exception. In sharp contrast to the formal sessions at head office, its meetings were full of debate and argument about strategies and tactics. Among other things it pushed for a 'new deal for secretaries'. The company, adopting a liberal position, or perhaps confident of its capacities for cooption, invited two of its members to join the EEO steering committee and later actually entered AUNTIE for a nationwide affirmative action award offered by the Federation of Business and Professional Women. Two senior secretaries' conferences were initiated by one of the divisions and led directly to a secretarial task force which reported in 1985. It recommended a number of fundamental changes. These included the gender-neutral measurement of skills, separation of the job grades of secretaries and managers, the expansion of career grades for secretaries, the targeting of a number of positions normally filled by new graduates for secretarial staff, training programs and in-house courses, and the use of the performance-appraisal and counselling process to identify secretarial staff with the interest and ability to fill these positions.

Despite the enthusiasm of AUNTIE and the support of some managers there was strong resistance. The personnel section had other plans for making secretarial staff more productive, while the accounting section worried that secretaries would soon be earning more than (male) invoice clerks. They could not acknowledge that any secretary could be worth more than a clerk! It is not clear how far the company ever intended to go but it did make some attempt to implement the proposals, using one of its divisions as a starting point. It accepted that the position-description guidelines should be used to break the nexus between secretaries' grades and those of their bosses. It added a personal assistant grade to the existing five grades of secretary and acknowledged that there was a serious bottleneck for secretarial staff in job grades 3 and 4.

The resultant changes, which are set out in Table 5.1, were a big disappointment. All employees are on the same grading system which goes from 1 to 15 and then leapfrogs to 99, representing the top-secret packages negotiated for senior executives. Secretaries still barely make it to the lowest of the career grades. Only one out of 54 secretaries was promoted to the new grade 6 and three into grade 5. The bottleneck remained and no changes were made in the overall hierarchy. They reproduced exactly the situation they were supposedly trying to change: the secretary to the managing director was given the one grade 6 and the secretaries to the three general managers all received grade 5s! Personnel thought there was 'something wrong' if a secretary to a junior manager earned more than a secretary to a senior manager, and were reluctant to distinguish between women working for the same grade of manager. This was considered an affront to the managers. Yet there were very obvious differences in what the three grade 5s did. According to my informants one was largely a typist, another was a 'traditional' secretary, while the third was involved in sensitive policy decisions as well as being responsible for the efficiency and morale of all the secretaries in the group. The personnel section, who resisted the changes, wanted to avoid the 'embarrassment' of having to rank individuals on what seemed to them a highly 'subjective' basis. Yet they routinely do this with the clerical and administrative positions. All the review achieved was to catch up with the market and make the wages offered more competitive at the lower end of the scale. At best, a secretary could now reach grade 6, which was the grade of entry for a new university graduate, and it was made clear that grade 6s would be restricted to the very top. Yet some grade 5s took administrative and policy responsibilities that far exceeded the range of many an experienced graduate.

AUNTIE's other recommendations about the training and promotion of secretaries into managerial positions, and the reservation of a proportion of such positions for them rather than graduates, were conveniently ignored. One secretary achieved a regrading from secretary to technical officer, and a word-processor coordinator was appointed—but she was expected to have dual role as a senior secretary. After continued pressure, some efforts were made to enable secretaries to visit the male-dominated production and mining sites.

Just as the review was completed the rug was pulled from under it by across-the-board retrenchments. The 54 secretarial positions were reduced to 40 and the likelihood of further reductions had serious implications for the senior secretaries. Personnel wanted to impose a 'team' arrangement which would prevent senior secretaries from being part of management and force them to pick up more routine typing and filing. They were locked in a power struggle with the liberal general manager, a North American, over this. He protested that his secretary was 'going to be a glorified typist because she is not going to be able to utilise any of her talents...The minute she tries to do something like that I am going to get severely criticised because it is distracting her from making sure she is available for all the other managers up here on this pool basis'.

At the time I visited in late 1986 a memo had gone out announcing that secretaries would be working for more than one person and would all be working collectively. Consequently they were meeting to reorganise the filing system, putting as many things as possible into one central file and reducing their own separate files. This was creating a lot of friction since it meant giving up some of their independence. Who was to set up the central file? Could

Table 5.1   Regrading of secretaries at Darling, 1986

Job Grade	Number of positions	% of positions	Salary* (at December 1985)
1	1	2	15 976
2	8	15	17 363
3	33	41	18 888
4	19	35	20 569
5	3	5	22 506
6	1	2	24 628
	54	100	

* Ranges from 80–110 per cent subject to individual negotiation

they get a kid on work experience? Can they find someone to put on the reception desk? Can they get a more efficient telephone system? Their access to juniors was diminished and there was concern that the one junior available would be treated as a lackey. The 'team' looks suspiciously like the return of the 'pool' in a new updated form. There is little chance that secretaries will be able to move into career positions or that secretarial work itself will be revalued, its skills acknowledged. It remains to be seen whether affirmative action legislation, which has come into effect since this study was completed, will have any effect on the situation of secretaries. Ironically, the company in which these experiments took place was sold less than a year later. The regrading procedures had not, at that stage, been introduced into any of the other divisions.

The public sector

The Department of Public Welfare has its new head office in western Sydney and a number of regional and district offices throughout New South Wales. All offices felt very different from their private enterprise equivalents. The atmosphere was less formal and dress more casual; the pressure of work, and perhaps its challenge and stimulation, were clearly less for most staff. There was more freedom to move around the building, to stop and observe the work process and to chat to people on the job. This was facilitated by landscaped office space. Efforts had been made to create a pleasant work environment. The space was divided by low screens, by plants and by non-standard furniture. The typing pools are the only section with open-plan layout, and they too have been 'humanised'. The new building allocated them more space, a special airconditioner and humidifier, a separate room for the printers, and a separate tea room for the operators to take regular breaks. Only the senior managers have closed-in offices: small interviewing rooms are available where privacy is required, and it was in one of these that most of the interviews were conducted. There were no time constraints and virtually no one seemed under pressure to get back to work.

One obvious difference from the private sector is the higher proportion of women in management. Women moved in in some numbers in the late 1970s and developed a number of strategies of power, many of them organised around femininity. Valerie, now a director, projects an upper-class, relaxed openness. Her desk has been replaced by a round table, filing cabinets are nowhere to be seen and the door is always open. She is rumoured to have affairs with men at the top, not to gain power but as an expression of her own status. Her mystique depends on distinguishing herself from secretaries, but she talks a lot about supporting other women, pushes EEO, and fought for the adoption of 'personal assistant' as a courtesy title.

A range of personal assistants, stenographers and typists are all paid on the stenographic scale. 'Personal assistant' is a courtesy title which is applied to those working for directors or bureau heads. They are the only ones who work in a one-to-one relationship with a 'boss' in the private sector sense. They carry enormous responsibility and in some cases hold a great deal of power of the gatekeeper variety. But despite a heavy workload they earn substantially less than their private sector equivalents. There is a considerable gap in status, if not in salary, between personal assistants and stenographers, who generally work for a section rather than for specific individuals. The stenographers are not given much responsibility, which at times creates resentment: 'You've got to get it out of your mind that there's secretarial work in the public service. There's just not...whereas in private enterprise, if you don't *think*, you're not wanted.'

Images of 'family' were frequently evoked to describe working relations. Betty, for example, described a group of people in her bureau who gave emotional and even financial support through shattered romances, marriage breakups and other traumas. 'It feels like family really. It is very close...and Garth [her boss]...is one of the family.' She cares enough about him to be preparing to move with him to another job in a regional office a long way from her home. 'That's the only reason. I don't find anything appealing out there other than working for him... he's so nice to work for. He's one of my best friends.' Another personal assistant, an older woman who definitely came within the 'dragon' range, emphasised that she was secretary to the position rather than the person, and that she worked with rather than for him. Though more formal and reserved than some of the others she had created a personal space and in some ways had more power than the secretaries in 'modern' egalitarian relationships.

In the absence of any formal delegation of 'secretary' it is often the clerical assistants (CAs) whose work most closely resembles that of secretaries. This is especially true in the country, where they act as office managers. They may be left in charge for six weeks or longer while their district officer is away and have to deal with all manner of client enquiries. The department recognises some of these anomalies and had taken steps to remedy them. For example, it set up spokeswomen's meetings to facilitate contact between the CAs and senior staff. Sitting in these meetings I was struck by their similarity to the senior secretaries' meetings I had attended in the private sector. Some had been secretaries or stenographers before they left the workforce to have children. They now find the CA's job more varied and interesting, despite the low pay. Yet they earn less than half of a district officer's salary and less than typists and stenographers. They have even had to train unemployed people on Community Employment grants who were earning more than *they* were.

While many large corporations were disbanding or transforming their typing pools by the 1970s, the department actually extended its use of them into word-processing pools. Until 1975 the branches and units had their own typists and stenographers. Now most work goes to one or other of the pools: repetitive work goes to the word-processing pool while standard forms and 'one-offs' go to the typing pool. Most staff dislike this arrangement. In the past, for example, typists had prepared affidavits from the files. The clerks now have to do more preliminary work while the typist has lost any sense of involvement in what is happening. This in turn limits their chances to get the experience that might enable them to skirt around the examination bar and find an alternative way into a clerk's position.

In 1981 there were attempts to break down the typing pools and to upgrade the secretaries by providing a larger range of job classifications. Treasury put its foot down and the pools stayed. With the move to the western suburbs the stenographers and some of the typists were distributed around the sections and the pools reduced and consolidated. They may shortly be phased out. The Public Service Board's 'Integrate' project, which was being negotiated with the union, involved the merging of the keyboard and lower clerical grades into a new classification called 'clerical officer'. The demise of the board, following the 1988 state elections in New South Wales, may bring an end to these plans, leaving each department to make its own separate arrangements.

However, the aim was to provide more flexibility and make possible the redesign of jobs in such a way as to widen people's work
experiences and minimise the risks of occupational injury. It was
proposed that a maximum of 20–50 per cent of a person's time
be spent using keyboard or stenography skills. While this would
not automatically break up the pools it would certainly ensure that
individuals spend no more than a part of their working time
there.

The women who work in the pools talk of camaraderie and
support. They defined them as 'home' as against the unknowns of
the larger department. 'Often we get blown up over the phone if
we can't answer any of the questions...Well, that's not our job.'
This comment, from a typist who works outside the pools, illustrates the sorts of anxieties the women have. A supervisor suggested that most would not survive outside the pools because 'they
can't make decisions and don't show much initiative'. How much
of this is cause and how much affect is not clear, but it certainly
creates difficulties for involving these women in EEO programs.
There have been efforts to bring down some of the barriers and
encourage contact between the typist and the person for whom
she is working. A start had been made with assertiveness training
workshops, but these had not been particularly well received. The
women either denied their need for such assistance or were cynical about its ability to change their structural position. Some saw it
as an effort by the feminist 'bosses' to appease their consciences or
deny the reality that most women in this position did not in fact
have any strong career ambitions. The spokeswomen commented
on the complacency of many of their colleagues who were not
prepared to voice their discontent or felt threatened by what they
experienced as pressure to change and progress.

The public sector differs from the private in that it has been
more susceptible to pressure from the unions and from organised
feminism to open up career opportunities and to improve working
conditions. The Public Service Association has been active in
taking up issues around occupational health, technology, restructuring and equal opportunities. Both federal and state governments are concerned about mass outbreaks of RSI and hope to
mitigate this by spreading keyboard work among more people,
each doing it for part of the day only. Private enterprise has been
more able to evade the financial responsibility by using temporary
and part-time workers and through lay-offs. Government departments, on the other hand, are obliged to put affected workers on
'light duties' and, since they cannot sack people, may not be in the
financial position to employ additional staff. In March 1987 the
federal government followed up changes foreshadowed by some

state governments in announcing a reorganisation of the keyboard staff, clerical assistants and the junior levels of the clerical/administrative grades. The present 48 different categories are to be integrated into one new structure with only five promotional levels. There should in the future be no formal or informal barriers to secretaries moving into administrative positions (*SMH* 12 March 1987). The proposal combines cost savings in more efficient work practices with a response to demands for the full implementation of EEO and concern about RSI and health problems associated with the new technology.

Jessie Street Institute

Universities and CAEs mirror the public service in their pay and conditions but differ from government departments in a number of ways. They have more 'secretaries' in a clearly identified and understood sense of the word; and there is considerable folklore about the 'departmental secretary' and her skills. Secretaries are more likely to have their own offices than they are elsewhere. Office landscaping has not penetrated far into tertiary education and would no doubt meet with enormous resistance from academics who, though typically spending little time in their offices, insist on maintaining them. The absence of typing pools in a clearcut spatially defined sense makes it difficult to draw a line between 'secretaries' and 'typists', and the term secretary is used in a more generic way than it is in the public service. The women may be scattered around a variety of rooms in the department, taking work from a central register which is clocked in and out. In some cases each secretary/typist is allocated a group of academics for whom she works. Even professors' secretaries may be included in this arrangement.

Secretaries at the Jessie Street Institute work in the central administration, the departments or the library. They tend to conform, in expectations and dress, to the department for which they work. Conservatism emerges from conservative departments and radicalism from radical ones. People from all sections were interviewed, with care being taken to include both 'hard science' and humanities disciplines in the sample. The division between administration and the departments is akin to the distinction between the head and regional offices of large companies. The first is conducted with more formality, is seen as the showpiece, and is centrally involved in policy-making. Senior secretaries take on substantial administrative responsibilities, organising graduation ceremonies and the like, for very low rates of pay and with minimal career opportunities. By some extraordinary blind spot their work is assessed as less skilled and responsible than that of the humblest clerk. They have few chances of promotion since to become an administrative officer they must have a degree. Though 'specialist experience' may be taken as alternative to a degree, secretarial experience is not so regarded. There has been little acknowledgement of the extent to which secretarial and administrative work overlap, and much of the latter is labelled secretarial and done on the cheap. Even where secretaries *have* taken out a degree they find it hard to progress very far up the ladder. There seems to be a discomfort in acknowledging that such a change of status is possible. To do so might threaten the whole existing career structure. However, this is changing dramatically. The EEO officer has been active in pursuing the interests of general staff, and focused on them in research reports. Militancy has increased, now with EEO principles as well as hard facts to support them. A high-level committee has been set up to consider regrading. As in other workplaces, there is resistance from the industrial relations and personnel areas.

The jobs of departmental secretaries vary with the size and type of department and the general outlook of its staff. In some places they work as secretary to the 'god' professor and may even construct themselves in this role when there is no such expectation— by attempting to take over the appointments diary and so on. This could be a strategy for distancing themselves from the pooling arrangements. Professors may conspire in this, being as keen as any business executive to have a secretary of 'their own'. Elsewhere they work for the department rather than the individual. The professor's work may or may not have priority. Such a position may give them more autonomy but it cannot be taken for granted. While some secretaries quite literally run the department, others spend most of their time copy-typing. A great deal depends on how the professor chooses to administer the department. The departmental secretaries were divided between those who said they worked for a boss (their professor or head of discipline), those who said they worked for a boss but 'did some work for a number of other people', and a smaller group who rejected the relational definition and said that they fulfilled a function for the department.

Most of the secretaries at Street live nearby and are married to professional men, including academics. The Institute is able to attract well-educated 'middle-class' women because of its location. Jobs are filled by word of mouth rather than by advertisement. Despite the low pay and lack of promotional opportunities, women like the closeness to home, the apparent flexibility in leave arrangements and the fact that there is less pressure than in the private sector. The lack of job descriptions gives the Institute a lot of flexibility. There is no career ladder and no system for rewarding individual merit. The institute sticks rigidly to the awards, ignoring the fact that these specify only minimum conditions. As in the private sector, salary is determined by the salary to which the boss is entitled. It is assumed that 'the work done by all secretaries to deputy bursars, deputy registrars and professors, for example, is the same and that it warrants a lower level of remuneration than that done by all secretaries to registrar, bursar, architect-planner and librarian—without the need to examine the work actually performed by those secretaries' (Wills, 1986: 147). The disdain for general staff is evident in the story that circulates that the governing board long resisted having a representative for fear that they might get 'somebody's secretary...or a groundsman!

Cutbacks in secretarial staff had already taken place before word processors came in. There has been an increased use of temporaries, casuals and part-timers. Senior secretaries now have less backup and are expected to take on additional work and to service a longer list of people. Word processors were seen as saviours by many academics and overworked secretaries.

Academics have been more willing than managers to use word processors and now have less need of typing support. This could free secretaries to take on administrative work or it could further reduce their numbers, leaving those remaining to spend more time on mundane tasks such as photocopying. They could be a return to the one-to-one relation to the head of department, as the only one who will retain the 'luxury' of secretarial assistance; or they could find themselves working collectively, whether or not they choose to. The outcomes will vary and will depend on local struggles concerning the allocation of tasks and resources.

Semi-public organisations: the unions

Run neither for private profit nor in the 'public' interest, the unions fall into a category of their own. One might expect that the working conditions of secretaries would be markedly better than elsewhere. Secretaries have been more willing to strike against unions than any other employer. This may say something about conditions, or it may illustrate a greater political consciousness or commitment. Unions are also much more easily embarrassed by such actions. To take up some of these questions it seemed wise to avoid the more 'macho' unions where cliches would have been inevitable, and seek out unions which had a high proportion of women members and officials and where there had been debate about feminist issues. As at Jessie Street, there was freedom of movement around the building, opportunities to participate in tea room conversations, collect gossip, and talk with a larger number of people than were formally interviewed.

The Workers' Association has a staff of around 100 of whom about half are union officials (officers) and the others are support staff—secretarial, clerical and maintenance people. The officers are elected for three-year terms and their duties and responsibilities are jealously guarded. There is a strong sense in the union that the officers should continue to see themselves as workers rather than as permanent union officials. Even the industrial officers are 'amateurs' rather than specialists with law degrees. While officers are temporary, the staff are permanent. There is thus a sharp divide between officers and staff, in a union that prides itself on its egalitarianism. The staff provide continuity but there are very limited opportunities for their promotion: they cannot, as in some other unions, move into research positions, let alone become organisers.

The senior secretaries are paid between 20 and 25 per cent over the basic rates, which is a lot less than they could earn in the private sector. If pay was the only consideration the union would never keep top staff. The women were highly committed to their jobs and found political or personal satisfaction for working for the union. Lower down the scale there were rumblings about the 20 per cent increment; the officers and senior secretaries were admanant not only that they earned it, but that it was still not nearly enough given what they do. Though it is union policy to advertise vacancies internally first, the senior positions are rarely filled from inside. This suggests that possible internal applicants are well aware of how hard the top staff work for the extra money.

There are no personal assistants at the Workers' Association, and much of the work of the senior secretaries involves taking minutes and preparing agendas, rather than working directly for bosses. 'Even though you work on a one-to-one basis with a senior officer, the executive is your first priority. Last year they had 42 meetings,' said one of them. Unlike Jessie Street, the union does not need graduates to fulfill these tasks. Some secretaries work entirely for associations or committees, their work largely unsupervised. In this office the grapevine pipes up quickly enough if anyone is abusing their hours or not pulling their weight.

Staff who have worked for the Association for a long time are fiercely loyal to it. They look back nostalgically to the days when it was more like 'a family' where their opinions were asked for and their policy advice respected. The last ten to fifteen years have seen it become much bigger and more bureaucratic. This means it has become more specialised and secretaries are restricted to a narrower range of work. 'Elsewhere you can go onto other things rather than be a secretary. Here it is a complete and utter impossibility. A lot of the jobs that were done by secretaries are now being done by officers at double the salary...Our salaries have slipped back...Now they are really a long way behind what is being paid outside and we are having trouble getting replacements for anyone who leaves.' The only exception to this is in the country where, as with the clerical assistants in government offices, they may find themselves operating as de facto officers, interviewing, dealing with welfare issues and urgent personal crises or left alone for long periods to run the office. Union work often appeals as offering involvement and an outlet for political interests. Many secretaries are disappointed at the limitations, the factionalism, and the attitude of some of the officers that because you are not elected you don't have a brain and can't have an opinion. Some feel that they have been deskilled and diminished as a result of the growth of specialist positions. They often link this with the arrival of new technology. As one of them put it: 'A lot of it has to do with technology and it is partly because the place has got bigger. Bigger than it needed to in my personal opinion. There's a feeling that you are no longer valued...some duties have been withered away from us...it's assumed we're not political and not capable of initiating anything...I just see technology is going to take away a lot of initiative that we have and a lot of job satisfactions that we have.'

The presence of clearcut factions, who may move in and out of power at election time, highlights a question that is present in all workplaces but is usually more difficult to bring out into the open: is a secretary's loyalty to a particular boss or to a position? One secretary commented: 'When the new lot came in there was a funny feeling that the staff weren't supposed to help them...It was stated quite openly...And I don't think that it's right to dictate to us...You have to adjust to the people that are elected.' The adjustment is easier for some officers and staff than for others and on occasions secretaries do ask for transfers. Most secretaries are careful to avoid direct political involvement and are often upset by faction fights and distressed by emotional scenes between officers. One officer made a distinction between personal and political loyalty: 'I think the secretaries are the ones that see and cope with the stress that the person suffers in the job...They've got to deal with people who I might have had a blue with the day before about a political issue...They need a very fine-tuned political maturity in terms of their dealings with people.' Secretaries are formally allocated to positions rather than officers. Unlike most of the business world, officers are not permitted to take 'their' secretary with them if they are re-elected to a more senior position (though they sometimes fiddle it). This places a limit on the intensity of the involvement and on the expectations they initially have of each other. The staffing section make no attempt to match up officer and staff: if there is a vacancy for a secretary it is thought more important to find someone who will get on with the other secretaries on the floor, whose opinion will be considered.

What is notable about the union is the strength of the opposition to new technology. There had been ongoing debate, not only on terms and conditions under which technology would be adopted, but whether it was actually necessary. As a result, only two word processors were to be found in the whole building, in the research and legal sections. All kinds of data that elsewhere would be computerised continues to be dealt with by hand. The opposition is not to do with technology per se. It was pointed out that the Association had 'really gone to town' on photocopiers, and there was no opposition to the computer and the setting up of an EDP section. The word processor became a symbol for fears about deskilling and unemployment. Predictions about its devastating effects were central to the radical politics of the late 1970s and would have been taken for granted by large sections of the union. There is also a belief that technology would enable officers to bypass staff and tap directly into the computer. The setting up of a technological change committee allowed these views to be forcefully stated. Staff were in a better position to voice their opinions than in most other workplaces. The fact that the management of the union is temporary (even though people may be re-elected and some do have continuity) means that there is a greater reliance on staff and in situations that do not directly involve the union membership, a willingness to defer to them or at least hear them. As 'amateurs' the union officers were less laware of the potential productivity gains that word-processing and office automation might bring.

Opposition to the word processor was not unanimous. Some secretaries fought hard for the two machines in existence and complained that the opposition had not even bothered to come and have a look at them. Their frustration is evident: 'I mean the place is antiquated...They do minutes and cut and paste reports. I call it playschool activity.' However the attitude to new technology remains cautious and there is considerable pride in existing skills. 'You're using a WP because you've got an inefficient secretary or the officer does not dictate properly. You'd be better sending your officer off to learn to dictate better.'

Union secretaries were more assertive about exercising their rights and expressing their views than most others. Some identified strongly as feminists and/or socialists; even where they did not there was a political sophistication that was rare elsewhere. Some had been active in the reform group which set out to challenge the right-wing control of the Federated Clerks' Union. 'Amongst the feminists are some of the toughest feminists in the women's movement...So in talking about feminism we're putting up a pretty hard-line barrier to judge people.' This is a union whose women members have fought hard for their rights to equality and an environment where sexual politics are routinely discussed. How does this affect secretaries?

Feminism itself is hotly debated and the factions may be seen as *within* feminism rather than between feminism and its opponents. The position of women's officer is a politically and emotionally charged one, representing different possibilities and priorities. It had been the focus of a vigorous electoral struggle, with groups fiercely for or against the previous incumbent, and opponents labelling each other as either separatist extremists or male-identified cop-outs. There is space here for a lot of misperceptions. While some of the secretaries had strong feelings about it most had avoided getting drawn in. Some managed to remain detached by regarding feminism as an issue for management rather than for them. They are cynical about how far it extends, or else they see women officers as officers first and feminists second, assuming they have more in common with male officers than female staff. One commented that they 'are preaching to the women who are already exceedingly well-educated...who really have no problems, well not a great deal of problems with childcare and their sort of situation at home would be one of a complete division of labour...They should direct themselves to the women who work in the factories...' Feminist officers are often frustrated at working with the more traditional, less flexible and somewhat stereotypical secretaries who are resistant to change. As the ones who had been pushing wider policy issues they may actually be more demanding of the secretaries than most other officers. Others complained that women officers were less willing than the men to delegate work.

There are significant differences between this and most other workplaces. Friendships and sexual liaisons, wider social interactions and to some extent a shared political commitment mount a challenge to the structural inequalities between officers and staff. 'One of the rather delightful aspects of working here is that you are on first-name basis to begin with...And you certainly don't have problems with coffee...You just don't have that power game in here at all. It is not condoned...' In the more male-dominated unions, by contrast there is still the expectation that the secretary can be called away from whatever else she is doing to make tea. But the structures do not go away: 'It is a pity that they don't carry that progressive attitude forward in other ways.' Though the atmosphere is relatively egalitarian there is a residual contempt among some of the officers. One staff member felt that 'the union isn't totally honest in that its private face is completely different from its public image'. They had threatened strike action over a salaries claim after the union had tried to redefine 'average weekly earnings' in such a way as to limit a pay rise. There had been some bitterness over the union using their own industrial officers against a group of women without access to industrial expertise.

Issues may not be satisfactorily resolved but they are more likely to come to the surface. This is helped by the existence of committees such as the staff and salaries committees (not to mention technological change) where secretaries can put their views. There had been fights around annual holidays and long service and maternity leave, with staff adamant that they should have the same conditions as officers. In the private sector such a demand would never be heard. Here they were sophisticated enough to take it to annual conference just when maternity leave conditions for the members were being debated. While the natural justice of the claim could not be disputed, and the officers were extremely sensitive to accusations of applying a double standard, they pointed out that conditions were already way ahead of those of most other secretarial workers. As one secretary summed it up: 'They are an employer and you are an employee...And you always face problems with the employer.'

Structures and discourses

Similar structural constraints were evident in all the organisations visited. Though some secretaries and employers had greater awareness of them than others, there was a limit to the extent to which individuals could 'choose' to operate outside them. The example of the Workers Association makes this particularly clear. The three discourses, master—slave, nanny/mother—child, and 'team', operate across all the workplaces but at different intensities and with different emphases. Some employers were 'traditional' in their use of secretaries while with others the secretaries had been successfully able to evoke the 'team' discourse. There is no necessary connection between income and job satisfaction. On the contrary, those secretaries who reported most satisfaction with their jobs were frequently receiving lower salaries than they could earn elsewhere.

It is not possible to generalise about the conditions of secretaries. The ways in which they experience themselves and their work are affected by a variety of factors including the whole ethos of the organisation. A variety of styles of masculinity were constructed across the workplaces, ranging from working-class brutality, gentlemanly sadism, paternalism, liberal rationality, socialist mateship and fraternal back-slapping. All are oppressive to secretaries, but not uniformly so. It is not helpful to rank them but rather to work out the strategies of resistance that each requires. It is not always the case that socialist or radical employers will be the most enlightened or that the private sector will be automatically the most backward. It was, for example, a private company that had tackled the issue of establishing secretaries' salaries independently of those of their bosses. In this case, it was liberal managers challenging traditional assumptions that brought about some change.

All the workplaces had been affected by technological change and the reorganisation of the labour process. Power struggles go on, not only between bosses and secretaries, but between managers, as to what role secretaries should have. Often bosses and secretaries unite in attempting to preserve a relationship that in some sense suits them both. Equal employment opportunity and affirmative action are now starting to hit the private sector as well as the public sector—again with differing results. It remains to be seen to what extent truly 'objective' measures of skill will be developed, how they will be applied, and how they will affect secretarial positions. Work value or 'comparable worth' rulings from the Arbitration Commission would provide a greater impetus for change than affirmative action functioning alone. But legislative changes and court rulings have to be adopted within particular workplace cultures and the extent and directions of change depends on concrete local struggles.

·6· Office 'ladies': training to be a secretary

This is a transition year. We hope you'll learn to
behave and dress as you would in an office... You
are not naughty little children but office *ladies*.

TAFE TEACHER

Grooming... a dirty word with the women's
movement but not with me.

JOAN FIELDING, OUTGOING HEAD OF SECRETARIAL STUDIES

The teachers of secretarial studies are in a rather different situation from most school teachers. Their subjects command little
respect and, with the possible exception of shorthand, have no
academic or technical status. Their trade colleagues in the colleges
of technical and further education often regard them as not 'real'
teachers in much the same way as secretaries are regarded as not
'real' workers. Typing teachers are assumed to have a particularly
easy time since all they are thought to do is supervise and walk
around the room correcting mistakes. Teachers are expected to
attend to the non-technical aspects of secretarial work, the social
skills which Griffin sums up as 'service with a smile' (1985: 124–28).
Their students will be judged less on their occupational skills
than on their femininity, defined in terms of appearance, fashion
awareness, clothes and taste.

Assuming that they have the interests of the students, as well as
their own interests in mind, how do teachers respond to this
situation? They may, of course, insist on the importance of the
skills they teach or attempt to have them revalued in professional
or technical terms. Or they may play down femininity, denying its
relevance to secretarial training, and emphasise gender-neutral
skills. But these 'solutions' are not much help in the short run.
Ninety-nine per cent of the students are female. In making their
transition from the school to the office they do have to learn to
negotiate sexuality and gender relations, not only with their peers
but in the adult world of work. The girls know this and are, for
the most part, keen to find clues for the construction of adult
femininity. The most popular teachers are the ones who engage

with the students' 'real-life' problems and who reveal something about themselves.

Traditionally the way in which teachers have solved the problem of how to gain identity and self-respect, both for themselves and their students, is to insist that what they are producing is 'young ladies'. Femininity and skill are welded together here in a construction that relies heavily on class imagery to confer status and respect. Middle-class femininity conveys a certain kind of 'presence' which balances submissiveness with authority, sexual attractiveness with dignity. Literacy, general knowledge and secretarial competence are considered important, but important in a taken-for-granted way. They are treated not so much as skills as characteristics which a lady has, along with a well-groomed appearance, a well-modulated voice, maturity, poise and grace and the ability to converse intelligently with managers. Office 'lady' with its dual overtones of gender and class encapsulates this ideal of a white and middle-class femininity.

The ideal is an important reference point in the construction of a segmented secretarial workforce. Anglo-Australian and middle-class girls take it on board fairly effortlessly as an extension of all they have previously learned. For those from non-English-speaking, Aboriginal or working-class backgrounds the world of the office is alien and unfamiliar and the socialisation process may involve an attempt to break down or transcend the existing cultural background. This results in explicit hostilities between staff and students. Not surprisingly, the middle-class groups are likely to move into the higher-status jobs as private secretaries and personal assistants, while the others may have difficulty in getting any kind of job at all. Unemployment for teenage women with secretarial qualifications is around 15 per cent, and heavily concentrated in country and outer suburban areas (Labour Force, February 1986).

The ability to present themselves as well groomed, articulate and confident affects not only what type of job the girls get but the type of organisation for whom they work. An Alfred Marks Bureau survey in England indicated that male managers prefer secretaries to come from a similar cultural background to their own (Griffin, 1985: 127–28). The head offices of prestigious companies such as Pacific Industries, Darling or Universal, are more interested in recruiting 'ladylike' staff than are the regional or suburban offices of manufacturers or retailers. An advertising agency will be looking for a different kind of staff from what a small engineering company or biscuit manufacturer in the western suburbs will be seeking. Students from working-class, and particularly from non-English-speaking backgrounds, go into government jobs precisely because there is less emphasis on appearance, personality and performing well at interviews. Middle-class students are more willing to put themselves through a series of interviews until they find the 'right' job, to explore various possibilities in the private sector and to see secretarial work as a stepping stone to 'something else'.

Each year in Australia more than 40 000 students enrol in secretarial and typing courses (based on Sweet, 1983; O'Neil, 1985). Technical education in Australia is largely in the hands of state government departments of TAFE. In New South Wales the secretarial curriculum is drawn up by the Secretarial Studies Department within the TAFE central office and taught in various technical colleges across the state. The bulk of the students are catered for either by these colleges or private business colleges, while a small minority take degree courses in tertiary institutions. Most come straight from school and typically they are sixteen to seventeen years old and have the School Certificate. There is also a large group of eighteen-year-olds who usually come in with the Higher School Certificate (HSC). Only a few have any intention of becoming full-blown secretaries.

The colleges do not create the segmented labour market but they shape it in important ways, particularly in connecting 'skills' with the cultural production of 'office ladies'. This may be part of the deliberate strategies of teachers or an unintended consequence of their teaching practice. By gearing their teaching to the training of professional secretaries, for example, they implicitly downgrade the majority of students even if their conscious aim is to make such training universally available. But middle-class femininity is not monolithic and teachers do not have one single approach or coherent strategy. Students come with a variety of backgrounds and abilities and have their own ideas of what they want from secretarial training: they are not pieces of plasticine. The colleges should be seen as construction sites on which various models of 'office lady' are worked out on the basis of interactions between teachers and students. Some groups will come close to the ideal while others resist it; in every case some kind of compromise will be reached.

Femininity is not simply imposed by teachers on unwilling students who 'resist'. The students have contradictory responses and may frequently change their minds about what they want, or accept some parts while rejecting others. Femininity is more than a list of character traits or appropriate behaviours and it is not simply grown into. Of course it may be argued that the girls have been learning 'femininity' from birth, that the social and cultural inputs are many and varied, and that the contribution of the colleges is merely a continuation of what they have learned at school. Some teachers believe that the girls learn more in their first six weeks in the workforce than they do in the whole year of 'let's pretend'. But they are there at an impressionable time in their lives as they make the transition from school to workplace and from the world of girlhood to the world of adult women.

In order to look at the ways in which gender and class structure the secretarial workforce at the point of entry, a number of the colleges were visited. They included six TAFE colleges (two in the western suburbs of Sydney, one each in northern, eastern and central Sydney, and New South Wales country) and a similar number of private colleges, all in Sydney. Classes in every subject were observed—shorthand and typing, business communication and clerical procedures, individual development and oral communication—in order to assess the 'informal' curriculum of femininity and social skills. This is taught not only in 'grooming and deportment', which takes up a only small number of total hours, but throughout the course. Even where there are token efforts to recognise change, the whole language of the curriculum reinforces the existing divisions between male managers and female secretaries. The boss is relentlessly referred to as a man and letters are addressed to 'Dear Sir'; the students are addressed as 'girls', even when an occasional boy is in the class.

TAFE teachers handed over sessions in their 'individual development' classes for the administration of a brief questionnaire. This was a way into discussing with the students their reasons for being there, their images of secretaries and their plans for the future. In both TAFE and the private colleges students' groups of three students from each stream were interviewed. Conversation ranged over what they thought of the courses, the teachers and the other students, as well as leisure activities, work expectations and their opinions about boys, sex, marriage and children. Given that they had every reason to associate us with the teachers they were remarkably forthcoming in expressing their opinions. In each class one volunteer was then asked to choose two others to participate. Talking to friendship groups and using class time undoubtedly helped. Where most other interviewees were anxious to preserve their anonymity these girls were keen to be 'in the book' and wanted their real names used. Some were interviewed again later in the course and a third time the following year when they had spent some time in the workforce.

Finally time was spent in staff rooms and talking with individual teachers. These interviews covered not only their thoughts about teaching but their own work histories. Some had wanted to be teachers in the first place and were denied entry through their lack of an academic education. Teaching secretarial studies was a way of achieving part of their original goal and for some a means of upward mobility. Many teachers could be earning a great deal more working as secretaries; but teaching can be combined with childcare, whereas with secretarial work this is more difficult. They welcome the part-time work, the shorter hours and the term breaks even if they are exploited. Given the fluctuating numbers of students between the beginning and end of a year they provide a flexible workforce. In the private colleges they are likely to be paid by the hour and under-employed, sent home when they are not needed. Their structural situation means they are likely to be conservative or passive in their outlook and do not want to rock the boat. Their own lives convey important messages to students about how to juggle home and work and about priorities and expectations.

Class and status divisions

The six TAFE colleges felt very different from each other as well as from the private system. The private colleges range from the large, prestigious metropolitan ones which provide for the elite to tiny suburban colleges which often take in students who would not survive in the TAFE system. I shall treat TAFE and the private colleges separately. The bulk of secretarial students in New South Wales are now catered for through the TAFE network. Until World War II the majority were in the hands of the private colleges. TAFE's initial courses in the 1930s were set up to give both men and women specific skills. Their first full secretarial course began in 1945—46 and by 1953 TAFE was attracting students away from the private schools and making 'middle-class femininity' available to girls from the working class. Formal streaming began in 1958 with the commencement both of an Advanced course and the first secretarial course in which shorthand was not compulsory. Students are placed in either the Certificate or Advanced course, depending on the outcome of intelligence tests and whether or not they have the HSC. Some colleges have special INTO (Introduction to Technical Occuations) classes for mature-age students, while the Commonwealth Employment Service (CES) finances a number of aboriginal students.

The TAFE colleges run a number of streams. While all include basic typing and office procedures, business and oral communication and some form of 'individual development' the more advanced will have either shorthand or bookkeeping or, in some cases, both. Typically there may be five or six classes of around 30 students, organised into three streams. Care is taken at the formal level to avoid differentiation. Rather than ranking the classes A, B, C, they are named after poets or precious stones or flowers or timbers. While the ranking of poets may be a subjective matter, in most cases the hierarchy is ruthlessly clearcut: cedar takes precedence over pine and orchids over daisies. The streaming is done by teachers on the basis of school results combined with tests on vocabulary, composition and mathematics. Teachers claim this is about '90 per cent accurate' and for the most part students cannot change streams, although some do drop down from the shorthand class. The students have little contact with those outside their own class.

Until the late 1950s a lot of girls came from selective high schools with the equivalent of six As in the old Intermediate Certificate. In the country it is still not unusual to find students with HSC aggregates of over 400. As these students started going to university in larger numbers TAFE began to offer its first secretarial courses without shorthand. Coinciding with the departure of brighter students to greener fields, the new courses attracted a predominantly working-class clientele. Many of those interviewed in the early weeks had not heard of typing pools and had no idea what a stenographer did; business administration was another world to them. Ability and class are conflated as in 'we don't get Level 1 English students any more, only lower-class girls who would once have worked in shops or factories'. Colleges in areas where the 'higher socioeconomic brackets' predominate put on more shorthand classes than those in the western suburbs. 'The girls we get would have worked in factories years ago,' said one teacher. Another spoke of the 'garbage we get now' while another referred disparagingly to their manners and behaviour. While their reference point was usually the decline in literacy or ability, the class connotations were unmistakable.

Teachers disagree on whether the HSC girls are, in fact, the best students. Some see the ideal student as the bright fifteen-year-old, who is enthusiastic, eager to learn and relatively easy to mould: these are the ones who have 'made a commitment' to be secretaries. The HSC girls may be more literate and have established more regular study habits, but for them it is a comedown to be doing a secretarial course. Shorthand was still regarded as the prestige subject, even though it has diminishing relevance in the workplace. Teachers claim that employers take it as evidence that they are getting more than a pretty face, a sign of 'grey matter up there'. But the department has reinforced this by testing girls on entry and putting the brighter ones into shorthand classes. It may be more accurate to say that employers see shorthand as a sign of diligence and attention to detail, rather than intelligence. As one teacher remarked, 'I don't know if they think about secretaries as being intelligent'. In the current reorganisation shorthand is being treated as an option rather than a core part of the diploma course and may become less significant in the ranking of students.

There are enormous differences in the way the streams are treated. The shorthand students are treated as young adults, frequently permitted to call the teacher by her first name, given responsibility and a degree of freedom. They are expected to get the pick of the jobs and because they are typically more middle-class the transition is smooth. Since there is little conflict between their backgrounds and the requirements of the office the teachers can simply build on what is already there. The bookkeeping students may be every bit as intelligent as the shorthand class but are defined as socially inferior: they need 'the rough edges knocked off'. Less hope is held out for the 'lower' streams which experience a direct continuity with school discipline. The teachers often encourage these students to leave early and are pleased if they can get any kind of an office job. Far from turning them into 'office ladies' teachers are glad if they can give them a few 'life skills'.

There is a strong correlation between the streams and the different sections of the labour market. There is regional variation too. The colleges in the western suburbs, catering for working-class girls from predominantly migrant backgrounds, are decidedly more regimented and prison-like. Hostility between staff and students is ongoing. 'Career path is a difficult concept for them. Many just want a job behind a typewriter,' says one teacher. Low academic achievement, poor speech and the inability to write and spell severely limit their employment prospects. Some will remain unemployed. Others are there to fill in time until a husband is chosen for them by their families.

If their class and cultural backgrounds are seen purely as handicaps it is not surprising that students will vent their anger in the classroom. Teachers recognise a link between their limited prospects and their rowdy behaviour, their determination to express who they are and to get some entertainment from the otherwise drab lives that restrict them. Heavy drinking and drug-taking or sexual adventures may be their reaction to strict controls at home. Despite all this teachers carry on teaching 'the course', often with minimal effort. Some, like Peg, are committed to helping the girls overcome at least some of the handicaps: 'They don't belong to any culture. They're culturally lost. It's not a class but a cultural gap. They might come from quite wealthy backgrounds but they are as rough as bags. They need to learn that the dialect of their peers is not acceptable in the office. I try to get them interested in words.' Peg says they come from girls' schools and convents and have not learnt to relate socially or sexually. They are not allowed out unescorted and it is assumed by their parents that they will marry the first man they date. Their chances of learning formal skills are limited by difficulties in their personal lives as they try to reconcile their parents' culture with elements of Australian culture. In one of the colleges girls from Greek and Lebanese backgrounds were enrolling for shorthand at night and getting the parents to drop them off and pick them up two or three nights a week. They spent the time in the canteen with the boys.

Their transition to office life will not exactly be easy and they often show aggression in the classroom. Marie talks about the importance of teaching them how to behave, via personal development, oral communication and office skills. Peg comments that 'they're so unenlightened about life that anything you teach is beneficial'. I heard her spend half a lesson patiently explaining why the phrase 'jesus christ' was not socially acceptable! She seeks to give them confidence and a role model, seeing their emotional development as a necessary preliminary to the learning of any office skills. She positions herself as mother, attempting to give them things that their own mothers were not able to give. They respond well though she says the weaning process is often painful.

Whatever their class backgrounds, students in the western suburbs had a limited view of what was possible for them. Even the top stream said they would be satisfied with fairly lowly public service jobs. I asked classes at a western suburbs TAFE why they were doing the course. Here are some of the answers they called out:

It's good careers for girls.
You get good jobs.
You can always step up in the office.
Girls can put up with the work.
It's clean work [compared with factory work, working at Kentucky Fried Chicken, hairdressing].
You wear nice clothes.
My mother decided I should come here.
There was nothing else to do.
I wanted to be a beautician. My mother talked me into coming here.
My mother said, do a secretarial course, or get out.
My dad said, you're going to tech.
I did typing as school for two years and I really like it.
I tried to get a job in a travel office but I couldn't so I decided to do the secretarial course because I had nothing else to do.
I wanted to be a vet but Mum didn't want me to go on.
I was doing accounts for a while. But it was pretty boring. I didn't know what to do so I decided that I wanted to do typing and shorthand and be a secretary.
She [mother] made me come here—threw me in here.
They say it was good for them so it's good for you.

I could have worked in a record company. Mum said that it wasn't a good job.

In all the colleges mothers are the decisive influence and it is their lives that the daughters are expected to copy or improve upon. The northern and eastern suburbs show a stronger air of confidence even among migrant and working-class girls. Government jobs are viewed with contempt and the girls believe they will be able to get the positions they want in private enterprise. They expect a secretarial course to be a stepping stone to other things, often with the help of family contacts. It did not occur to them to choose secretarial work because it was 'clean' for they had never thought they might work anywhere 'dirty'. The city students tried to be more sophisticated and were often ashamed or defensive about their choice. They were aware that students in business studies, computing and mass communications courses referred to them as 'raving idiots' and they often deceived their friends about what they were doing.

Aboriginal students are concentrated in country areas and their special needs have been recognised with the creation of separate classes to deal with specific problems of cultural difference, poor English and lack of literacy. Students say that without this special class they would not remain in the course. They get ranked last behind even the other classes doing the same stream, which tends to reinforce the image of inadequacy. The CES pays them twice what the other students' tertiary education allowance (TEAS) does and this creates additional hostility from the whites. Given the racism, particularly in the country, and already high unemployment there, the majority will not get jobs without special assistance. They will go into the public service or find employment among their own people with one or other of the Aboriginal agencies. Rarely will they work as private secretaries.

The colleges are no melting pot. A disparate range of people are thrown in and subjected to a socialisation process. They come out the other end in a number of more refined categories, ranging from cream to skim milk. These categories fit well with a segmental labour market and a fragmented labour process. But it is not a neat functional fit. Employers may carp about illiteracy, scruffiness or lack of punctuality but to some extent they have to deploy what they get. They have not rushed to offer secretaries monetary rewards for conforming more nearly to their ideals. In times of high unemployment they can pick and choose more. But there are shortages and bottlenecks. Employers cannot simply snap their fingers and have the colleges turn out exactly what they want.

Modernisation

'Grooming and deportment' used to be a standard part of secretarial training. In the 1970s there were major battles in TAFE
between traditionalists and feminists over whether it should continue. The leading 'traditionalist' was Joan Fielding who, after a
brief career as a secretary in the 1940s, moved through the TAFE
system to became head of Secretarial Studies. For more than two
decades she dominated the curriculum and produced many of the
textbooks. *Australian Secretarial Practice* (Fielding, 1969) was originally published in the USA in 1934 and was still widely used in
the 1970s (Taylor, 1982: 14–15). Mrs Fielding's ideas about what
a secretary should be remained fixed in the 1940s: '...graciousness
is one of the greatest attributes any woman can have...and buying a silk scarf for the boss's wife is an important part of the
job...' Feminists wanted to replace grooming with gender-neutral
'life skills' and to emphasise technical proficiency. The 'individual
development' courses that emerged in the 1970s were something
of a compromise, blending beauty and fashion, hair and nail care
with apparently neutral subjects like diet, psychology and human
relationships. Debate continues on both the status of secretarial
skills and the ways in which gender may or may not be taken into
account in the teaching process.

A review of the TAFE system was completed in 1983 and since
then there has been some reform. Pilot programs were set up in
26 courses in 1984 in an attempt to create a more flexible unit
structure. But change has been slow and difficult to implement
and often runs into resistance from teachers whose knowledge of
the workplace may be dated. They are now required to have at
least five years' work experience, which brings them into line with
other technical college teachers. Teachers are often wary of new
technology and are threatened by the development of word-
processing and computing. Since shorthand is the most skilled
and prestigious teaching subject, they fear their own jobs are at
stake. Any fundamental reorganisation of secretarial work may
conflict with their industrial position. A consideration of secretarial
studies in relation to apprenticeships also runs into trouble with
those teachers who consider their students 'superior' to the 'trade
boys'. Under the proposed changes, students would be able to
pick and choose which skills they wanted to learn.

In each of the colleges there was a handful of teachers with
broadly feminist sympathies and these were the ones who were
the keenest to talk about change. Esther, a head teacher, often
takes holiday office jobs and is aware that people behave differently towards her once they realise she is a teacher. Teaching is
prestigious, whereas 'a secretary could be practically anybody'.

She would like to see proper standards, a certificate akin to that which apprentices get. A secretary should be valued for her occupational skills. As it is, she says, the most unlikely students often get jobs because the employer likes the look of them. In her view everyone should be mindful of appearance and personal hygiene but there should be no place for sex in the office. She admits that the beauty therapist can give good practical advice—if you prepare them tongue in cheek! At her college 'grooming and deportment' is an optional extra which was put on after normal hours!

Other teachers echo these themes. Some argue that a year is too long and that it would be better to teach a four- or five-month skills-oriented course, though this would not be directly comparable with a three years' apprenticeship. They believe shorthand is a waste of time and are frustrated that they still have to teach on manual typewriters. There is strong support for 'individual development' being treated as an option rather than a compulsory course. Nancy tells her students that typing is a useful personal skill for when they go to university in the hope that they might see new possibilities in their lives. And she introduces them to transactional analysis in an effort to develop some self-awareness. Teachers like Nancy believe the problem of low self-esteem must be addressed if secretaries are to develop confidence and a capacity for critical thinking. They frequently spoke about the 'Cinderella complex' and argue that as long as women fear independence they will prefer to work for men so they can have a daddy figure to look after them.

Mother—daughter relations underlie and structure teacher—student relations in the colleges. The mothers are preparing the daughters for their final step into the adult heterosexual world. While some teachers take on this role quite self-consciously, others specifically try to avoid it as smothering or controlling. In the inner city there has been a move away from the classroom situation to divide the students up into small groups and to simulate the office more closely. A counsellor there argues that teachers have to let go of mothering and treat the students as adult women. It is ironic that they have to prepare their charges for adult heterosexual life in the context of a single sex group, particularly as most of the girls have come from coeducational schools. Some teachers think that 'only if boys do the course will the girls work out they are not at work to be handmaidens'. They say that male students 'tidy up a class remarkably. The girls become a lot more mature a lot more quickly. They are less clucky'. The logic of degendering secretarial studies would be that it would become attractive to male students.

The retirement of Mrs Fielding and the appointment of a new head of school at TAFE has seen a determined push towards professionalism The name of the school has been changed from Secretarial Studies to Office Administration and the next few years should see a change of emphasis from shorthand and book-keeping to communications and computing. There is a recognition that secretaries need more managerial skills than in the past, including computer accounting and an ability to use microcom-puters. Methods like 'Sight and Sound' could revolutionise typing-teaching, with implications for teaching jobs. With less time spent on shorthand and typing more time would be available for learning other skills. The possibility of a merger with 'Business Studies' is there, though teachers fear losing their separate identity and being swallowed up.

Many in the TAFE system want to extend professionalism fur-ther, with more tertiary courses and diplomas that are acceptable as part of a degree structure. While some teachers want to abandon any reference to femininity, others believe the 'dress for success' literature may be usefully included in the new 'Presenting for Life' course. Various constructions of femininity now alternately blend with and contradict each other.

The private colleges

In addition to the state system there are a number of private colleges, which claim to be more in touch with current business realities. Some are run commercially offering specialised six- to eight-week courses. The majority are run as non-profit organisa-tions and have since the 1970s been 'government-approved', run-ning similar courses to TAFE. Government subsidies and controls here parallel the structure in the private school system. The colleges range from the tiny suburban establishments of one or two rooms through to the prestigious Metropolitan Business Col-lege (MBC) founded in the 1890s and now by far the largest city college and recognised as leader in the field. While MBC attracts the academically able, the private colleges as a whole cater for many who are unable to cope in the TAFE system. They sell themselves as offering individual tuition, firmer discipline and closer contact with business realities. Because they are smaller, they have less rigid streaming than TAFE and a lower dropout rate. Fees make a big difference, for the contract here is primarily with the parents. The students are generally divided according to age rather than ability and the classes are thus more mixed. There is little sense of rivalry between streams and friendships form across classes. The emphasis is on testing and feedback on individual performance rather than keeping up with or identifying with the class.

Where the suburban colleges are quite spartan, MBC occupies a plush inner-city space. It has a large reception area with plants, expensive lamps, substantial leather armchairs and the emblem, in gold letters, adorning brown fabric walls. Part of the staff's job is to 'sell' secretarial training. Brochures are glossy and highly produced and they have a video which is shown in New South Wales country as well as city schools. Secretarial work is aggressively 'marketed' as a career 'which has just taken off', and its pleasures are emphasised: MBC graduates will work with top people, the brains of the company, and get to know a lot of confidential information.

At MBC the advanced students study economics and law and the teaching is pitched at a higher level than classes at the TAFE colleges. Business communication was taught by a man who commanded absolute attention. He was authoritative and energetic, with structured spaces for student participation, usually through a show of hands, and extremely businesslike. He talked to them about open and closed punctuation and the importance of being flexible enough to follow the firm's policy rather than sticking to what is formally correct. There was stress on pleasing the boss (always a man), and doing it the company's way when you find out what that is. His routine language was of exams and assessment, as in 'Two parts, heading and reference, I'll let you leave out, and I'll take no marks from you. But I ask you to think twice about doing it'. The students laughed at his jokes and were surprisingly keen; any talking was about the content of the lesson.

In the private college 'g and d' is still routinely taught. One such course, called 'Total Woman', is organised around the themes of sight, smell, sound and touch. The teacher, in her thirties, was heavily made up, with dyed-blonde hair, lots of jewellery and very high heels. She warned the girls that since they could be competing with hundreds for other jobs they must package themselves appealingly:

> If you had to choose between a brown paper parcel and a very pretty one—which would you choose? Which would you be attracted to? That's what it's about—turning yourself from a brown paper parcel into one with all the trimmings... You have to get your outside package into top shape—through self-discipline, a positive attitude, a willingness to succeed.
>
> I can tell just looking at you which girls really like themselves, have self-esteem. And I can tell the girls who are hiding behind their hair—I wonder, what are they hiding?
>
> Some of you may have the same hairstyle you had two years ago—You wouldn't be like that with your clothes. Always change and adapt... even if it's just a slight change...

The girls are told they must dress to please everyone—themselves, other girls and of course, men.

> You have to have the same attitude to dressing for college or work as you would for a party—just the style of dress is different. You have to have a strict routine, to make an effort. You have to be pleasing to the boss and others at work. You have to wear the right clothes...and for work they should be understated. Later in the course we will teach you planning your wardrobe...grooming is from top to toe, and you have to work at it...

A major task for the Total Woman is controlling her female body which is ever on the brink of uncontrollability and needs extensive cleaning and deodorising to prevent it smelling. She must learn to speak clearly and grammatically and train herself to lower her pitch—a high-pitched voice grates. She must read to improve her mind and especially to converse on men's topics: 'A successful lady knows what has happened in Europe—just on the surface— you don't have to have an in-depth knowledge. She knows what's happening in sports—she can talk about that too. That will make you a Total Woman.' Unfortunately I had to leave before finding out how touch contributed to the Total Woman.

This course is consistent with 'traditional' femininity in that it is concerned with looking, smelling, sounding and behaving like a lady. But sexuality and sexual assertiveness are pushed more strongly than they would once have been. The 'Total Woman' comes close to Helen Gurley Brown's *Cosmo* girl: stylish, ambitious and sexually playful. She shares the feminists' interest in careers and assertiveness but uses her sexuality more deliberately to achieve her ends. She sees herself as part of a world in which sex is perceived, by both men and women, as part of the reward of being at the top or of working with those who are. Yet the *Cosmo* woman has to work hard on her looks and attractiveness, and learn to play all sorts of games in order to get what she wants from men, whether at work or at home. For students the attraction of grooming and deportment classes is that they get a professional to take them through what they read in the magazines.

The 'personal development' course, at the same college, takes more of a liberal feminist approach than does 'grooming and deportment'. But it is very different from TAFE-style feminism. Here the latest insights of the personal growth movement are applied to help students set their own individual goals and plan strategies for achieving them. Meditation and relaxation techniques are combined with creative fantasy and the use of positive affirmations. Life is divided into categories (physical, social, mental, self-awareness, family and financial) and goals are set in each through the use of visualisations in which 'all thoughts of limitations are to be banished from your mind'. I watched the class do an exercise in which they were asked to visualise themselves in three years' time and then to write down where they were and how they had got there. One could imagine a TAFE class going into complete uproar if asked to perform a similar exercise but this group did it with remarkably little fuss and enjoyed them-selves. Their dreams included overseas trips, luxury cars, pres-tigious jobs and smart clothes. The following is typical:

> Lisa is standing in the sun outside a terrace house in Surry Hills, still blonde, hair longer and she is far skinnier. Before her is parked a little 1957 Model Jaguar...She got her diploma, a job in the travel industry came quickly. After a few months she rebels and leaves with a large pay packet. She proceeds to get a new job as a highly paid business manager...She makes a happy little home with the two guys she lives with.
> Life is fun, the job is OK, the house is a hobby and she is busy motivating herself. She is saving her brain out for a trip overseas...

It is these aspirations rather than marriage and family that were validated by the teacher. The new 'office lady' has her personal agenda well worked out and is in no sense passive, subservient or without personal ambition. She is confident in both her profes-sional skills and her sexuality. The influence of feminism is evident here but it is coming not through a demand for elite professional courses, as in TAFE, but through incorporation into 'progressive' management strategies. Women can be Winners too if they play their cards right.

Sexuality and resistance

Not all the girls are interested in *Cosmo* sophistication or think it matches their image of secretaries. They are caught up with 'girl culture', with their relationships with their close female friends and the activities of the peer group. While not uninterested in clothes, femininity or heterosexuality, they want to work out their own styles rather than unilaterally accept the ones the teachers put up. Secretaries' clothes are seen as neither glamorous nor casual nor smart:

> *Who ticked secretaries wear fashion clothes?*
> (Laughter) You're joking! No they don't.
> They have to look nice enough.
> They only wear silk shirts and tailored skirts.
> Your have to be sophisticated in a legal office.
>
> *How should ordinary secretaries dress?*
> Not fashion clothes. Suitable clothes: a skirt, not really high shoes, a blouse.

It's not fashion, that's not suited for work.
It's not a uniform like a factory. You can choose what you wear.
You wear a uniform in a bank but it's better than a factory or a nurses' uniform.
They wear glasses with their hair up.
They wear nice clothes...not jeans or slacks.
Straight skirt. Blouse.
Neat and tidy.
A skirt and top.
Respectable.
A tailored look—it shows you're efficient.
Would you like that?
No. It's too dressed up.
What would you prefer?
Being trendy.
Saturdays are different. You dress way out to go out.
Fashionable. Trendy. Fix your hair. Wear long earrings.

Clothes are second only to boyfriends in their conversations with each other. The two often go together as in, 'well, I went out with this spunky guy and I wore...' Only in some of the private colleges was there any interest in *Vogue* sophistication, cream linen dresses and so on. This makes sense. Very few of these students are likely to have the incomes, or move in the social worlds, where high fashion is appropriate. They do not want to wear 'office' clothes until they have to, and resist the idea that they should start forming disciplined habits *now*. They do not want to dress like secretaries, in blouses and skirts and low-heeled shoes. They find work clothes boring and prefer to spend their limited money on punk, brightly coloured, 'outrageous' clothes. Their preferred style is casual and many come to college in jeans or cotton pants and tee shirts. Some say they'd rather be wearing shorts and sandshoes.

The girls know that appearances will affect their job chances but they do not want to think about the possibility of sexual interactions at work. 'Work' is still largely an unknown world of adults into which they have not yet been fully initiated. While they want friendly relations in the office it is not seen as a place to meet boyfriends or husbands: you meet men 'somewhere else'. They do not have to be ear-bashed about the desirability of forming relations with men. They take it for granted, just as they take marriage for granted, as what life is about. But they may resist the terms and the timing. And it is their female peer group that gives them the confidence to resist as well as providing an audience.

Both middle- and working-class girls resist the teachers' injunctions to dress and behave like 'ladies', although their resistance takes different forms and has different consequences. At one college the 'top' stream had been pushed into inviting the carpentry boys to a lunchtime sausage sizzle to thank them for making some footstools. Intended as a practice session in playing hostess, both the boys and the girls had to be frogmarched there, and once there refused to talk to each other. It may be that the boys were regarded as too young, or of the wrong social background, but the major reason seems to have been the sense of being under observation and possible ridicule by adults. One student reflected later:

> The BBQ was just so tacky. They were just off the air. It was like some American thing: someone's got to fall in love with a carpentry guy to give it a happy ending. We knew most of the guys from school anyway and could easily have got to know them ourselves if we wanted to. . .I don't know why the teachers pushed it. Perhaps they were bored. . .They were trying to make the whole tech one big happy family. Everyone was just there for the free hot dogs and steak sandwiches.

The sausage sizzle was a flop primarily because the teachers were there and would not leave. The girls were not rejecting 'femininity' or opposite sex relationships, but objecting to what they saw as unwarranted 'interference' in their extracurricular activities. In the classroom, they were cooperative and intent on passing their exams. This is why the teachers could take an interest in their social life in the first place: the 'lower' strands in this college had not been invited to the barbeque! In the private colleges and the 'higher' TAFE streams resistance is limited. The students may be fed up or bored but they are prepared to put up with the college in order to get their certificate or diploma.

In staffroom conversations the teachers regularly labelled classes or individual students as 'troublemakers' and they proceeded to live the part (Samuel, 1983: 374). These were usually the younger working-class girls who were not thought bright enough to do shorthand or bookkeeping. They were not bothered about being excluded from shorthand and a lot of their resistance was to subjects they considered irrelevant, among which they included just about everything except typing. There was also a continuous struggle with the teachers over the 'office ladies' mould. According to teachers:

> There's been a fair bit of trouble over dress. We let it go for a month and then when we told them it wouldn't do they objected. . .But they have to be young ladies. . .not rowdy and running around like kids, not smoking and no loitering. . .
>
> We teach them how to be in an office every day, how to dress, to present for an interview. . .and not to be aggressive. A lot of girls are aggressive now and they have to learn not to be. They may think they are great outside and then find in the office they are a little nobody.

They have to learn to live in a world where you don't get what you want all the time. Our job is to make them understand that.

This contrasts with the liberal feminist style of places like MBC, where the girls learn that they can be assertive, use their femininity to their advantage, and get what they want. Of course MBC, and the 'troublemakers' in the western suburbs TAFE colleges, mark two extremes. In between, girls from a variety of class backgrounds are educated together. The 'office lady' routine, with its connotations of subservience, represents an *outdated* middle-class femininity and a blurring of the class boundaries. The girls are socialised into what may be described as a 'lower middle-class' culture. They are being taught to be subordinate.

The main signs of resistance came from the 'lower' TAFE streams, where it took the form of high levels of absenteeism, returning late for classes, aggressively calling the teacher 'Miss' rather than using her name, conspicuously ignoring what the teacher was saying, giggling, maintaining continuously high levels of background noise, yelling at each other across the room, wearing jeans and sandshoes, doing each others' hair and applying make-up during class, reading excerpts from *Dolly*, typing letters to each other, smoking in the toilets, loitering in the corridors, skylarking around, and occasional acts of vandalism. Like Lin Samuel's group of school-resisters, they 'tried on' a variety of patterns of behaviour to see what they could get away with (1983: 370—73). This included the assertion of a decidedly 'unladylike' sexuality. They refer to the boys as sex objects, discussing loudly who is cute or spunky or well endowed. Such 'rampant' displays of sexuality can easily put the teachers off balance and make them anxious that the situation will get 'out of control'. While it may be part of their task to 'prepare' the girls for adult heterosexual relationships the college timetables ensure that boys and girls are separated and that meal breaks do not coincide.

Resistance comes from those sections of the working class who have not already been incorporated into 'lower middle-class' culture. To them the 'lady' represents a removal of freedom and the imposition of an alien identity. They are not merely resisting the teachers but adjusting to the contradictory expectations of their parents, who may in some ill-defined way want social mobility for their daughters. The girls have difficult ground to traverse in working out their adult identities. Unfortunately for many of them, the patterns they try out have detrimental effects on their academic performance and prevent them from completing their courses. The outcome is not merely a failure of socialisation. A complex set of interactions between the individual girl, the college and her family and peers explains how it is that these particular working-class girls end up with the lowest clerical jobs and a lifetime of insecure part-time work.

Is it meaningful to refer to opposition to teachers as resistance? One of the dangers here is that any sign of life at all may be labelled that mystical thing, Resistance, which feminists and socialists are so desperate to find. By definition, wherever there is power there will be some form of resistance or how else would we know that power was operating? Where only the top classes are afforded official recognition, the others inevitably find alternative ways of gaining identity and self-respect (Hawkins, 1982: 7; Connell et al. 1982: 82−88). A student told me about one girl who 'got so frustrated she used to pull the keys off the typewriters. One day she flushed them down the toilet. They [the teachers] knew the keys had gone missing but they didn't know where. She did it to get attention. She hated one of the teachers so much she used to phone her up at home at two o'clock in the morning.' Given the low expectations and negative attitudes towards girls, any assertion of uniqueness makes some kind of sense. Such 'resistance' is spasmodic and individualistic and the most positive identity they can construct is as rowdy and fun-loving. The group provides an audience as well as support in dealing with boredom and alienation. Teachers deal with rowdiness in a number of ways: by locking classrooms at lunchtime, splitting up classes or advising students to get out and try to get jobs.

Debbie provides a good example of a working-class femininity which shares some things with (lower) middle-class femininity but also makes very different assumptions about the world. Teachers held out little hope for her class, defining them as rowdies and no-hopers. I spoke to her near the beginning and towards the end of her course and again at her home a year later when she was in the workforce. She is an attractive-looking girl, tall and willowy with long blonde hair, and a warm, friendly manner. At first sight she could easily fit the stereotype of the office lady. She is hardly a rebel. But from the beginning she was unhappy with aspects of college discipline that a middle-class person would take for granted, and expressed a lot of hostility to the teachers:

> You want to do something else and they want you to listen. They get you into trouble just like at school. Once we came back fifteen minutes late from a drive at lunchtime and we were in big trouble... We played up because we were bored.
> If we are late they lock us out and sometimes we get blown up... If you take days off they sometimes phone home and check up on you. It is exactly the same as school in that respect.

Like the students in Moran's study, their aim was to maximise the time spent pursuing their own interests, not necessarily to disrupt the class or to give the teachers a hard time (Moran, 1985: 7).

Debbie liked the freedom to smoke and to leave the building at lunchtime, but also felt it was her own business whether she was late or took days off. She placed limits on the legitimate areas of control. Debbie was not out to disrupt the class just for the sake of it. She enjoyed being in an all-girls class because 'we concentrate better...and talk about personal things', whereas the boys at school had been 'stupid'. She was looking for relevance but was unable find much in the course that addressed what she saw as her problems. She complained there was endless discussion of topics that had no interest to her and she hated spelling tests and clerical procedures. The only teacher she warmed to was the typing teacher: 'We could tell her anything, talk about our problems...with boyfriends and that.' She was going out to lots of parties and discos and running into some friction with her parents over being late home. She left in October because she knew she wasn't getting anywhere.

When I met Debbie again the following year she was working as an office assistant in a small engineering company on very low wages. It is a safe bet that she had been selected on the basis of her looks. She was working with seven males and getting a lot of harassment, particularly from the boss who kept trying to touch her and has made explicit sexual demands. She wears jeans to work deliberately to desexualise herself. Looking back she concedes that if she had stayed and got the diploma she might have got a better job and not be trapped in her current situation but still feels that the only useful part of the course was typing. Her sense of being trapped in an unpleasant job serves to reinforce her plan to place family concerns ahead of work. The boyfriend's car was parked prominently in the street outside her house and it was clear from her parents' teasing that he spent most of his time there. Marriage, she agreed, was on the horizon, 'not a long way off...but a while...about four years time'.

Not all students achieve even a semblance of 'middle-class femininity' nor are they 'meant' to. But all are ranked in accordance with this gender and class ideal, their futures linked with their conformity. The ideal cannot simply be abolished but it can be modified to allow for greater assertiveness and self-worth. So far it is the top private colleges that have been most active in constructing an alternative 'strong' femininity. Whether it will 'catch on' in TAFE remains to be seen. While a number of teachers were willing to talk to their students about self-esteem and boyfriend management, few were able to take this far in a radical direction.

Feminist strategies are still organised around denying the relevance of gender difference, playing down sexuality, replacing 'femininity' with personhood, and insisting on a proper recognition of skills. The impact of feminism had been to reduce the 'grooming and deportment' components or to make them voluntary. Yet students generally enjoy the material on femininity because they want to know how to succeed in the adult heterosexual world. It is no 'solution' simply to deprive them of this knowledge, leaving them to pick up what they can from their peer groups and from women's magazines. An updated 'grooming and deportment' course could be the most effective place to introduce critical ideas about gender relations. Fashion and beauty could be taught in the context of the patriarchal world with which the girls will have to engage. A critical stance does not have to be moralistic or involve a denial of pleasure. It may talk instead of the pleasures involved in subverting existing structures, opening up the possibility that of new powers and new pleasures.

Subjectivity and consciousness

Secretarial students are not in any sense a 'subculture'. Even within the same college or the same stream, group identity is weak. Unless they happened to go to school together they do not have much time to get to know each other and their identification with their class was limited. A year later students could barely remember what stream they were in and had forgotten the names of most of the teachers. This does not suggest a high degree of involvement and points up how much of a transition time it is.

Far from being at loggerheads with their parents, most students remain close to them, sharing their value system and relying heavily on their advice. Mum was overwhelmingly the main influence on the decision to do a secretarial course and it was her reasons they internalise: it's a stepping stone to that mysterious 'something else'; it's a good job for girls; it's easy to change jobs; there'll always *be* jobs; it's better than working in a shop; it's clean; do it while you figure out what you really want to do. Often there had been disagreements with Mum, as she gently talked them out of air hostessing or hairdressing. Surprisingly few students said that secretarial work was their first preference: hairdressing was seen as 'fun' and 'more creative'. The other occupations they found attractive were childcare worker and vet's assistant, both of which involved 'helping people'. They also liked the idea of 'personal assistant' not because it carried higher status (few actually understood what it meant) but because it conveyed the idea of helping someone.

Though students voiced the idea that 'girls can do anything' it was an empty phrase. They felt no necessity to explain why, if this were so, they were doing secretarial studies, or why secretarial studies remained almost entirely female. If anything they were impatient with 'dumb' questions about gender. To them the answers were self-evident: this is how the world is supposed to be. The image of girls 'doing anything' was associated with trade courses rather than preparation for management. They could more easily see girls doing panel-beating than accountancy. That a girl might think of herself as a pilot rather than an an air hostess was greeted with mirth or horror: to be a pilot required brains and/or strength which they seemed satisfied to allocate to men. Some thought that girls are not 'allowed' to be pilots and were surprised to hear that woman pilots exist.

Boys who did hairdressing, fashion or secretarial courses were regarded as 'pretty peculiar'. The few boys in secretarial studies did seem ultra-slow or were doing the course with some other career interest, such as journalism or the police, firmly in mind. They had no image of themselves as secretaries. Their presence served as a reminder that this is still a female sphere. The girls typically said, it's sissy for boys, they've got better things to do; guys are supposed to be the boss; men don't feel threatened by women secretaries. They suggested it would hurt the boys' egos to be seen to be doing women's work... 'you'd certainly be unlikely to get the beach guys'.

Virtually all said they will leave the workforce while their children are small but then return. The model they have in front of them is of fairly continuous part-time work once the children have gone to school. There was also a near consensus on the subject of sex before marriage. Most took it for granted that you will have sex with your boyfriend and believe it would be insane not to check out sexual compatibility before marriage. Some had discussed this with their mothers who agreed with them. While a counter-view exists it is not given any firm expression. Sex was always discussed in the context of 'relationships': only 'tarts' would admit to casual sex.

As a group the students have conventional ideas about marriage and family life but are not necessarily romantic about it. As Sue Lees (1986) found in her study of English teenagers, marriage is often regarded as something you end up with after you have lived. They cannot envisage *not* getting married and they see marriage as being for ever. It is the only alternative is to be marginalised as a lonely old maid. When a teacher talked to them about being divorced they said 'but you don't *look* divorced'. Their picture of a divorced woman was 'cranky, old and sad'. Rather than making a positive choice to get married, they make a negative one to avoid being left on the shelf. What is important therefore is to find a guy who is all right. This is what Adrienne Rich (1983) refers to as 'compulsory' heterosexuality. In the absence of choice, she argues, women will have no collective power to determine the meaning and place of sexuality in their lives.

Many of the girls are pragmatists who reason that marriage will get them away from home and give them a taste of freedom. While they may share their parents' values they bicker over such things as what time they have to be home at night. Many deeply resent their continuing economic dependence, with which some parents bait them. 'If you don't like it you can move out', they say, and the girls know that is not economically possible. But they take for granted that the husband will impose new limits on their freedom and have the power to enforce those limits. This was particularly true of the women from migrant family backgrounds. The only major differences among the girls are about the age at which they wish to marry and the number of children they want. While we might expect to connect this with what stream they are in, and their likely job prospects, such links are hard to establish. The main differentiating factor is whether or not they currently have a steady boyfriend. Those with a boyfriend are more likely to be thinking of marriage in the next two or three years than those without.

What is in the forefront of their minds is enjoying the precious years until marriage. A surprising number talk of postponing marriage until their 'late twenties'. As Lees comments, when you are fifteen ten years seems a lifetime away (1986: 95). While boyfriends are a subject of continuous conversation and planning, they do not seem amenable to fantasy—or at least not fantasies that can be readily shared. Sex is not talked about in the context of fun or adventure. The girls' 'public' fantasies are above all about travel, followed by cars, clothes, jobs and flats. Secretarial work has frequently been chosen because they believe it will enable them to travel. The travel bug was shared by Aborigines, Greeks, Italians and Lebanese students, by city and country students, by those in the western suburbs and those on the north shore. The travel industry is also the most favoured place to work—along with advertising and the media. It was mentioned even by students who knew the reality for them was likely to be banks or the public service or perhaps the dole. Three Greek students I followed into the workforce were overjoyed to discover that the public service could actually mean working in travel. They had been unaware of the state tourist commissions. Students saw industries rather than particular occupations as glamorous. Thus a student could say, 'I couldn't care if I was just a tea-girl for *Vogue*, to say I worked for *Vogue*'.

They had no illusions that most typing jobs would be other than routine and boring. 'It's OK in the morning when you're fresh but tiring by late afternoon.' Though they were keen to learn the word processor and complained that not enough time was allocated to it, they did not report any kind of 'addictive' fascination. Other subjects are seen as a welcome relief from the typewriter and students say they wish to avoid jobs that involve typing all day. The idea of 'helping' has some resonance, for while it suggests subordination it also suggests flexibility, variety and personal interaction. They wanted a direct and individual relation with a 'boss', who they hope will look after them. They expressed a preference for a man, fearing that a woman would make you work harder. There were echoes here of the mother—daughter relationship, for undoubtedly it is mothers rather than fathers who impose homework or domestic chores. One girl said that working with a man would be 'a nice change from here. All the teachers are female and I'm sick of 'em'. Others volunteered that a typing pool would be boring because there would be no men in it. Yet female friendships are important, and far from having one closed group they were learning to develop a number. They feel intensely the loss of their old school friends and were having to learn to renegotiate their relationships with them as well as forming new circles further afield.

For secretarial studies students in the 1980s the picture is not so very different from that of their predecessors earlier in the century. They are preparing for highly sex-typed jobs with limited opportunities for advancement and virtually no career scale. While they now expect to be in the paid workforce for much of their lives they continue to place greater emphasis on marriage and children. While a certain amount is being done to encourage greater assertiveness and to open up career options, the colleges do not operate in a vacuum. The shape of the workforce is also affected by specific changes in the labour market, in supply and demand, in technology and work processes and in the structure of the economy. It is to these factors that I turn next.

·7· Constructing the workforce

> The people who taught me said I should stay on and sit for university entrance. But father wanted to keep the family together and he was about to be transferred...So I left school at fourteen and a half. Interestingly enough the next one to me, who was male, went on to university...

> By the time I finished my degree I was married and there weren't too many jobs around for a 22-year-old married woman who just had this vague Arts degree...I thought I would just get a secretarial job until I got pregnant—but I didn't get pregnant straight away did I?.

> I had a male secretary once. He was a clerk who came from the Air Force and I discovered one day, quite by accident, that he wrote shorthand and he typed...I didn't have a secretary at the time and he was one of those guys who was quite happy to fill a secretarial role...He was an effeminate sort of person and he appeared to enjoy the subservient role. He was one of those people who always wanted to help you.

In the space of a few decades the secretarial workforce underwent a sex-change. Until the late nineteenth century most secretaries were men; by 1930 the majority were women and by the 1950s male secretaries were considered strange, as the third quotation above demonstrates. Although a few men have moved back into the area in recent times, 'secretary' remains one of the most heavily gender-typed of occupations. Demand and supply-side structures interact in significant ways to produce a gendered secretarial workforce. These interactions are mediated by changing definitions of secretaries and amplified by the decisions of the statisticians on how to count and classify them. A central theme of this chapter is, therefore, the ways in which 'secretary' is constructed in official statistics.

Structures of both demand and supply are important in determining the shape of the labour market (Rubery, 1978). Company takeovers, rationalisation procedures, new technology and the employers' drives for efficiency and flexibility bring continuous changes in the demand for types and quantities of labour. Other factors influence supply, independently of demand. Willingness to work as a secretary depends on one's perceptions of its gender-appropriateness as well as more material considerations such as marital status, domestic situation, the availability of childcare or the choice of alternative employment. It may be argued that men made themselves unavailable for secretarial work because more favourable opportunities opened up elsewhere; at the same time, there was a growing supply of educated women who needed to work and were, by and large, blocked from entering other professions. Such women have typically perceived themselves as having a choice between teaching, nursing or secretarial work. There is still a reluctance to consider non-traditional occupations.

Secretarial work is seen as so 'traditionally' women's work that it is hard to remember how recent, and in some senses partial, this development is. Until after 1900 it was men's work and it meant something very different for what it typically means today. 'Feminisation' occurred in conjunction with a major shift in the meaning and status of 'secretary'. This shift is signified by the three definitions offered by the Oxford English Dictionary (1979):

> One who is entrusted with private or secret matters; one whose office is to write for another, especially one who is employed to conduct correspondence, to keep records and (usually) to transact other business for another person or for a society, corporation or public body.

> Private secretary—a secretary employed by a minister of state or other high official for the personal correspondence connected with his official positions. Also applied to a secretary in the employ of a particular person (as distinguished from the secretary to a society etc).

> A person employed to help deal with correspondence, typing, filling and similar routine work.

The first of these definitions invokes the older meaning which lives on in titles like Secretary of State, Company, Union, Club or Press Secretary. It usually appears in capitals and still signifies largely male preserves. Stalin wielded tyrannical power as 'General Secretary' of the Communist Party while, closer to home, the New South Wales chief minister was, in colonial times referred to as the 'Chief Secretary'. Men who are Secretaries in the 'old' sense are often impatient or uncomfortable about comparing themselves with 'small s' secretaries. One, a Union Secretary, went out of his way to stress that he was of equal status to the President. The double meaning is important for understanding both men's and women's relation to secretarial work.

The second Oxford definition indicates a transition of meaning. 'Private secretaries' fall between the other two definitions. As assistants to senior managers they still act as officers of the company or organisation but their continuity with secretaries in the original sense goes largely unacknowledged and they are, for counting purposes, usually included with typists and stenographers. The third one more accurately conveys what most contemporary secretaries do and is female more or less by definition. These changes did not take place overnight. They happened gradually over half a century and are still continuing. As typing becomes 'keyboarding' and associated with the power of the computer, for example, it once again becomes compatible with masculinity.

Australian women trickled into secretarial work at a time when clerical workers overall numbered hundreds rather than thousands. With the development of the tertiary sector, the demand for secretarial workers expanded and the proportion of women grew rapidly. In the 1890s private business colleges got into full swing and by 1911 the greater number of their students, in all states, were women (Jones, 1967: 247−50; Jarrett, 1982: 87−88). The last of the New South Wales colonial censuses in 1901 recorded 400 women typists while eight women worked as secretaries for religious societies and five for dentists! The first definition was still being used.

By the turn of the century, 'secretary' was already beginning to carry a broader meaning. The variety of meanings produced by the federal statisticians are summarised in Table 7.1. In an attempt to clarify the situation the first two national censuses replaced 'secretary' with 'officer in a public company', a small group which remained predominantly male. Women increased from 12 per cent of the category in 1911 to 19 per cent by 1921. Typists and stenographers were included in the general categories of 'office caretaker, keeper, attendant' and 'clerk, cashier, accountant undefined'. The proportion of women in the latter category rose from 27 per cent in 1911 to 35 per cent by 1921 and it is safe to assume that a many of them were typists, stenographers and private secretaries.

Of all the components of what we now call secretarial work telephony was the first to be designated as feminine (Kingston, 1975: 93). Typing took a little longer as it was at first considered to require not only manual dexterity but some practical knowledge of the material being processed (Fitzsimmons, 1980: 24). As typewriters came into general use, in the first decade of the twentieth century, typing became accepted as a women's subject. Shorthand retained for longer a masculine image, but before World War I had already become paired with typing to create the feminine job classification of shorthand-typiste.

Women did not simply replace men. The development of a more sophisticated economy involved the creation of a range of *new* jobs; and this coincided with the availability of a large new literate female workforce, in need of jobs. Rather than being treated as apprentices gaining an overall knowledge of the business, women were restricted to the lower levels of typically larger bureaucratic structures. Yet they did retain some initiative and independence. The 'private secretary' was at the top of the pyramid of female office workers, differentiated from the stenographers and typists beneath her. Until at least the 1960s this was for women virtually the only path, if a rare one, into management. It continues to hold out this hope in areas such as advertising, publishing and personnel. Those with ambitions in these areas would usually now acquire professional qualifications but still take on secretarial work to 'gain experience'. It is debatable how often this path does take them into management and how often it simply consolidates their position as secretaries. The woman arts graduate who is unable to move on is still a common phenomenon among secretaries.

Though men continued to engage in secretarial work in the interwar period, their proportion steadily declined. The feminine 'typiste' came to be used in the 1920s to distinguish 'women's work' (a practice continued into the 1950s). The statisticians caught up with this terminology and, in the 1933 census, published detailed tables for the category 'typiste, office machinist'. Men were absent by definition from this category and there was no alternative grouping of male typists in which they could be included. Since advertisements for typists (without the 'e') routinely appeared in the classifieds it is hard to believe that no men at all had typing as a major component of their work. Along with the growth in the numbers of 'typistes' the 1933 census registered a large-scale movement of women into other clerical jobs. About a third of the 100000 clerks in Australia were women—almost as many as those working as typistes (39000). The census still showed nearly twice as many male as female secretaries but the overall numbers were relatively small. The description of the category as 'secretaries and organizers' indicates that 'secretary' standing alone can no longer be assumed to convey its original meaning (see Table 7.1).

Between 1933 and 1947 the gender ratios in the 'secretary' category were reversed and the number of women almost doubled that of the men (7400 to 4700). But 1947 is the last year in which 'secretary' is listed as a distinct occupational category. By this time the meaning was shifting decisively away from the secretary as executive officer towards the secretary as personal assistant and senior stenographer. In the late 1940s the term 'secretary' started to be used in the classifieds to convey the latter group: before that

Table 7.1 **Proportions of men and women in selected 'secretarial' occupations as classified in ABS census data**

Year	Classification	Women	Men	% Women
1911	Office caretaker, keeper attendant	362	1206	23
	Officer of public company, society	103	719	12.5
	Clerk, cashier, accountant, undefined	1718	4586	27.3
1921	Office caretaker, keeper, attendant	452	1788	14
	Officer of public company, society	658	2793	19
	Clerk, cashier, accountant, undefined	6884	12888	34.8
1933	Secretary and organiser	797	1274	38.5
	Typist, office machinist	38921	Nil	100
1947	Secretary	7400	4700	61
	Typist and shorthand writer	71000	245	100
1966	Stenographer and typist	130689	—	100
	Receptionist, female	10692	—	100
1981	Stenographer and typist	97983	820	99.2

time typist or shorthand typist had been more typically used (see Table 7.2). The statisticians were obviously concerned that company secretaries and the like might get confused with the humbler typing varieties. Rather than making any effort to distinguish private secretaries as a professional group they conflated them into the category of 'typists and shorthand writers'. From a masculinist viewpoint what these groups have in common as 'women workers' is, perhaps, of greater significance than what distinguishes them. It is thus difficult to look at the demographic characteristics of career secretaries separately, or to say much about the class and status differences within this broader group.

In the 1947 census men could again be counted among typists and stenographers but their numbers were small: 245 compared with some 71000 women. The coders were given a great deal of flexibility and were allowed to take gender into account in deciding in which category to place people. Men who did shorthand or

Table 7.2   Job advertisements in the categories of typist/clerk, stenographer, receptionist/typist and secretary, 1936–71

	Typ/clerk	Stenog	Recept/typ	Secretary
1936	8	4	–	–
1940	–	6	–	–
1946	30	36	–	12
1956	84	63	7	14
1966	124	92	26	76
1971	184	126	84	204

Source: Compiled from *Sydney Morning Herald*, Saturday classified advertisments, week including 19 May

typewriting (and there were still a large number of them in the public service) were more likely to be recoded as clerks. The 'typist, stenographer' category was constituted in statistical discourse, as a feminine one. In 1961 and 1971 men were again formally ruled out by definition. In 1976, perhaps with some recognition of the sexism of the categories, they were permitted to return, but by then male stenographers had become virtually unthinkable. Only 1201 men appeared in the group, reducing to 820 in 1981. If 'shorthand typist' was a category reserved for women so too was 'receptionist'. So that there could be no mistake about this the 1976 and 1981 censuses actually labelled the group 'receptionist, female'. A man, by definition, could not be a receptionist and would have to be placed in some other category.

One might have expected that with the advent of sex discrimination legislation and affirmative action programs the statisticians would stop using gender as a criterion of job classification. At the 1986 census 'sex' was no longer available to processors to help them work out the correct occupational category, though it is admitted that 'in the last resort' the chief supervisor may refer to it. They have dropped the cruder versions, whereby jobs were male or female by definition, but gender bias remains in a subtler form, through definitions of 'skill'. Under the new ASCO coding system people are supposed to be coded according to their 'most skilled' task. Although secretaries may be virtually office managers, such skills are not acknowledged and they are still ranked with stenographers and typists, and behind a range of clerks and receptionists.

Supply-side considerations

What sort of women become secretaries and what draws them into secretarial work? Literacy is obviously important and it is significant how many senior secretaries had aspirations of becoming teachers. Had they been male there is little doubt that many of them would have gone on to higher education and entered the professions. Elaine, who left school in 1950 sums this up:

> You don't get many young secretaries any more. Anybody who has got any brains goes to university or gets some professional training...But there was no question of my getting to university because my parents had no money and you went out to work as soon as possible. I was damn lucky to get even as far as Junior—it was only because some school teacher went to see mum and dad and said, you can't just send her to business college straight from primary school you know. They relented and I went to college for two years and did a commercial junior.

Fifteen years later women had similar stories:

> I wanted to be a music teacher but there was no money to go off and train and I was at home looking after my younger brothers and sisters.
> I would not do that again. I would go to uni. In fact the deal was that I would do this when my husband finished...But two children and no money later I can't. We could not afford to live on one income and pay a mortgage.
> My father was a fireman and my mother was a secretary—she has worked all her life. I was brighter than my brother at school but they wanted him to be an engineer and me to be a secretary. I can remember thinking, 'is that all they want of me?' and feeling a little bit disappointed...I would have gone teaching.

From the 1940s to the present, their stories are much the same: limited options and the reluctance of their families to educate them further. Mothers seem to have been the strongest influence in channelling them into secretarial work as 'something to fall back on'. Teaching and nursing were seen as the only alternatives and some had tried those as well:

> I wanted to get out of school. I hated school so much...The teachers...were all very elderly and strait-laced...I did my business college course and went to work and got thoroughly bored to sobs. I went back and did my matriculation at night and then I was still bored to sobs with office work. So I went nursing for a couple of years...but I went back to secretarial because there was more money. You know, I didn't like teaching, I didn't like school. The choices were office work and nursing. I tried them both and I didn't like either of them so I got married.
> Through mishap I suppose I started my working life nursing and I didn't finish. It was four years' training in those days and I only did one and a half. Then I just fell into office work. It sounded like 'wham' after emptying bedpans.

In the early part of the century the salaries of secretaries were roughly comparable with those of teachers and nurses (Lowe, 1987: 156).

Since the 1920s, secretarial salaries have steadily dropped behind the other two.

Those who make it into secretarial jobs are not only female and literate, they generally conform to the cultural criterion of white, heterosexual attractiveness. Women who do not match up—Aboriginal and ethnic minorities, lesbians, feminists, older women or working-class women who have not been sufficiently incorporated into middle-class culture, are marginalised unless they can find some way of conforming. This may involve suppressing their sexuality, or their age or their politics; or adopting the values of an alien culture. A 'feminine' sexual identity is enforced through office practices, most obviously codes of dress and behaviour. Women are judged on 'feminine' characteristics like charm, poise, courtesy, personality and appearance.

Women from non-English-speaking countries now make up more than 12 per cent of those with secretarial qualifications, falling mid-way between women with trade or health qualifications (ABS labour force survey, February 1986). This is consistent with a status hierarchy in which nursing and other jobs in the health sector are rated more highly and the trades jobs are ranked lower than secretarial work. These women are also concentrated at the lower end of the scale as keyboard operators or clerical assistants. Students from migrant backgrounds now form a sizable pro-portion of secretarial studies classes, over 50 per cent in some colleges. The small group of Aboriginal secretaries denied direct discrimination but had clearly had little choice about their em-ployment. Sheila and most of her friends had gone into the Queensland Public Service when they left school: 'You couldn't just leave one job and walk into any kind of a job you wanted...there weren't too many jobs available...You had no choice where you went to. They just said, this group goes to the Main Roads Department and this group to the Treasury...'

Typists and stenographers make up a young workforce. It has consistently had a higher proportion of employees aged under 25 than has the total employed female workforce. Not surprisingly it also has more single people. Amongst the over 25s there is also a higher proportion of women who are unmarried, separated or divorced (Sweet, 1983). Career secretaries are particularly likely to be single. In prewar days women were expected to resign on marriage, a practice that was continued in many workplaces until the late 1960s. As a result most had left the workforce before reaching the status of private secretary. But how do we explain the continuation of this trend?

Secretarial work remains a full-time occupation almost by defi-nition. Secretaries work long and irregular hours, which are diffi-cult to combine with caring for small children. Senior secretaries with young children have to be able to give watertight guarantees that childcare problems will not interfere with their work. Despite anti-discrimination legislation most bosses consider it madness not to check this out carefully at the interview. Secretaries need to be very committed to their jobs, to have bosses who are willing to be a bit flexible, or to have extremely sympathetic mothers, husbands or neighbours. This explains why so many ex-secretaries go back into the workforce in job categories lower down the scale. Part-time secretarial (as distinct from typing or clerical) jobs are few and far between. There has, however, been an increase in temporary employment, especially in service industries, and a move towards subcontracting to agencies.

By moving out to the suburbs employers have been able to tap the pool of married women who are willing to work for lower rates of pay in order to have jobs close to home. Both state and federal governments have supported retraining programs for such women. Nepean CAE introduced an associate diploma course in secretarial studies for women who have been out of the workforce for some time, while the federal government included access to secretarial courses under its Participation and Equity Program (PEP). The right-wing Federated Clerks' Union, which should be representing such workers, actually wanted the federal government to pay its married women members $40 a week to leave the workforce in a campaign to create new jobs (*Australian* 3 January 1980).

Commentators have consistently pointed out that the occupation is oversupplied, especially with juniors. Basing his calculations on Victoria, O'Neil (1985) estimated a notional supply level of 10 per cent per annum, while Sweet (1983) placed it at 14.5 per cent of the workforce in 1981. This is greater than for any other occupation in Australia. Unemployment rates for those with typing qualifications are much higher than for women with other qualifications, at 9.6 per cent compared with 5.7 per cent (ABS, Labour Force, February 1986) and more closely resemble those among women with no post-school qualifications. Despite such evidence, it may be argued that the oversupply problem has been exaggerated, for secretarial courses deliberately train for a wider range of occupations. Grendt (1982) followed up a sample of 1979 students from TAFE secretarial studies courses in New South Wales and found most had moved fairly smoothly into the workforce. Twenty-eight per cent of country respondents compared with 7 per cent from the metropolitan area were unemployed. Not only is the rate of unemployment among the recently trained lower than rates of supply would lead one to expect, but they seem to get jobs which use their skills, irrespective of the title of their job.

While there may be some oversupply at the junior level it is not maintained through an intermediate period and does not produce an adequate supply at the advanced level.

High wastage rates among the 25–34 age group are only partly attributable to flows out of the workforce for child-rearing purposes. Sweet (1983) suggests that it is single rather than married women in this age group who leave, and that low salary and limited prospects are the cause. The income advantage which teenage typists have over employed teenage females as a whole drops away sharply in the early twenties. Juniors earn around 10 per cent above the average for young women, whereas adults earn slightly less than the average wage for women in non-managerial occupations (ABS, Comparative wage rates, May 1986). There is a move from secretarial into clerical and administrative fields and non-quantifiable losses to tertiary study and non-traditional areas of employment. In 1977 'secretary' was made an acceptable immigration category in an effort to increase the supply. The shortage of top secretaries has finally forced companies to pay higher salaries, and by 1986 salary packages of around $30 000 were not uncommon.

Changes in the workforce

The relative size of the secretarial workforce grew steadily between 1933 and 1961. It appears to have fallen slowly in the next twenty years and risen again slightly in the early 1980s (Table 7.3). But secretaries are not just sitting at their desks waiting to be counted and classified. In identifying them we are dependent on the rules and grading practices developed by the official statistics bureaucracies. On current definitions more than 99 per cent of secretarial workers are female and they number anything between 20 000 and 250 000 in Australia. The Department of Employment and Industrial Relations was clearly tryng to define career secretaries when it gave an estimate of 20 000. All the other figures are for the broader typist/stenographer category and show a lot of variation. They numbered 98 000 in the 1981 census but nearly doubled that (185 000) in the Labour Force survey of the same year. The 1986 census revises these figures upwards to 250 000 but is based on new grading procedures and is meant to be more precise in its classifications.

In May 1986 the Australian Bureau of Statistics coded everyone in the labour force survey twice, in order to allow direct comparisons between the old and the new systems. 'ASCO' found 260 900 people in the 'stenographers and typists' category, which was 25 per cent more than the old system counted. The size of this difference, in coding the same sample, indicates some of the problems involved in counting secretaries. While 5 per cent had been reclassified as 'receptionists', just over a quarter had previously been placed in the residual category of 'other clerical workers' (Labour Force Survey, ABS, May 1986). As a 'problem' category, the number of secretaries fluctuates wildly according to apparently minor changes in rules or coding procedures. Arguments about levels of unemployment or the effects of new technology have to be considered with this in mind.

There has been much debate about the extent to which new technology and/or the recession have reduced the demand for secretarial and keyboard workers. The sheer difficulty of interpreting the statistical data should caution against any rash predictions. Hall, for example, estimated that in the decade 1971–81 the number of typists and stenographers was reduced by one-half (1985: 52). There was undoubtedly a sharp decline in the late 1970s, when word processors were introduced on a large scale. But the apparently big drop of about 43 per cent between the 1976 and 1981 censuses was largely a byproduct of coding changes and new occupational categories. Word-processor and VDU operators were reclassified as office machine operators, and clerk typist as clerical workers. After 1976 coders were given less flexibility and are not allowed to take gender into account in determining a person's occupational category. As a result the 'dump' categories ballooned and a particularly large one for women was 'other clerical'. In the 1978 labour force statistics 'other clerical' went up by more than 11 per cent at the same time as 'stenographers and typists' went down by around 15 per cent. It seems from comparisons with labour force surveys that perhaps as many as half again of the 'typists and stenographers' in the 1981 census were put in the 'other clerical' category on the basis that typing was not their main duty.

Richard Sweet (1983) has argued that the main decline in demand came not in the second but in the first half of the 1970s and was heavily concentrated among teenagers. The aggregate figures, he says, mask an increasing demand for older typists during the same period. The 1970s saw an important restructuring of demand with respect to age, level of experience, industry, state and hours of work. Employment became ever more concentrated in New South Wales and Victoria as companies centralised their administrative functions in their headquarters states. As the computerisation of invoice production in warehouses and statement production in banking reduced the need for copy typists and office juniors, employers were looking rather for people with experience and flexibility (Sweet, 1983).

Technological change and company rationalisation have affected juniors and routine keyboard workers more seriously than senior secretaries. While individual organisations have shed jobs, the aggregate figures have remained stable. The sharp decline in the period 1977−78 should be seen in the context of the gradual, relative long-term decline in the 'typists, secretaries and stenographers' group as a proportion of the female workforce which has taken place since the 1960s (Table 7.3). Both the 'decline' of typists and stenographers in the late 1970s and their apparent increase in the 1980s are largely attributable to coding changes. The use of the ASCO code 1986 made possible the 'unpacking' and reclassification of the 'other clerical' group. Since 1986 there may have been a slight increase in the proportion of secretarial workers. There has been a decline in relative weekly earnings for 'typists and stenographers' alongside, surprisingly, a small increase in the rates of juniors (Table 7.4). It is possible that juniors are starting to be employed on tasks that would once have been given to more experienced workers. Executive secretaries remain in short supply and are finally starting to receive higher rates of pay.

Table 7.3   Typists, secretaries and stenographers as a proportion of the female workforce, 1933−86

	Female typists etc (000s)	Employed women (000s)	Typists etc as % of empl women
1933 (census)	38.9	629.2	6.2
1947	70.7	717.2	9.9
1961	125.5	1059.2	11.8
1966	162.8	1434.6	11.3
1966 (labour force)	178.2	1458.2	12.2
1971	203.1	1803.0	11.3
1974	215.9	2008.1	10.8
1975	215.8	2020.8	10.7
1976	220.5	2061.5	10.7
1977	211.8	2128.6	10.0
1978 (old series)	208.9	2154.4	9.7
1978 (new series)	180.7	2154.4	8.4
1979	176.6	2157.4	8.2
1980	180.9	2298.5	7.9
1981	179.8	2335.8	7.7
1982	179.9	2335.0	7.7
1983	184.8	2337.4	7.9
1984	198.5	2449.9	8.1
1986 (labour force, CCLO)	205.8	2657.8	7.7
1986 (labour force, ASCO)	256.0	2657.8	9.6
1986 (census)	247.6	2561.6	9.7

ASCO: Australian standard classification of occupations
CCLO: Classification and classified list of occupations

Table 7.4 Changing differentials between stenographer/typists/ secretaries and all female, full-time non-managerial employees

	1976	1978	1980	1983	1985
Steno/typ/secs					
Adults	144	175	204	278	315
Juniors	97	121	138	189	203
All occupations					
Adults	144	177	210	295	341
Juniors	96	117	136	179	198
Steno/typ/secs as % all occupations					
Adults	100.0	98.9	97.1	94.2	92.4
Juniors	101.0	103.4	101.5	105.6	102.5

They may well be constructed as a separate category in future occupational statistics. It is likely that higher pay at the top end, increased demand and greater emphasis on 'professionalism' will attract men to the occupation. This has started in the United States but has not yet affected Australia significantly.

Male secretaries

The strong associations of 'secretary' with femininity have a number of implications for men doing broadly secretarial work. First, they are rarely called secretaries, hence the number of men in the area is difficult to establish and the extent to which secretarial work has been feminised has been overemphasised. Second, men who work as secretaries are assumed to have some 'problem' with their masculinity. What 'real' man would want to be subservient let alone helpful! Third, any 'feminised' occupation is presumed to draw homosexual men: fashion, hairdressing, entertainment and more recently nursing are cases in point. A firm connection is made between gender and sexual preference and the stronger the sex-styping the stronger the resulting stereotype. This raises questions about the ways in which the stereotype does structure the 'reality'.

There has been speculation about whether men will move into secretarial work in the way they have into nursing. Newspapers love to discover the occasional brave man who is doing a secretarial course. In fact, they have been discovering them every few months since at least 1968! (*Sun-Herald* 10 November 1968). In 1973 when employers faced the prospect of equal pay, we were told that Caulfield Institute had just enrolled their first male in a

secretarial postgraduate course (*Australian*, 4 March); that Stella
Cornelius has a male personal assistant (*SMH* 14 March); and that
such men were earning nearly twice as much as the women and
saw their jobs as stepping stones to more important careers (*SMH*
7 February). With the introduction of equal pay we were informed
that 'the first male secretaries are sharpening their pencils to lead
the men's lib march down the corridors of power' and that they
were 'edging out board-room blondes'. One of their number
allegedly commented: 'Female secretaries are two a penny. Men
beat them for efficiency and stability...We don't fall pregnant
and don't come and go' (*Sun-Herald* 9 January 1977). A year later
it was 'Take a letter MR Jones' (*Sun-Herald* 5 March 1977). In
1982 a policeman was chosen as Queensland's Secretary of the
Year: as the *Herald* put it, 'Sergeant Greg takes on the girls and
cops it sweet'. He had started twenty years earlier as a foot
patrolman and gone on to become assistant to the police com-
missioner. With admirable secretarial tact he commented, 'the
police in Queensland have received a lot of unwarranted criticism
lately and I hope my award can do a little bit to help our cause'.
(*SMH* 22 April 1982). He had obviously not bargained on the
Fitzgerald Inquiry!

If 'male secretaries' are largely a newspaper fiction so too are
gays. The *Sun-Herald*, in an article entitled 'Sex changes in the
typing pool' (July 1982) described the unhappy experience of
Ashley before he joined the safety of the public service: '"It was
disastrous", he said. "The boss tried to chase me around the desk.
I left after only three-and-a-half-weeks".' It is actually a good deal
easier to find gay nurses than gay secretaries: and even in nursing
gays are a minority. There is no reason to believe that gay men
are congregated in secretarial work. Even in the gay community
where, if we followed American trends, we might expect to find
them, they are few and far between. A gay lawyer, with a high
proportion of gay clients, told me he had advertised widely for a
male secretary and had not been able to find anyone suitably
qualified. He thought that even if they existed the law was probably
too staid for them. A spokesman for the Gay Business Association
in Sydney suggested that gay men would be attracted to something
more flamboyant: for them secretary represents dowdy, respect-
ble clothes and long hours of drudgery. If they go into office
work, they were much more likely to be working as receptionists
or switchboard operators than as secretaries.

For gay men secretarial work may represent not feminine but
masculine qualities. Steve grew up in a country town and wanted to
be a court or Hansard reporter, he explained, to reconcile his
sexuality with 'something masculine'. When he did not get the
necessary speeds he joined the State Rail Authority which had also

retained a masculine image and it was only when he became dissatisfied with the promotional prospects there that he became willing to consider secretarial work in the private sector.

Men have, in fact, continued to work in the area, particularly in the public sector. Through to World War II advertisements for typists specified gender and a number of men were employed as typist/clerks. Until that time the majority of secretaries, as distinct from stenographers, were still men. For them stenographic work was the start rather than the end of a career. The only way young men could get promotion in the public service was by going to nightschool and studying either shorthand or accountancy. Shorthand was taken as proof of extra ability. Men who talked to Ros Byrne about their secretarial experiences included the permanent head and assistant secretary of Commonwealth government departments, senior management of major newspapers, and office managers (1982: 10).

Solly noted in the 1970 edition of her text that 'in industries where secretaries are required to represent their employers, in factories or on construction sites, and in strictly masculine provinces, male secretaries are in great demand...they are frequently employed in the legal field, in purchasing, mining, the oil and rubber industries, public utilities and in the newspaper field' (Solly et al., 1970: 6–7). Men have learned stenographic skills in the armed forces and police and for journalism. They have continued to use them in government organisations such as the State Rail Authority which in the past insisted that all their junior recruits learn to type and right through until 1970 required shorthand as a qualification for its clerks.

Until 1960 the New South Wales court reporters were all men though women had taken over the typing side. In what seems a strange division of labour the reporter takes down the proceedings in shorthand and dictates them direct to the typist. In the late 1950s the men tried to prevent the women from getting equal pay by getting them banned from doing vicious murders or rape cases, as well as from country travel. As one woman recalled, 'we said we had been doing them for years and were not delicate little maidens'. A typist said that many of the women actually enjoy the country travel as a rest from domestic responsibilities. Men have dropped out over the last ten years and by 1986 made up only fifteen out of 109 reporters. The work apparently became less attractive to them after equal pay, because they could no longer experience themselves as 'the breadwinner' earning more than women.

Many managers 'could not imagine' having a man as a secretary and it is quite possible that male applicants face discrimination. Once in they, like male nurses, receive very favourable treatment and the 'discrimination' works to their advantage. Since it is 'unimaginable' that men might be secretaries they are paid more and they move quickly up the career ladder. A professor spoke warmly of his 'technical officer' who, 'to my delight writes letters almost in the words I would have used'. He relies on him for 'higher-level secretarial tasks' and sees a future for a lot more men in these positions. Male secretaries earn about 20 per cent more than their female counterparts, a figure that directly parallels the differential for full-time workers overall (Comparative wage rates, ABS, May 1986). The self-confidence and assertiveness of Raoul, the male secretary described in Chapter 3, thus has a solid financial basis. The higher rate cannot be explained in terms of the different occupational distributions of men and women, and can only signify that the men are receiving more favourable treatment and taking over some of the senior positions. June, a personal assistant who had been to a seminar on this subject organised by Rydges, reported that American secretaries were extremely worried by such developments and are trying to keep men out. June's own firm of chartered accountants had recently taken on a male 'temp' and it was, she observed, 'absolutely fascinating the way that he was treated differently'.

Men are rarely called secretaries. They are described as a personal or research assistant, sometimes simply assistant, a computer operator, or a trainee of some kind. It was only by dropping the label 'male secretaries' that it became possible to locate men in these positions. We would frequently hear that there *had* been a man in this company or department who did secretarial work but had now moved on. After much time and effort we would trace him through a variety of different workplaces and eventually find him somewhere well up the managerial scale, looking back over his secretarial period as a temporary episode in his career. What they have in common is that they are never intending to stay in these jobs for very long; they are using them to gain experience.

Tim works in the family law firm. He tells close friends that he is a secretary but otherwise describes himself as a legal clerk. He picked up typing while working in a bank and works from a dictaphone. He does not do shorthand. His brother and sister, both soliciters, say he is the best secretary they have had because he wants to know exactly what each piece of work is about. He behaves as though he were one of the legal staff and does not see himself staying in the job. He is currently doing an accountancy course. At Rialto, a small real estate agency, young men are being taken on as trainees provided they are willing to learn to type. Raymond, the owner, prefers men because they are more likely to have cars and are better able to collect rent from stroppy tenants.

But he believes that in future the secretarial components of the work will be merged with that of sales staff.

Philip agreed to talk to me after a woman friend of his saw the advertisement for 'male secretaries' and volunteered him. He had not identified himself as a secretary until that time because his job description says he is a 'marketing assistant'. Now in his early twenties, he had started work in a bank and had taken it on himself to learn to type when he found he kept making mistakes on bank cheques and international drafts. The teacher told him '...not to bother too much about spacing and so on because I won't be using that in my role...She assumed I was not going to be a secretary'. After leaving the bank he had taken a series of temporary jobs and was now working for a small pharmaceutical company. What does he do? 'Basically it is to look after the managing director. I run after him, and organise him, keep his desk tidy, make sure he goes to appointments...Get things done that he should do and doesn't get time for.' Though he replaced a woman who did a lot of typing, he does not use his typing skills at work: 'I've heard said that the girl that is doing typing now has had to do more because I'm there...He [the boss] didn't even ask me if I could type...he just assumed I didn't. So he must have taken me on on the basis of other attributes.' Phillip has taken the job to get marketing experience and plans to do a marketing certificate at the University of New South Wales. Despite his lack of a science or pharmacy degree he is being groomed for a long-term position in the company. But he does not see a future there and it is unlikely that he will be part of the secretarial workforce for much longer.

Men have *always* maintained a presence, albeit a minority one, in secretarial work; the reason this cannot be seen is because of the gendered nature of the cultural construction of 'secretary'. Men can and do type, though they often decline to do so at work, for fear of losing their status or their masculinity, or out of a concern to protect jobs. While secretaries have shown some resistance to their bosses using keyboards many are using word processors or wanting access to them. Henry, a solicitor, did a typing course so that he could modify documents 'without the manual handwritten requests and all the rigmarole you have to go through before you have it in a form that it is acceptable to the women who use the word processor'.

The question is not how to get *more* men into secretarial work but the terms on which they come in. Since clerical jobs increasingly require the use of a keyboard the old distinction between clerical and secretarial work is, in any case, breaking down. The danger for women is that men will take over the best-paid, most prestigious jobs; that the old vertical division of labour will be replaced by a horizontal one in which women are restricted to the bottom rungs. It will be necessary to deconstruct the category 'secretary' to ensure that it does not continue to be used to limit the areas available to women.

•8• Technology and power

It would be difficult to imagine the office without typewriters, telephones and filing cabinets. These technologies were adopted in the late nineteenth century coinciding with the movement of women into secretarial work. They have been central to the definition of what a secretary *is*, and to the construction of the boss—secretary relationship. The basic pattern laid down by the 1920s has remained unchanged in its essentials despite regular technological advances. Long before word processors, technology had the capacity to make the boss—secretary relationship archaic. But it was not until the 1970s, with the prospect of automation, that a dramatic upheaval in the social relations of the office was promised or threatened. To understand why the boss—secretary relationship continues to be normatively constructed around male power and female subordination and why, despite automation, it may still be preserved we have to consider the meanings attached to technology, the struggles around these meanings and the potentials attached to technology.

It was through technology that a sharp division between men's and women's jobs in the office was created and maintained. Technology was implicated in the construction of the 'secretarial' as a category separate from clerical and administrative work. Typewriters were defined as appropriate for women by being associated with feminine interests and skills: sewing, playing the piano, the nimble fingers that were supposed to result from these activities. Before long they were considered appropriate *only* for women. Women and typewriters were synonymous—'lady typewriters' were people not machines. If it became hard to think of men doing secretarial work, it was hard to think of women in the office doing anything else, so firmly did they seem to be attached to their typewriters. Keyboard workers were thus kept separate from the promotional structures and women restricted to the lower ranks of clerical work. In the public service this was ratified by separate male and female grades. Once the division was established it was possible to elaborate further on the nature of 'men's' or 'women's' work. Thus it was that grooming and poise, a constant smile and a willingness to manage office tensions were drummed into generations of secretarial students as a central part of their training.

Gender is more fundamental to the 'labour process' than most of the literature allows. A number of studies have pointed to the associations between masculinity and machinery and the importance of sexual symbolism in constructing gender relations

(Cockburn, 1983, 1986; Game & Pringle, 1983). Technology does not 'cause' changes in the labour process in an unmediated way. Its existence is inseparable from the meanings and symbols attached to it. These representations did not begin with 'automation' but have a long history. Office technology, like technologies of production, war and leisure, constructs gender around relations of domination and subordination. New technology is shown as offering bosses an almost superhuman power and control which is equated with masculine virility and power (Plate 3). It enhances men's power, enables them (quite literally) to tap into the sources of greater power and has an explicitly sexual and phallic dimension (Plate 4). If men are represented as the masters of technology, women are its servants. Technology does not empower them but reinforces their powerlessness and dependence on men. Their role is to operate the technology on the master's behalf. Women and technology are both there to serve men as well as to please and titillate them.

Images of secretaries and technology may be read in terms of fetishism. Psychoanalytic insights suggest that men unconsciously perceive women as being castrated and hence as creating the possibility of their own (symbolic) castration. In order to relieve the castration anxiety that this sets up, men symbolically return the phallus in the form of fetish objects. Through a process of disavowal they simultaneously deny the woman's 'castration', and punish her for her 'lack'. This is a familiar theme in pornography where whips, high heels, long cigarette holders and so on function as fetish objects. The 'sexy secretary' images are an extension of the pornographic images. The high heels, long legs and short skirts express an ambivalence between what is always 'in place' and something that must be anxiously repeated. The fetish taps into men's anxiety about castration and sexual difference as well as normalising that difference. The conventions of pornography carry over to representations of technology. Far from being replaced by technology, secretaries are 'empowered' by the computerised gadgetry that is given to them by men (Plates 5 and 6).

All of this suggests that technology is an active part of fantasies around the boss–secretary relationship. In a toned down way, even the old typewriter can be seen as a phallic object. It is 'given' to women by men and in some sense 'completes' them (Plate 6). With it they serve men more effectively. Secretaries are invariably represented beside a typewriter. They are rarely permitted to escape from these objects. To do so would reveal their 'lack' which is perceived to make them unfit for promotional positions. (Or perhaps, even more terrifying, it would reveal that they lack nothing.) While the typewriter is a placid object, the computer is more dangerous to 'give' to women in this way. They might steal it and use it to their own ends. While typewriters are attributed to women, men have retained control of computer keyboards and a distinction is made between mere word processors and personal computers.

Technology and the labour process

Technological change is usually discussed in relation to questions of unemployment, deskilling, new health hazards and 'proletarianisation', its tendency to reduce previously 'middle-class' groups to the level of the working class. Gender does not take priority in these debates. The agenda is set elsewhere and the question of gender arises only in 'quantitative' terms, as in whether women are in greater danger than men of being deskilled or unemployed, whether they are being proletarianised at a faster rate, or whether they are contracting more work-related illnesses.

Two broad approaches have been taken on the directions of technological change. The first, strongly influenced by Braverman's work (1974), emphasises the battle for control between capital and labour, the deskilling of the majority of workers and the extreme polarisation of the class structure. In this framework, the majority of secretaries are part of a growing 'white-collar proletariat' while a minority become hyperskilled and close ranks with management. The second puts the more optimistic case that computer-based technology marks a fundamental break with the past and creates the possibility for ending the existing fragmentation and reintegrating the labour process. There is said to be no longer any need for the functional specialisation or centralisation of work. Feminist approaches have cut across these two, with socialist feminists taking the first as their starting point while liberal feminism takes much from the second.

'Labour process' is a term that derives from factory production. In Marxist usage it refers to the process whereby labour, technology and raw materials are drawn together to create commodities and generate surplus value. This is a decidedly masculine domain and the frame of reference is the struggle for control between capital and labour. When the term is applied to office work it is usually to signify that the office has become more like the factory and that office staff are part of an enlarged working class. Here I use it broadly, to signify that secretarial work has to be taken seriously as *work*, with its own labour process and its own distinct skills. I want to remove it from its earlier theoretical context and argue that the labour process is structured as much by gender and sexuality as it is by struggles around ownership and control of the means of production. The two are, of course,

Plate 3 Advertisements for office technology are directed towards a male viewer and, as these examples show, are obsessed with 'power and control'. There is some ambiguity about whether the power is in the machine or the buyer—they are mutually reinforcing. The computer is represented as an extension of masculine power but also plays a significant role in constructing it. There is clearly some anxiety around who has control: the computer seems to settle it.

177

Are you a computer virgin?

DEC HAS A POT OF GOLD AT THE END OF THIS RAINBOW

Plate 4   The two images above develop the connections between computers, power, and sexual potency. The top one plays on masculine anxieties about the impotence, even castration, that threaten if he does not come to terms with computers. The lower one is reassuring: the phallus is connected up, via the keyboard strategically perched on the lap, with the power of the computer, thus magnifying its original power many times over.

When it comes to fax, we've got the legs.

Plate 5   Two fetishistic images, one glaringly obvious, the other more discreet. The message is clear: women/secretaries lack the phallus, but men can give them a substitute in the form of technology (and high heels).

"MY BOSS GAVE ME A WORDPLEX"

Modern Office, September 1982

Plate 6 These images continue the theme of technology as a gift that men give to women. Smiling secretaries bask in the glow of masculine power and magnanimity. Both secretaries and technology appear as men's possessions, a measure of their worth, the objects as well as the basis of men's power and control. The secretaries are there to operate men's machines and to service men—in ways that are, by implication, rather intimate.

interrelated. Gender constructions are class-specific: never more so than in the kind of 'middle-class' femininity that is required of secretaries (whether they are actually 'middle-class' is another matter). Class power is frequently represented as a form of masculine sexual power and prestige: 'having' a secretary both signifies power and facilities its exercise. Far from being marginal to the labour process, sexuality is a primary organising feature. The boss—secretary relationship is just one of the more obvious examples of the ways in which the labour process is sexualised.

In the decades before 1970 the most widely discussed piece of technology was the dictaphone. Bosses found it difficult to accept this one as empowering when it threatened to take their secretaries away from them. In the United States it was linked to the establishment of typing pools as early as the 1920s. Both developments came later in Australia. Even when electronic machines became available in the late 1950s their market penetration was slow (*AFR* 16 November 1961). Managers preferred to dictate to a stenographer/secretary or write their work out in longhand, and pools consisted of stenographers and copy typists rather than audio-typists.

The recession of 1960—61 brought pressure to make offices more efficient. This period marked the beginning of a gradual long-term decline in the relative proportion of secretarial workers. Managers were shocked at the speed at which office staff had grown and at the dramatic increases in costs. For example, by 1961 a business letter cost between 7/6d and 30/-, escalating to $7 by 1964 (*Sunday Telegraph* 31 May 1964). Cost-reducing measures included the standardisation of paper, the use of window-faced envelopes, and the gradual adoption of 'open punctuation' by which commas, the indentation of paragraphs, the underlining of addresses and so on could be omitted. Dictaphones were taken more seriously in the 1960s. Companies which used them claimed to have reduced the number of typists by as much as 50 per cent. One company reported that a 'pool' of four stenographers and eight typists had been reduced to five typists (*AFR* 16 November 1961). Caltex, which leant heavily on the audio system, claimed to manage with only five private secretaries for the top directors and senior executives. But resistance remained strong and the case had to be reargued throughout the 1960s (*Rydges* December 1969). In the end it was staff shortages rather than cost savings that encouraged their adoption. Stenographers began to be replaced by 'audio-typists' who were described as the new cinderellas of the office, turned into 'battery birds' (*sic*) by the conditions in the dictating pools (*Mirror* 11 May 1971).

Dictaphones do not have to be used in a pool situation. As it became clear that the dictaphone need not replace the secretary, bosses showed more interest. When small hand-held dictaphones became available, in the 1970s, senior managers used them to make their own secretaries more productive. The manufacturers now appealed specifically to those who had retained their sec-retaries. In a direct appeal to megalomaniac fantasies they argued, for example, that an executive can put his ideas down in longhand at a maximum speed of about 15 wpm, dictate to a secretary at twice that rate, and to a machine at 60 wpm after a few days' practice. The manager can dictate when and where it suits him, at whatever speed he likes. He does not have to call for a relief when his secretary is ill, on holiday or at lunch. She can transcribe faster from the machine than from her notes, particularly if she is not a particularly proficient shorthand writer (*Modern Office Adminis-tration* March 1973). All of this appealed to a masculine ideal of machine-like efficiency and limitless energy. In this literature management is allocated almost mystical powers and secretaries are presumed to be either silly or slow or out to lunch! These putdowns are facilitated by the relentless use of 'girl'.

The early 1970s saw a continuing shortage of secretaries and stenographers, with older women coaxed back into the workforce ('Plenty of office jobs for old girls', said the *Sunday Telegraph* 10 June 1973). In November 1973 a pay rise flowed on to women clerks from the 1972 'equal pay' decision. Although the *Daily Mirror* assured its readers that 'Sexy Secs won't find themselves out of a job because of this week's equal pay breakthrough' (29 November 1973) both the shortage of staff and rising rates of pay were forcing managers to think about productivity. The 1974 recession brought further pressure for staff savings. Junior and unskilled staff were cut back and the 'status symbol' secretary was pronounced a luxury. Interest in the dictaphone merged at this stage with the new possibilities of the word processor and mini-computer.

As the dictaphone came into general use, stenographers could have been phased out. But they were not. Managers developed various strategies to keep their secretaries and to avoid using the pools. They argued, for example, the need to preserve confiden-tiality which, they said, was at risk if a document had to go outside the office. To justify retaining the services of a stenographer she was frequently relabelled a secretary and given other tasks such as answering the telephone. The term 'steno-sec' came into being. Shorthand remained useful for jotting down telephone messages but was really only required for taking minutes of meetings.

The use of the dictaphone meant that the secretary spent less time actually in the company of her boss. The time spent taking shorthand was freed for other things. Secretaries may regret losing their speeds but they are often impatient with bosses who want to use shorthand. They regard it as a waste of time. That they can ill afford the time is a good indication of the increases in work pressure since the 1960s. If the boss can dictate more, the secretary is expected to type more. Because she is more productive she may be expected to work for more than one boss, or to do a little 'extra' typing for other people. By the late 1960s there was a new image of secretaries as 'Girl Fridays', jacks-of-all-trades and general dogsbodies. In terms of pay rates, they lost ground to ledger machinists, key punch operators and receptionists (*Rydges* July 1968). In larger offices receptionists took over duties that had previously fallen to secretaries. There was a general blurring of the tasks of secretary, stenographer and receptionist and any of them could be referred to as a secretary. 'Secretary' came to be synonomous with the middle rather than the top of the range.

The distinction between a secretary and a typist was once clear-cut. The secretary had an office and telephone of her own, while typists were relegated to the pool, sitting in rows rather like a schoolroom, with a supervisor at the front. By the 1960s there was dissatisfaction with pools. It was felt that they produced poor-quality work and that greater contact was needed between the typist and the 'author'. First in private enterprise and belatedly in the public service the pools were phased out or modified. In the 1970s 'landscaped' offices homogenised the working conditions for a range of office staff including management.

Perhaps the most underestimated piece of technology to slink in in the 1960s was the photocopier. One of the earliest places to use it was the Probate Office where it was extremely useful for copying wills and other papers and quickly displaced a number of straight copy typists (*Sunday Telegraph* 26 March 1960). The photocopier saved a great deal of retyping. Documents could be edited with white-out and scissors and paste and then copied: the corrections were invisible. They also removed the need to go through the laborious process of making multiple carbon copies and thus enabled all typing to be done more quickly. (Though even in the late 1980s there are secretaries who still churn out a carbon on the *printer*—old habits die hard!) The work of the remaining typists was now similar to that of 'steno-secs'.

The photocopier created work as well as saving it. It became possible to reproduce papers, articles, minutes and so on on a scale never dreamed of. Where people once might have shared copies, or looked at the office copy, they now expect to have their own. A university professor described how he marks out news-paper articles nearly every day and has his secretary copy and distribute them to every pigeonhole in the department. In the past she would have been expected, at most, to clip and have the file available in the office for those interested. While it is an obvious task to pass on to the office junior, it often falls to the secretary. The Secretarial Studies Review conducted by NSW TAFE 1982–83 found that the photocopier is the most frequently used piece of equipment by secretaries and personal assistants alike (*Modern Office* August 1984: 26).

Automation

Office automation began in the 1960s when mainframe computers took over many routine clerical functions. The Foundation for Australian Resources estimated that by 1978 150 000 low-grade clerical jobs had been abolished in Australia as a result of computerisation and about 24 000 created (*AFR* 18 December 1978). While this did not directly affect secretaries it disrupted the existing office pyramid. Secretaries were deprived of a sense of having layers of clerical assistants below them. In much the same way, the status of tellers and examiners was changed when the banks computerised and ledger machinists were no longer required in the branches. Instead of being a position commanding some respect, based on overall knowledge and experience, telling became one of the most junior (Game & Pringle, 1983).

The fully automated office involves a variety of technologies working in tandem to provide almost instant information, decision-making facilities and communications. Taken to its limits, it would mean the end of the secretarial workforce as we know it. The boss–secretary fantasy is replaced here with another masculine fantasy of complete omnipotence and autonomy. There would be:

> ...no secretaries, filing clerks, mail sorters, receptionists, switchboard operators. There would be no need for mail sorters because there would be no paper mail, just electronic messages flashing around the globe...In this fully automated office there would be just a lot of managers sitting at terminals calling up information on their screens, their decisions translated into digital data by speech recognition systems so it can stored and transmitted as text to other people sitting at other terminals...(*Australian* 25 November 1985)

Such developments are in their infancy. Gradually people are becoming aware of the way in which word processors link in with data bases, telex, facsimile machines, telephones and so on to provide a unified system. While the components of this system are firmly in place it may be another decade before the full effects are felt.

The earliest memory typewriters in the 1960s were based on a paper tape. They were considered useful for reproducing names and addresses but were never popular. The first 'editor type-writers', which appeared in the mid-1970s, were magnetic card machines, devoid of both screen and printer. High labour costs, combined with improvements in the technology, a fall in prices, and aggressive marketing strategies of the suppliers to ensure that word processors penetrated the Australian market very rapidly. By the late 1970s there was much concern about their employment implications. Linda Rubenstein, in a paper to the first Women and Labour Conference in Sydney in 1977, estimated that they would allow staff cuts of 50 per cent and make vast numbers of typists, stenographers and secretaries redundant (1978). In April 1978 they were claimed to have already displaced 20 000 typists in Sydney alone (Adele Horin, *NT* 3 April). The general manager of Westaff boasted that a word processor used to full capacity could replace up to 25 typists! (*Age* 12 May 1980). There were many attempts to establish the average displacement ratio. For a time 1:4 was a generally accepted figure. After an initial panic, these estimates were revised downwards and ratios of 2:1 or 3:1 became more common. Word processors have also created a lot of new work, as documents such as handbooks and manuals were typed onto the computer to provide a data base which could be routinely updated. Since the early 1980s attention has shifted from unemployment to changes in the nature of the work.

Outside the multinationals the most dramatic changes in the labour processes surrounding secretarial work have taken place in large law firms. Legal work, with its large volume of repetitive documents and requirement of complete accuracy, was an obvious candidate for the word processor. Large firms have been best able to take advantage of this by creating teams of full-time word-processor operators, who work in shifts, getting material ready for court the following morning. Reception and telephone duties are carried out by a small number of clerical assistants. Though such word-processor operators are highly paid, they do not have the status once afforded legal secretaries. The kinds of legal knowledge they pick up on the job will no longer be used, because their contact with clients, and familiarity with particular cases, will be minimised. The computer affects not only typing but accounting and billing procedures and hence modifies the work of secretaries in all professional offices. The work of medical secretaries has changed most, as bills and reminder notices, which were once a big part of their job, are now sent out automatically.

In Britain word-processing was still, by 1983, limited to typing pools rather than secretarial offices and was having little impact on secretaries except in the prestigious offices of multinational companies based in London (Softley, 1985: 229–30). In Australia, by contrast, they were soon used in small offices and by individual secretaries typing 'one-offs'. A typist completes a rough draft much more speedily than she can produce perfect copy. A speed of 60 wpm may easily be reduced to 10 wpm if she has to interpret information accurately or under pressure. Once corrections became easy to make accuracy counted for little and the rate of keystrokes could be increased. As the price came down it made sense, from a management viewpoint, for almost any kind of typing to be done on word processors. Over two-thirds of the senior secretaries interviewed either had a word processor on their desks or made use of one.

IBM: exception or rule?

If we want to get a sense of the 'paperless office' then IBM is an interesting case study, for of all organisations it has advanced furthest in this direction. Unfortunately it refused to cooperate with our study beyond one interview in the personnel department. What follows is based on published sources and informal conversations with people who have either worked for, or had dealings with, the company.

IBM introduced word processors in 1970 in the form of magnetic typewriters. Initially they tried to make a clear division between 'correspondence' or 'word-processing' secretaries and 'administrative' secretaries and have all routine typing done by the former in a central word-processing centre. Because of interpersonal conflicts and lack of job satisfaction among the operators they moved to smaller word-processing centres. These were later supplemented by 'one-person stations' on the executive floor and areas such as personnel, which require confidentiality. They established an exchange system between the various locations to cope with the peaks and troughs. The success of such a system requires rapport between the operators, and since they were now isolated from each other, the company provided recreational and sporting facilities to encourage good social relations (Coffey & Dunphy, 1982: 3−9).

In the late 1970s IBM converted from magnetic-card typewriters to visual display terminals. The next technical step was to link all stations to a central computer, enabling users at any location to link in. This provides the basis of an electronic mail network by which documents can be transferred between any two terminals in the system. It makes exchanges possible throughout the country and internationally via satellite. While IBM have retained their secretaries, the technology is available for much of the work to be performed at home or, for that matter, in South East Asia. Publishing workers have long been familiar with the practice of sending non-urgent work to places like Hong Kong to by typeset and printed. Satellite communications make it perfectly feasible to turn a job around within 24 hours regardless of distance. So far this option has been restricted to labour-intensive and repetitive work, but it could be taken further. There is no need for secretaries to be physically present in the office.

IBM now boasts a system called PROFS which sends and receives information on computer screens, keeps personal electronic diaries, helps compose letters and memos and finds vital documents. It is possible to schedule company meetings simply by typing in the names of the people you want to be present, together with a range of times and dates. PROFS will check everyone's diary and rapidly tell you the most convenient times and available rooms. A few more keystrokes will book the room and send everyone involved a memo. In addition there is PhoneMail which digitises voice messages and stores them in the computer for later retrieval, and DISOSS, a vast electronic filing system.

While this is not the blueprint for the future, it does offer some general pointers. Despite careful selection of staff, regular sackings, a ban on unions and a system designed to minimise organised workplace opposition, there has been a lot of staff discontent at IBM. The overall number of secretarial positions has been cut dramatically and anecdotal evidence suggests that executives do not all favour the 'rational efficiency' model of masculinity. Some have fought to keep their personal secretaries and resisted learning keyboards skills. Neither are staff happy with the degree of monitoring that takes place when the system is fully in operation. The precise details of everyone's diary is, in principle, instantly available.

The division between correspondence and administrative secretaries at IBM has caused problems. The former found the transition easiest, perhaps because they were learning new skills and are valued because these skills are in short supply. The administrative secretaries have an identity problem. They could become part of management or be reduced to the role of receptionist or clerical assistant. While both groups retain personal relations with executives for whom they work, they lose the direct relationship with a 'boss', and come under the direction of a coordinator of secretarial services. Problems are meant to be taken to the immediate superior and there is no structure for group discussion.

Secretarial jobs will be further eroded with the advent of phone mail and electronic filing. It has been estimated that the average organisation wastes 65c out of every dollar spent on record-making and filing. Most organisations keep 70 per cent more records than are needed; 85 per cent of records are never referred to and 95 per cent of all references are made to records less than three years old (*AFR* 13 September 1982). Gary Nash from IBM points to estimates that there are eight filing drawers containing 18 000 documents for each white-collar worker. A survey indicated that about one-quarter of an office worker's time is wasted looking for information (*The Chartered Accountant in Australia* July 1983: 41). Filing has thus been earmarked for productivity gains with the use of electronic systems. Once telex messages can be delivered direct to executive terminals, internal messengers and filing clerks will be redundant (West, 1982: 68).

The executive's fantasy is a machine that transmits the human voice onto a screen, bypassing the keyboard altogether. Such equipment could be available by the end of the century. Plessey have a telephone which digitises a human voice and displays it as a waveform on the screen so that the speaker can edit speeches, deleting words or changing their order by touching the appropriate part of the screen. There are currently difficulties in producing a system that can recognise a variety of voices and reliably translate them into electronic data. If and when such a system is developed office automation will take a quantum leap. Integrated Services Digital Network (ISDN) already allows data, voice text and image transmission over a single link and Telecom has introduced such systems in Melbourne and Sydney.

The new forces of production mount a fundamental challenge to the old social relations of secretarial work. But they are being introduced at different speeds in different contexts with many different currents of resistance. It is unlikely that any uniformity will result. What is striking at the moment is how *different* the majority of workplaces are from IBM. As a computer company and a large multinational, IBM has an interest in presenting a high-tech image. Others will adopt the technology in a more piecemeal way, and will proceed more cautiously. Word-processor operators have largely replaced typists (disappearing category) but the majority of secretaries have been retained, with word-processing simply added to their duties. The 'administrative assistant' has not taken off, probably because management find it difficult to specify what it is, other than typing, that secretaries actually do!

New jobs in information-processing will not automatically be considered women's work. Softley (1985: 235—36) notes the increase in male word-processor operators in the USA, and a loosening of the traditional association of keyboarding with women. With schools teaching computer skills, both sexes should, in principle, learn the keyboard. But moves to break down the existing sexual division of labour and to treat men and women as interchangeable in the workforce are contradicted by discourses that eroticise difference. The gender outcomes still have to be negotiated.

Pleasures and hazards

Much of what secretaries describe as pleasure at work is pleasure in exercising skills; much displeasure is in being forced to do boring, repetitive, unskilled work. Where 'skill' is often poorly defined, questions about what gives pleasure are a useful way of unlocking our preconceptions. What seems 'boring' to the outsider may generate intense pleasure to the person doing the work.

Old skills have undoubtedly been lost as a result of new technology. Shorthand skills are disintegrating through lack of use, while the typist's skill in producing perfect copy is irrelevant when word processors automatically indent, justify, tabulate, paginate and correct mistakes. More time is spent keying in and less on handling paper and layout. Dissatisfaction is highest in the pools and lowest among secretaries who see the word processor as a helpful adjunct to their work. Secretaries are usually keen to minimise the time they spend typing and do not seek their primary work satisfaction in this area. Softley's study of word-processor operators in England found that 72 per cent derived more satisfaction from their work after word-processing was introduced and that none were less satisfied. She concedes that any who were dissatisfied may have left (1985: 230−31). The secretaries in my sample who used a word processor generally felt they had gained a useful skill and valuable time-saver. They had got over the 'novelty' effect and still enjoyed its capacities. Their main grievances were the limited training, the expectation that they would immediately be able to perform miracles, and increased work pressure. Only a small proportion had refused to learn, mostly older women close to retirement.

A minority of the sample had contracted repetitive strain injury or RSI. This is the collective name, used in Australia, for muscle and tendon injuries resulting from the continuous movements demanded by numerous kinds of repetitive work. It includes tenosynovitis, carpal tunnel syndrome and other injuries connected with over-use of the hand, arm, neck and shoulder muscles. In the United States these are usually now called Cumulative Trauma Disorder (CTD). While such symptoms have long been present in other parts of the world they reached such epidemic proportions in Australia that they came to be known as 'Kangaroo Paw'.

At the time of the interviews there was much public debate on the subject and most secretaries had something to say about it. They were aware of the importance of ergonomic furniture, of desks and tables being the correct height. They knew they were supposed to take regular rest breaks but were scathing about the possibility of implementation. The responsibility for taking breaks was placed on the operators. Managers had made little attempt to restructure their own schedules in order to allow for such breaks and the operators felt unable to stop in the middle of something that was needed urgently. Their other frequent complaints were that managers were more likely to hand in appallingly produced first copy, on the assumption that changes were easy to make; they expected more drafts; they underestimated the time it still takes to make changes and print out new copies. This creates all-round pressure as well as pressure to increase the rate of key-strokes.

It might be expected that full-time word-processor operators would be more vulnerable to RSI than secretaries who are performing a range of tasks. However, a study of workers at the Australian National University in Canberra indicated that private secretaries were as vulnerable as full-time word-processor operators, and both groups had a higher incidence than did typists or stenographers (Bammer, 1986). As the ones who take final responsibility for a job being completed secretaries, in a sense, carry the stress of the whole office.

RSI has been perceived as the 'Australian' disease on the basis that its symptoms have been more widely reported and discussed here. Yet working conditions are not obviously different from comparable countries like Britain and the United States. International comparisons are difficult to make because of the variety of ways of measuring both workloads and musculoskeletal problems. It may be that Australian businessmen have worked their secretaries harder and failed to acknowledge the skills of senior secretaries. While this does not correspond with the international image of the Australian worker as being 'slack', it should be remembered that that image is based on *male* workers. Colder air-conditioning, fluoride in the water supply, and a larger intake of aspirin have been put forward as alternative explanations. There is much speculation and little hard fact about what might cause the differences.

The one striking difference between Australia and a number of other countries is that in Australia musculoskeletal injuries are considered compensable by law. Such injuries are thus more likely to be reported and have been the subject of numerous court cases in which theories about the nature of the injury and its causes are aired. In the United States, by contrast, employees may wait two years for a case to be heard. In the meantime they risk being fired from their jobs and having nothing to live on. While similar injuries have been documented in Japan, they are never the subject of compensation claims. Employers generally pick up the medical bills but admit no liability. In Australia RSI victims have successfully claimed workers' compensation payments for total or (if fit for light duties) partial incapacity. In the first RSI damages case to go to a Supreme Court jury, Mrs Dawn Crick received a settlement of $154 531 after the Commonwealth government was found guilty of negligence in failing to provide her with a safe place to work (*SMH* 13 February 1986). Mrs Crick, like most RSI sufferers, was a process worker. Though the 'typical' RSI sufferer has been portrayed as the female keyboard worker, the majority of claimants have been process workers and a high proportion (35.7 per cent in 1984) have been men. In 1983–84 there were 1288 compensation claims (excluding Western Australia and the Northern Territory) from clerical workers compared with 3726 from tradesmen, process workers and labourers (Worksafe Australia, 1986:27–29). Nevertheless the rate among clerical workers increased fivefold between 1981 and 1984, and it did appear to correlate with the introduction of word processors.

The cost of RSI to employers and insurance companies has been enormous. At Telecom alone the costs amounted to $15.5 million over five years, which included $1.8 million of medical costs (Hocking, 1987: 220). The difficulty of clearly identifying the symptoms leaves the way open to accusations of 'malingering'. Mrs Crick was subjected to strenuous cross-examination during a five-day trial in which the jury viewed films taken of her secretly, which showed her patting a horse and out on a shopping trip. When these tactics failed, psychiatrists were called in to try to establish that RSI is an hysterical symptom, and hence not 'real'. The best known was Dr Yolanda Lucire who argued that RSI is a not an injury but an occupational neurosis or hysterical conversion symptom. She said that 'the texts which claim that epidemics of hysteria no longer occur on the scale of those in the 19th century may have to be rewritten in the light of the Australian experience' (1986: 325). For good measure she added in an interview that for women RSI was a way out of the 'tacky office affair' ('PM', 21 November 1985). Lucire's evidence was at first rejected by the Queensland Workers' Compensation Board (*AFR* 20 November 1985), but similar arguments have repeatedly been put and are starting to find acceptance. Dr Robert Spillane, for example, has put the view that the disease was created by doctors (*Australian* 25 March 1986). Other medical evidence suggests that changes do take place in the muscle tissue as a result of injury (*SMH* 10 May 1988). The debate goes on.

Given that 'psychological' theories have been used against RSI sufferers in court, it has been difficult for their supporters to analyse the mental and social factors. RSI is brought on by 'stress' in a generalised and psychological sense and not simply by the absolute numbers of keystrokes performed. In Telecom, for example, the telephonists were the most affected, followed by the clerical workers and the telegraphists. This order is the inverse of the keystroke rates. The new technology had a particularly negative impact on the environment of the telephonists, making the work more routine, with less customer contact, and in a context of planned redundancies (Hocking, 1987: 22). Whole sections or departments go down with RSI in something like a 'domino' effect. If one person goes sick and is not replaced there is obviously pressure on those remaining, but along with this, fear and then panic set in as the disease spreads. Far from receiving the sympathy of their colleagues, RSI sufferers are often abused as freeloaders. This is exacerbated where they are put on light duties and are seen to be having an 'easy time' compared with the others.

RSI is often regarded as a psychosomatic protest against boring, monotonous, repetitive work. Yet 'stress' may equally be present in interesting, absorbing work: it is just not registered as 'stress'. In Foskey's alternative account (1987) RSI sufferers are portrayed not as victims but as analogous to athletes straining for the best performance possible. Many workers actually derive pleasure from going as fast as they can and from 'racing the machine'. While older manual and electric typewriters set limits to this possibility, the new electronic keyboards mean it is literally impossible to outpace the machine. It is thought that short fast bursts may be even more damaging than long stretches on the machines. The onset of RSI may therefore be very sudden. There is a growing awareness that the 'work ethic' itself contributes to RSI; it is 'good' workers who are most susceptible and those who understand how to relax and to pace themselves who are most likely to survive.

Nearly 4000 compensation claims were made between 1981 and 1985. Thereafter the figures began to decline and by 1987 the *Medical Journal of Australia* pronounced the epidemic to be 'over' (7 September 1987: 213). While one would expect the figures to drop as safety measures were implemented and people became more careful, it has also become more difficult to claim compensation. In March 1987 a keyboard operator with the Taxation Department lost a landmark case before the Supreme Court. The government, intent on ensuring it did not lose another 'negligence' case, spent over $1 million collecting evidence and expert witnesses. On this occasion evidence was accepted that RSI could be attributed to mass hysteria, and that the diagnosis actually encouraged victims to believe they were ill (CCH Australia Limited, 1987, 50–279). The price of recognising psychological factors has been to cut compensation payments.

Proletarianisation?

Neo-marxists have used the concept of 'proletarianisation' to refer to the deterioration of pay and working conditions of clerical workers relative to manual workers (e.g. Braverman, 1974; Abercrombie and Urry, 1983; Crompton and Jones, 1984; Cuneo, 1985). Davies (1982) applies the term specifically to secretarial workers. She argues that the 'proletarianisation' of secretaries happened in two stages, both very closely associated with the application of new technology. In the period of mechanisation in the early part of the century, women moved in and the occupation lost its standing as a training ground for management. In the period of automation, starting in the 1960s, secretaries gradually lost their craft skills and were reduced to the status of other low-level office workers.

In a recent critique of this literature Graham Lowe (1987) reveals some fatal flaws, including the tendency to view clerks as a homogeneous group, the failure to consider men and women separately, and the reliance on aggregate data rather than looking at specific organisations or analysing individual work histories. The situation is more complex than the 'proletarianisation' thesis suggests and the impact of new technology is extremely varied. Lowe chides Crompton and Jones for reverting to the 'opaque lexicon' of the proletarianisation thesis when their data suggests alternative explanations (1987: 165). If clerks are a heterogeneous group, then so too are secretaries. Moreover, any decline in their status is not necessarily brought about by 'proletarianisation' or mediated by technology. Other explanations can be offered.

English feminists Jane Barker and Hazel Downing (1980) have suggested that secretaries use their femininity to some degree as a buffer against direct exploitation; that automation destroys some oppressive features of the boss—secretary relationship only to create an increased possibility of exploitation. It is argued here that, on the contrary, their loss of status derived from shifts in the structure of femininity. Rather than being 'proletarianised' they lost some of their status as 'ladies' and were thrown into the mass category of 'girls'. This happened via a process of sexualisation rather than through loss of control over the 'means of production'.

The declining status of secretaries was being discussed in the 1950s and 60s well before the new technology directly affected them, and it was mediated by the sexualisation process: 'In brief the social picture is one of extraordinarily rapid levelling, to the disadvantage of those members of the workforce who take the trouble to acquire specific qualifications. The future of the senior secretary is merely part of a general problem' (*AFR* 25 February 1958). The rapid expansion of the tertiary sector created a labour shortage which meant that jobs were advertised as 'secretarial' as a way of attracting staff. Executives were criticised for bestowing continuing favours on their personal stenographers, including 'the fictitious title of secretary' (*Rydges* September 1968). According to Mrs Gilroy, director of schools at Hales Secretarial College, 'many girls described and paid as secretaries are no more than inexperienced junior stenographers' (*Sunday Telegraph* 17 October 1971). By the 1980s young women straight out of college were given the title of 'junior secretary'.

The word 'secretary' is used to cover a range of workers, some of whose conditions of work have changed markedly. While there may have been a decline in status it is not clear that this amounts to 'proletarianisation'. The proletarianisation of a group implies that it has lost the skills or resources that placed it outside the working class. Secretaries retain skills and initiatives and, in some contexts, considerable power. It is romanticising to claim that 50 years ago they were in a stronger position. The significant changes are not so much a loss of skills as the sexualisation of the occupation. Whether secretarial work is experienced as a move up or down depends largely on a person's class background. Working-class students experience secretarial work as a step up from the shop or factory jobs they might otherwise have taken. It is women from middle-class backgrounds who are more likely to be aware of the loss of status. Many who might once have taken up secretarial work are finding new opportunities in higher education and in professional, administrative and clerical work. Those remaining may view secretarial work with some contempt.

The proletarianisation theorists assume that class is based on occupation and that the class location of an occupational group can be inferred from its changing market and work situations. Behind the proletarianisation issue is the question of where secretaries are located in the class structure. How accurate an indicator of class is occupation? While its centrality has been taken for granted for men the opposite is the case for women. Those who reject the proletarianisation thesis generally do so on the dubious grounds that women take their class position primarily from their husbands or that in some vague way occupation matters 'less' to them. On these criteria, secretarial work could not be proletarianised if it were done by the wives or daughters of 'middle-class' men (West, 1978). But men and women do not appear as gendered subjects in patriarchal relations and as gender-neutral 'people' in capitalist relations. They are always gendered and hence their experience of class will be very different. To understand what class means for secretaries, we need to situate class in the context of patriarchal relations.

•9• Class, status and gender

> Yet because women are women, they constantly
> cross over the boundaries between jobs. As they
> move in and out of paid employment, they may span
> a wide variety of different occupations... Women
> simply cannot afford the same sense of class as men,
> for the reality of their lives constantly contradicts it.
>
> *PHILLIPS, 1987: 65*

> Women may be reviewed as a subordinate class in
> relation to men, but they take on the status of their
> husbands, they carry out domestic labour and
> childcare, and enter the workforce within the
> material conditions provided by their husband's
> command of income and property.
>
> *CASS, 1978: 34*

> The gender category is, like the class category, a
> construction of more than one type of
> practice... Class and patriarchy are forms of
> structuring that can be discovered in the same
> practices at the same time.
>
> *CONNELL, 1983: 75, 77*

Secretaries raise in an acute way the difficulties that class theorists have had in assigning class positions to women. Market capacity
and place in the social division of labour are usually taken as the
main indicator of men's class positions, but it is not so clear that
the same criteria apply for women. The division between mental
and manual labour is generally held to mark out a broad division
between middle and working classes. This has some application to
men but it makes less sense in relation to women's occupations,
since a relatively small proportion of women are involved in
'manual' work. In any case the term 'secretary' encompasses a
broad range of workers. Because it is seen as an acceptable thing
for a woman to do, women from all classes may be automatically
channelled into it. The status of the occupation has often been
measured by the 'middle class' backgrounds of the majority of its
members. The influx of working-class women is used as evidence
that the work is becoming 'proletarianised', as if this were cause
rather than effect. Gender is implicated in the construction of
class and status categories.

Do secretaries as an occupational grouping form part of an identifiable class and if so, which one? Do the same criteria apply for determining the class and status allocation of 'men's' and 'women's' occupations? Do women, as individuals, take their class identity from their own occupation or from that of their husbands? Is the unit of class analysis the individual or the family? If the latter, is its position derived purely from the male breadwinner or does the woman's occupation also contribute to it? Do individuals have only one or a variety of class identifications? Do women change their 'class' when they move in and out of the paid work-force? Do they have more in common as a group than the class or status differences that divide them?

It is notorious that class theory treats women as marginal. While some writers attempt to justify this as an accurate account of patriarchal realities others seem barely aware that they have done it (Crompton and Mann, 1986). In mainstream writing there has been relatively little exploration of the intersection of patriarchal and class structures. Erik Wright, for example, a leading Marxist theorist, has developed sophisticated criteria for defining 'class locations' but has consistently ignored gender (1976; 1985). As Delphy and Leonard point out, class has acquired 'the linguistic right to be *the* social hierarchy' (1986: 60). Class is seen as the primary social division while other inequalities struggle to be seen as either social or systematic. In the dominant discourses the social division of labour is restricted to that between and among employees, employers and the self-employed, while the family is somehow excluded from the domain of the social (or the public) entirely. Structural inequalities between husbands and wives are passed over as relatively trivial forms of stratification. While class and status embody, in themselves, the notions of power and inequality, gender does not. Feminists have put a lot of energy into contesting existing class analyses and attempting to modify them (Smith, 1983). In the process they have often drawn analogies with class or insisted that women have distinct class positions.

Feminists first challenged the idea that women take their class position from their fathers or husbands. They insisted that the individual rather than the family was the unit of class analysis and that it should not be assumed that family members hold the same class position (Cass, 1978; West, 1978; Delphy, 1984). The idea that class centres on occupation was maintained here, whether based on Marxist definitions in terms of relation to the means of production or more Weberian accounts which emphasise market position. Some writers kept to the family as the basic unit but insisted that its position was determined by the contributions of both husband and wife (Britten and Heath, 1983).

Radical feminists argued that gender divisions are more funda-mental than class divisions as they had been conceptualised to date, and that gender itself may be a form of class. Shulamith Firestone spoke of 'sex classes' based on biological difference and reinforced by ideology. Others have emphasised the ways in which 'sex class' relations have been historically constituted. In particular, attention has been drawn to the omission of domestic labour from analysis of class. Both Christine Delphy (1984) and Bettina Cass (1978) have argued that women share a common class position as domestic labourers. Differences between women are conceptualised not as class but as status divisions. Rather than taking them as given, Cass examined the historical processes that constructed 'sex classes' in Australia, arguing that women's domestic work takes place in the sphere of consumption and that their prestige and lifestyle depend on the economic class of the men to whom they are attached. 'Working class', 'middle class' or 'upper class' are here treated as status affiliations which may be withdrawn in the event of separation, divorce or the death of their husbands. Their own market capacity will typically be lower because they have placed marriage and motherhood ahead of equipping themselves for the labour force (Cass, 1978: 18–20).

It has proved difficult to build on such accounts. They excite discussion for a brief period, and then disappear, only to resurface in a slightly modified form. Sylvia Walby has returned to similar themes, arguing that class analysis has failed to incorporate 'the structured positions associated with the domestic division of labour' (1986a: 27). It does not count housework as an occupation, and glosses over inequalities between husbands and wives. In a sophisticated analysis, she suggests that housewives and husbands (though not men and women) can be conceptualised as classes (1986a: 33–35); that the relations of production are the same, whatever the position of the husband, and that differences between housewives are merely quantitative differences in standard of living.

The trouble with such accounts is that they leave men and women simultaneously in at least two separate class positions without specifying the relationship between them. I am not satisfied that any of these analyses provide a suitable starting point for an account of class either for women in general or for secretaries in particular. They have not had much impact on the dominant discourses, and this is not only because of the sexism of the (mostly male) Marxists and Weberians who talk about class (Crompton and Mann, 1986). I prefer to retain the everyday language of upper or ruling class, middle and working class whatever problems there may be with these categorisations.

I understand classes neither as collections of individuals nor of families but as very broad groups that draw their livelihood from a particular relation to the means of production or have access to similar market capacities. All members of the group do not need to participate directly in production or the labour market to qualify for membership. If this were the case not only a lot of women but all children, pensioners and unemployed persons would be disqualified from class membership. Neither do we have to assume that individual class members are equal or that class has the same meaning for them. The working class consists broadly of those whose livelihood depends wholly on the sale of labour power; the bourgeoisie and their associates own or control the means of production; and the middle class are defined by their position *between* these groups. The middle class may possess small-scale capital (the old petit bourgeoisie) or capital in the form of qualifications or skills which are exercised on behalf of capital and rewarded accordingly. It may be objected that these definitions centre on men; that what is being described here is a male class system to which women are marginal or connected only by their relations with men. But it may be argued that class is structured by patriarchal as well as capitalist relations: it is not possible to produce a neat theory of class that fits women in.

The problem with class theory is not that it treats women as peripheral to the class structure but that it takes their marginality for granted rather than analysing it. In some ways the feminist critique of class theory has not gone far enough. Feminists have challenged its obvious sexism but overlooked its more fundamental phallocentricity. While it is admitted, for example, that the working class is deeply segmented along the lines of gender and race, it is too frequently accepted that the experience of white males in some sense constitutes the class. Class theory has been developed with only men in mind and then presented as gender-neutral and universally applicable. Various attempts have been made to 'get the categories right' so they will be able to account for both men and women. This is handled either by locating men and women in sex-based classes or establishing economic (or 'social') classes that in principle may accommodate both on the same criteria. The possibility that 'classes' might be based on two genders rather than one is excluded. For example, by adopting the individual as the unit of class analysis we remove the obvious sexism involved in defining women by their place in the family; but we deny the ways in which the 'individual' is constructed as masculine. Sociologists from Marx onwards have talked about the worker and 'his' wife and family, leaving us in no doubt about the gender of the worker. Such assumptions are not challenged merely by insisting that women are workers too. This should alert us to the fact that men's relation to the class system is also gendered, mediated by their construction as 'breadwinners' and by a sexual division of labour which allocates them comparatively favoured places in the occupational structure. To argue individual versus family is to miss the point.

Once the issue of phallocentricity has been identified we can start to reconstruct class theory in ways that draw to the surface rather than suppress the assumptions about gender. Class analysis can still be used to illuminate the social position of secretaries, by providing not a grand theory but insights, fragments, clues. It would certainly be possible to construct a class system that was logically coherent and theoretically consistent. But what would be the point if it did not square up in any way with people's experience? We may need to give up the search for grand theory and the pursuit of 'water-tight' definitions and consider the ways in which class has been shaped by structures other than the highly abstract 'mode of production'. Class is more than a collection of occupational groupings or of individuals with a shared rank in a distribution of specified goodies. If we shift the emphasis from classificatory exercises to look at meaning and experience, then questions about people's social origins, their families, lifestyle, culture and consciousness come into the picture. The *meaning* of terms like working and middle class changes constantly and they have meant different things for women than for men.

In a variety of works Anthony Giddens has developed the idea of 'structuration' to refer to the processes whereby 'economic' classes become social structures (1973; 1979; 1984). The concern here is with the practices which condition or shape class formation. As E.P. Thompson observed, class is a cultural phenomenon. The working class makes and remakes itself; and while it does so in the context of a set of economic relations it is not reducible to them (Thompson, 1968). Once this shift has been made issues like whether the individual or the family is the unit, or about direct versus 'indirect' relation to the means of production, become less important. It becomes possible to situate class in a wider pattern of social relations in which gender, sexuality and the sexual division of labour are extremely important. Ted Willis, the regional manager of a hardware company, expressed this quite succinctly. His father and three of the four brothers are 'in hardware' while his three daughters are all secretaries: 'so I have got the girls going in one direction and the men going in another!' Not only the relations of production and the labour market, but living standards, housing, consumption patterns, social relations, culture and lifestyles are major influences on class structuration. Rather than taking production and consumption as opposites we will consider the way in which this division is set up and its links with the domestic division of labour (Pringle, 1983).

Classes are always already gendered while men and women experience their gender in class terms. We need therefore to situate class in the context of patriarchal relations. It is as if there were not one set of class locations but two, superimposed on each other and obviously meshing. More is involved here than acknowledging that there are divisions *within* classes. Obviously there are also segmentations based on race and ethnicity, at the very least. The question is, how would class analysis be transformed if the two genders were both equally recognised and women did not appear only with reference to men, as being similar to or different from men? Class has different meanings for men and women and cannot be separated from these gender meanings. A 'proletarian' woman never occupies an identical class space to that of a 'proletarian' man even though they may have been subject to many of the same processes. These processes will have a different meaning depending on the gender. We have noted for example how for women clerical workers proletarianisation went along with 'engirl-ment'—these women were reduced to a common status as 'girls' rather than 'workers'.

Gender and class have been subject to processes of mutual definition. Anne Phillips (1987) describes the way the nineteenth-century middle class defined itself partly by having 'its' women cultivate 'ladylike' qualities and removing them from the paid workforce. The class division between women who worked outside the home and those who did not was stark. By the early twentieth century, as more occupations became open to middle-class women, it was marital status rather than class that determined whether women entered paid work. Single women joined the workforce and those who were married mostly did not, particularly when they had children. It is only since World War II, with a growing proportion of women in the paid workforce, that it has made much sense to concentrate on occupational divisions as a major component of their class position. Phillips (1987: 61) argues that while women's jobs are now more stratified than they used to be, women may actually be much less divided by class than they were in the past. What determines whether a woman works is not class or income but marital status and the age of her children.

Giddens offers some recognition of the importance of patriarchal relations and the sexual division of labour for understanding women's class position. In a much-quoted passage he argues that since women 'still have to await their liberation from the family, it remains the case in capitalist societies that female workers are largely peripheral to the class system; or, expressed differently, women are in a sense the 'underclass' of the white collar sector' (1973: 288). Women constitute such an underclass because they are excluded from the primary labour market as a result of a lack of perceived skills, interruptions in labour force participation and sexist stereotyping. Giddens restricts himself to a few rather patronising comments but it is possible to draw out some underlying themes. Patriarchal relations do not simply make women peripheral to the class system but structure the labour market and the labour process and are thus directly implicated in men's and women's class situations. Giddens stresses the manual/non-manual division as the dividing line between middle and working class. He treats this as an objective distinction that can be applied to positions in the labour process regardless of gender. Yet at another level he recognises that the gender of those usually doing a job affects its class character. He treats low-level clerical work as 'non-manual' and hence 'middle-class' regardless of the fact that the workers are as subject to the machine and have as little control over the labour process as do most factory workers; their work involves monotonous, repetitive tasks and their wages and working conditions are comparable. Were it predominantly men in these occupations, he would have to pronounce them working-class. It is because they are women that he is able to reject the proletarianisation thesis. It is assumed here that the changes matter less for women who take their class and status from their husbands rather than their jobs. It is worth noting here that the distinction between manual and *mental* labour has been transformed into one between manual and *non*-manual. In this negative definition of women's clerical work there is a backhand recognition that these jobs do not command more mental ability than the manual ones.

Rather surprisingly, Giddens goes on to stress the importance of women clerical workers as a kind of buffer zone. Because the bulk of clerical workers are women, the decline in clerical salaries and conditions is less traumatic. If these workers were male there would be more tensions, with the group fighting harder to maintain a separate identity and better pay and conditions. As it is, the clerical and skilled manual workers intermarry; social mobility is mostly short-range and largely restricted to movement between these groups.

Though Giddens officially minimises the active role of women in the class structure his use of the term 'underclass' is also interesting. Clerical workers may not be working-class but it would seem they do not quite make it into the middle class either. 'Underclass' is conceptually important to Giddens, particularly in relation to the ethnic and cultural differences which divide the working class, and concentrate the groups affected into the lowest-paid occupations and the chronic unemployed (1977: 112). He has left it to others to explore the idea in relation to female clerical workers. Rosemary Crompton, for example, discusses the numerous ways in which this particular underclass services the 'service class' (1986). She restricts the latter to the professional, administrative and managerial levels of white-collar work, the people who carry out the functions of capital without necessarily owning it. Crompton reckons they make up nearly a quarter of the employed population in Britain and are overwhelmingly male (1986: 122−23). Lower clerical workers provide the backup support which enables this class to exercise authority and control. She argues that the existence of the 'service class' depends, at a number of levels, on 'arrangements' relating to the gender division of labour (Crompton, 1986: 126).

Crompton, unlike Giddens, locates clerical workers as part of a diversified working class. She reiterates that it is no longer meaningful to draw a sharp distinction between manual and mental workers and that the distinction, anyway, is not a useful way of classifying women. In relation to low-level clerical workers at least, I find her argument convincing. To suggest that because these jobs are white-collar they are middle-class is misleading, based as it seems to be on status theories of occupational prestige. This begs the question of whether clerical workers can be seen as a unified occupational group with a shared class background. There is an ongoing boundary dispute, not only about where the class lines should be drawn but about what constitutes the buffer zone.

Secretaries: a class of their own?

Where do secretaries fit into this analysis? Are they part of this mass of lower-level clerical workers? I think not. One of the interesting things about secretaries is that they do not fit easily into the 'proletarianisation' thesis. As has frequently been pointed out, one of the difficulties with analysis of clerical workers is that adequate distinctions between different categories are rarely made (Walby, 1986a: 28). Official statistics bundle typists, stenographers and secretaries in together as if working for the chief executive is much of a muchness with being in the typing pool. Secretaries as a group are so diverse it would be hard to allocate them a single class location. If anything a line can be drawn down the middle, between the lower ranks who merge with the clerical 'proletariat' and the private and executive secretaries who blend in with management. While some secretarial positions are becoming routine and deskilled, others are becoming professionalised and may be on the boundary of Crompton's 'service class'. If any group acts as a buffer between the classes it is not clerical workers as a whole but particular groups such as secretaries. Giddens' argument about underclasses and buffer zones applies better to the senior secretaries than it does to the mass of lower-level clerical and secretarial workers.

It is secretaries who most immediately service management and create the preconditions for their bosses' advancement. They are in positions of trust and authority. Much of the pleasure of the job may be in the sense of being close to the centre of power, participating in decision-making, having confidential knowledge, having power to act on the bosses' behalf or control access to him or her. Secretaries have complex alignments with management based on both skills and interpersonal relations and mutual emotional dependencies. The promotional structure is deceptive as it depends not only on training or experience but the acquisition of 'middle-class' (meaning ladylike) habits, based on poise, manners, charm and so on. But they cannot simply be treated as the 'lackeys' of management. Their exploitation is based on having a tentative and temporary membership of the service class. They may earn little more than the lower clericals from whom they proudly distinguish themselves; but their long and irregular hours are perceived not as exploitation so much as a sign of their professional status. As office wives they may have considerable class power over subordinate staff. Gerald Robbins, from Pacific Industries, recalled that for the young men the secretary to the departmental manager was 'a pretty powerful and slightly distant role...They approached her with a fair amount of caution'. Many of the senior secretaries are regarded as 'dragons' and treated with awe. They know how to put people in their place. They may be simultaneously dominant and subordinate. In Wright's terms secretaries have considerable 'organisation assets' even though they are exploited (1985). Their position is analogous to that of governesses, ladies' companions and spinster aunts in the nine-teenth-century upper middle class (rather than servants who, though they might also identify with the interests of their masters are more clearly of a different class). Robbins, asked if he considered his secretary his social equal, translated it into a question of whether he would take her to his club. After a long pause he decided that he would take her to the one with the more general membership, but not to the smaller elite one. This seemed to indicate a status inequality but not a major class difference.

It is not easy to distinguish between the 'true' secretary or the boss's personal assistant and those engaged almost exclusively on routine paper work. McNally argues that two entirely different groups of employees carry out these functions (1979: 49), but there are difficulties with this. The old hierarchy has not been replaced by two clearcut tiers. Instead there is a large amorphous collection of 'secretaries' who do not fit easily into either group. Gwen, who is about to retire, comments:

> Secretaries are not refined like they used to be...Everybody seems to be calling somebody their secretary now. Originally it was just the top

managers that had secretaries...There's a lot of managerial staff that
don't have the need for a secretary and yet turn around and say of any
office girl, she is my secretary...Everyone now advertises for a
secretary...but they are probably doing half a dozen other people's
work too...Every Tom, Dick and Harry are doing it nowadays. I think
that it has spoiled the image of a secretary...

The second problem is that the same women move in and out of
both categories. Does this mean that they change their class position each time? Women who have been private secretaries before
their marriages return to more junior, temporary and part-time
jobs. Employers take advantage of their experience while paying
them lower rates. This clouds the hierarchy for women, making it
clear how inadequate the occupational structure is alone for status
rankings or, it might be argued, for class position. Basic elements
in class definition, labour power and market capacities, are not
gender-neutral. Women's labour power is perceived by employers
as qualitatively different from men's. The occupational structure
is not gender-neutral but affected by status considerations.

Many of the tensions among women in the workplace stem
from the fact that they are caught between several different
pecking orders. Status drawn from the formal occupational hierarchy may be in contradiction with the status that derives from
their value to various different men, specifically bosses and husbands, or their general status as heterosexually attractive women.
'Successful woman' involves some combination of all these; but
they do not always easily mesh. Images of class are important here
for it is 'bourgeois' femininity that is being constructed in the
office. The English secretary has long been held to signify status
based on accent, style, poise and literacy, and having a 'classy'
secretary is seen actually to improve the boss's status rather than
merely reflect it. Projecting oneself as a 'lady' is an important part
of establishing a status position and exercising authority.

Whether secretaries take their class position 'directly' from their
occupation or 'indirectly' from their husbands may not be the
issue. If, as I have suggested, secretaries are relationally defined,
their class position may be constructed in relation to both work
and home, in terms of both bosses and husbands. The emphasis
on processes that *construct* occupations reminds us of the importance of discourse in giving meaning to 'raw' economic data. This
shifts the attention from class structure (a three-dimensional
model) to the ways we construct places for ourselves in a variety of
discourses around class. The problems here are similar to the
ones already noted with gender. There is a certain 'fixity' of class
identity which can only partly be explained by the argument that
class is 'trans-discursive', that there is sufficient overlap in discourses on class to provide continuity. While it may be easier to

shift one's core class identity than one's core gender identity, there appears to be something deeper operating here than a collection of discursive practices—even granted that discourse does shape the way in which we identify and experience class relations.

Kate Millett argued in *Sexual Politics* that 'the female has fewer permanent class associations than does the male. Economic dependency renders her affiliations with any class a tangential, vicarious, and temporary matter' (1972: 38). Women will identify with the men that support them but have, she says, much less of an investment in the class system. The point is an important one. However, I think she overestimates the extent to which women 'transcend' the class system or share a common position as a 'dependency class'; and she underestimates the strength of women's class affiliations. Women are more than vicariously linked to the class structure, though their links are different from men's, and must be balanced against their common identities as 'women'.

Given the ways in which women do move in and out of paid employment and across a range of occupations it can be argued that their class identities are more *fragmented* than men's. It has often been noted that masculine identity is more bounded, that men experience themselves as centred subjects, masters of their own destiny. This may apply more readily to middle- and upper-class men but to a degree it structures masculinity across all classes. Men's sense of themselves as autonomous, rational subjects is linked to a continuity of class experience, based on the fact that they they do not typically move in and out of the workforce or change occupations (unless defined as unemployed—and this is assumed to have disastrous psychological consequences for them). Even if they are subordinated at work, they can experience themselves as superior to women, who are less in control of their occupational lives, and may draw directly on women's services to create the conditions for their own sense of autonomy and independence from mundane rituals. For men, having a secretary of their own has traditionally signified the move from lower to middle management and hence the service class proper. It is now possible to see the ways in which different class experiences contribute to these different subjectivities. Women, defined relationally, are more aware that unified subjectivity is an illusion: they are familiar with the experience of being 'decentred' and do not need to feel at the centre of the universe in order to feel whole. Their egos are not threatened in the same ways that men's are. This is not to say that they have no class identity but that it has a different place in their subjectivity overall.

The secretaries in my sample did not have much to say about class. Where there was class awareness it was mostly from those who were conscious of mobility upwards or downwards. Women

from 'traditional' manual working-class backgrounds knew they
had gone 'up' in the world. Those from upper middle-class
backgrounds often considered they were slumming it and sought
to avoid the connotations of 'secretary', passing it off as a temporary aberration. Even in the union interviews there was little discussion of class. The division between bosses and secretaries was
played down by both groups. In a context of egalitarianism it was
not on for officers to be seen to be building a middle-class position.
It is a genuinely more open environment and there is pressure for
officials and staff to see each other as equals. But there is some
awkwardness about the extent to which they mix. The divisions
exist structurally and there are tensions around salaries, holidays,
maternity leave and other differentials in working conditions.

The secretaries' blank response to questions about class may
indicate 'fragmented' class identities and genuine confusion about
where to locate themselves and within which discourse. If secretaries
are part of a 'buffer zone' we would not expect them to identify clearly
with any class. A number said they must be 'working-class' because
they 'worked', while others seemed to think it was divisive to raise the
issue of class and close to dodge it. This was consistent with their
responsibility as secretaries to smooth over anything awkward or
embarassing.

For both men and women class identity comes from a variety of
sources. No one ever entirely escapes from their class of origin
which is constructed not only by 'father's occupation' (or even
mother's occupation) but various cultural practices and social institutions. In considering secretaries' experience of class we do
need to take into account more than the occupation: their own
social backgrounds and that of their spouses are important in the
construction of class as well as gender identity. Whether 'secretaries' as a group have a distinctive class identity will ultimately
be an empirical question of whether there is a 'fit' between work
and other aspects of their lives. I have already suggested limits to
this in the occupational sphere: women who have been secretaries
frequently cross over into lower clerical, sales and even factory
work when they return to the workforce after the birth of children.
This is not to say there is no correlation between current occupation and other indicators of class. There is typically a close
relationship between occupation and family in the class identities
of secretaries.

Family and class

Secretaries marry men from a variety of occupations and class
backgrounds, ranging from unskilled manual workers to high-

level professional, managerial and administrative staff. While one would not want to assume that they automatically shared the class position and status of their husbands, it would be silly not to take it into account. Many of the managers interviewed had wives, mothers and daughters who were either doing or had done secretarial work. In a patriarchal society it is inevitable that women will be defined as much through marriage as through their work. But it is not so easy to put the relevant factors into a blender and come up with a homogeneous class position. Women's circumstances shift and change, depending on parental whims, the comings and goings of husbands and children, the contradictions of attempting to operate in several arenas at the same time. Whatever their experience of class it is a distinctively female experience, very much backgrounded against being a woman. As the following examples illustrate, there is generally a correspondence between family background, spouse and 'place' in the secretarial ladder.

Roslyn Grenfall, now in her early forties, is secretary to a top bureaucrat. Her father was a banker and she comes from a secure upper middle-class background. Her two brothers went to university and she herself had wanted to become a teacher but her father said 'you'll be an old maid if you teach' and channelled her into secretarial work. She married another banker and sent her two children to top private schools. After her divorce she did finally go to university and is currently completing a higher degree. She says she is now quite happy to become an old maid and teach. She has always hated secretarial work which she says is 'not a career, it's a job', which she now does for the money. 'It is not what I really am. This isn't my life. I'd be off the Gap if it was. I always used to escape into Shakespeare. My projects are at home... I'm not a secretary really. You are interviewing me in that role.' Yet she, like a number of her friends who went to university, is still working in an office and cannot seem to find her way out. She cannot understands this except to say, 'We really did grow up to be...like our mothers'.

Shirley Benson is also secretary to a top bureaucrat. A woman in her fifties, she is married to an engineer and has three adult children, all of whom are tertiary-educated. She speaks of marriage as her vocation and has no hesitation in placing family ahead of work. She has no further career aspirations, yet she is is doing a senior administrative job on a very low secretarial salary. Senior staff rather guiltily recognise this to be a scandal. She does it because the job is close to home and fits in with her family responsibilities. It was family that prevented her from placing herself on a career path and restricted her for a long time to part-time jobe that gave her 'some extra money and a bit of satisfaction if you like'.

Hedda Styles, in her thirties and secretary to a college professor, is married to a struggling professional and has two young children. She says she works out of necessity. She is very committed to building their dream home, adding a swimming pool and sending the children to private schools. She never wanted to be a secretary and in fact hoped to be a PE teacher but then, 'with upheavals at school, changes from one school system to another, I just didn't get the grades I needed and so I ended up in an office'. She has just returned to the full-time workforce after ten years as a part-timer since the birth of their first child. She is only intending to do it for three years. She sees her security more in promoting her husband's career. She does all his typing for him and is pretty obviously the motivating factor in boosting his publication record.

Val now works for a personnel manager, after previously working for a long time with her husband in a family business. She is now divorced and her two children are at university. Though called a secretary, her work is identical to what is elsewhere done by 'personnel officers' and indeed in her previous job she was called a 'personnel and training officer'. She is now keen to get some qualifications and move up the scale.

Janine is called a secretary but spends most of her time on the telephone dealing with customer services. She is extremely knowledgeable about the products she is dealing with and takes substantial responsibility for public relations in the company. Her boss knows he has got a gem and also that she is not adequately rewarded for what she does. She feels used but will stay on in her current position until she collects her superannuation. Janine lives in the western suburbs with her husband who works for himself as an electrician. She does his books. Her 'luxury' is employing a cleaning lady once a week.

Gail is married with three school-age children and is secretary to a branch manager. She left school at fourteen and learned typing on the job. She was out of the workforce for ten years and since then has done a variety of part-time jobs as a demonstrator and telephonist. She is married to a builder who works very long hours. She herself gets up at 5 or 6 am to do the washing and ironing. She says the kids are happy for her to be working because they know they will be fed and clothed better.

Marilyn is secretary to the general manager of the same company that Gail works for. Though she has four children she says she has always worked because her husband brings home a fairly mediocre wage. Where he is in and out of the workforce as a labourer and factory worker, she is proud of the fact that she stays in jobs for longish periods—never less than two years and in one case seven. She does not like her current job but is holding out for the superannuation.

Sylvia is married to a teacher. She worked to put him through university and the deal was that he would do the same for her. But now they have two young children to support and they could not afford to live on one income and pay a mortgage. She works for a white-collar union and socialises with professionals rather than secretarial staff.

The private secretaries in my sample were more likely than the 'lower secretarial' group to have middle-class backgrounds and, if they were married (28 per cent were not), it was predominantly to professional and managerial (that is 'service class') men. Thirty-six per cent of those married were married to such men. The 'lower secretarial' group were overwhelmingly working-class in their backgrounds, typically married to men in clerical or administrative positions, or from the working class. Prandy's empirical analysis of recent British data may be interpreted similarly. He found that female clerks in banks and the civil service were three or four times more likely to have husbands in professional or managerial occupations than semi- or unskilled manual jobs. The reverse was true for wages clerks, cashiers and routine clerks, who were more likely to be married to the latter groups (Prandy, 1986: 141).

Table 9.1   Social backgrounds and partners' occupations of secretarial workers

	Higher secretarial			Lower secretarial		
	No	%	% of those married	No	%	% of those married
Partner's occupation						
Service class	27	25	36	2	5	8
Clerical/lower admin	24	23	32	13	32	52
Small business	13	12	17	4	9	16
Skilled manual	7	7	9	4	9	16
Unskilled manual	5	4	6	2	5	8
No partner	31	29		17	40	
Total	107	100	100	42	100	100
Family background						
Upper middle class	24	22				
Salaried lower Middle class	25	24		7		12
Small business	14	13		5		18
Skilled working class	27	25		15		35
Unskilled working class	17	16		15		35
Total	107	100		42		100

'Higher secretarial' includes personal assistants, secretaries and stenographers. 'Lower secretarial' includes typists, full-time word-processor operators and clerical assistants.
These figures have been compiled out of the interview data. Subjects were asked about their class backgrounds and husbands' occupations but did not always answer in very precise terms. Both parents' occupations were requested but not always gained. Often a judgement has been made about family background based on the general tenor of the conversation.

An important reason given for including the occupations of married women in class analysis is the significant number of situations where wives appear to be in higher-class occupations than their husbands. In a British study, Britten and Heath (1983) argued it is distorting to treat a family's class position as determined by the male head of household alone. Using the manual/non-manual boundary as the line of cleavage between working and middle class they presented an account of a class system in which large numbers of middle-class women appear to be married to manual working-class men. At a 'gut' level this argument was never very convincing. In a longer study McRae (1986) has distinguished between 'genuine' cross-class families and the fakes which she considers have been put up by Britten and Heath. The genuine cases are the ones where manual men are married to women in professional and semi-professional work. She places senior secretaries squarely in this category, but not the majority of keyboard workers.

The secretaries in my sample were mostly married to men of a very similar class background to their bosses—though this does not mean that the secretary is the social equal of either boss or husband. The only way in which they could be part of cross-class families is if we abandoned the traditional demarcation and re-labelled them working-class. But we cannot have it both ways. If we see secretarial work as proletarianised then there are an awful lot of cross-class marriages to men in all sections of the middle class. If on the other hand, we place secretaries, in occupational terms, on the lower edge of the middle class, then the vast majority marry into that class, to men in higher-status occupations than themselves. The tendencies towards proletarianisation are seen more clearly with the lower secretarial workers. The vast majority of these come from the working class and 52 per cent of those married have married men in lower middle-class occupations. It would seem that genuine cross-class families are relatively few though there is considerable movement within different parts of classes.

Cross-class theorists have mostly been concerned with situations where the wife is of superior status. If the husband is superior, the wife's status is assumed not to affect the status of the family as a whole. If she can pull him up, why can she not also bring him down? One secretary I spoke to was married to a senior bureaucrat. As his wife she operated as his hostess, on occasions greeting as equals people to whom she was subordinate at work. While it might be acceptable for 'middle management' to have their wives working as secretaries, senior managers were decidedly uncomfortable about it. It clearly reflected on their own status to have their wives working in 'inferior' jobs.

The college secretaries are stereotyped as 'north shore house-wives'. This simultaneously acknowledges and denies that they are in a situation that is structurally very different from that of their husbands. The presumption of a shared class position between husband and wife enables their gender inequality to be passed over. The stereotype conveys 'middle-classness', along with the idea that they are not serious workers and do not need the money, which in turn rationalises the payment of low wages. At the same time they are 'housewives' who, it is said, kowtow to their bosses in much the same way they do to their husband. It is the combination of middle class ('north shore') and housewife that makes these women subservient to the establishment, conservative politically and unwilling to make a fuss about their working conditions. In suburban locations, a class-based identity outside work connected with work-based cultures, and whole clusters of secretaries were married to men in specific occupations. For example, at the Institute it was professionals, while at Malvern it was self-employed tradesmen, usually builders. The women at Malvern had often been in business with their husbands and still usually did the books for them. These groupings contribute to the overall work-based culture and its class overtones, as well as determining the qualities and experience that these women bring to bear on their jobs. Class position does not derive purely from occupation; it still has to be constructed in concrete social relations and a variety of locations, of which the workplace is only one.

Where does this leave single women? It is too simple to say that their class is based on occupation alone. As with the married women, their own background will be an important component of class position and their family of origin may retain a greater significance than for those women who marry and have children. Lack of a husband may signify a lesser social status, particularly for a woman of middle-class origins, but it is not clear that it affects her class location. Unmarried secretaries over the age of say, 30, who are dependent on their salaries, may be perceived as a lower middle class; married women in equivalent occupational grades may be located higher up in the middle class if married to service-class men. While this does not follow automatically, such marriages create opportunities for the construction of upper middle-class places which a single women does not have. She may construct such a place for herself, but she will find it more difficult and require slightly different strategies.

A higher proportion of career secretaries remain unmarried than women in most other groups. It is this group who are most likely to give the self-sacrificing devotion that we associate with the 'office wife' and whose position remains similar to that of unmarried middle-class women a century ago. Like the governesses and spinster aunts they retain membership of the middle class but hover on its edges. They frequently take fewer initiatives to construct for themselves an alternative identity. Dianna, now in her forties and secretary to the general manager of a large corporation says: 'I think it's probably easier being a single person because you don't have the demands of another person at home... It's somehow easier to sacrifice one person's enjoyment than a couple's.' What this means is that she does not create the kind of social presence that would establish a stronger middle-class identity. Historically it is this group who have constituted the occupation as lower middle class in a cultural sense. But single women do not necessarily behave in this way. They have a variety of alternative strategies for establishing a social identity, including the acquisition of friendship networks, institutional or political connections, or 'cultural capital' in the form of participation in the arts. Lesbian secretaries also follow these strategies; their class position will change only if, as a result of discriminatory practices, their employment prospects are reduced.

While the economic sets the broad contours of class relations, class is created out of the relationships between work and other dimensions of people's lives. Men and women experience these relations rather differently. In order to understand the differences we need to explore the divisions between work and home, public and private life, and production and consumption. The first of each of these pairs is generally associated with the world of the masculine and positively evaluated. Home, private life and the sphere of consumption have a more shadowy existence and are associated with the feminine. This way of ordering the world as a series of opposites is based on masculine experience. For women there is more blurring and blending. These different meanings are important in the construction of gendered class and status groupings and will be considered in the following chapter.

·10· Work and home

> There is something very Australian about it...like gathering in the kitchen at a party while all the men are outside...Well it still happens....Like the other day there were about six of us talking in the files and Penelope walked up and said, 'this always reminds me of the back fence, hanging out the washing'. The files operate as a barrier so the way we cope with that is to lean over it all the time so we can all stand around.
>
> *CLERK AT JESSIE STREET*

> I sort of operate on three or four different levels. I don't like personal things intruding while I'm at work...When I finish work that's it. Once I pick up my daughter I stop being 'Lesley the secretary' and start being 'Mummy'. When she's gone to bed I become myself, 'Lesley the person'. I spend night after night reading the manual because I don't have time to do that at work. I love work. And doing work at home is different from doing it at work, naturally. If I were a man it would be considered normal. I was called a workaholic yesterday and I'm still trying to figure out if I've been insulted.
>
> *SECRETARY AT PACIFIC INDUSTRIES*

Work and home, public and private spheres: these are the familiar and well-worn categories which we use to talk about the main divisions in our lives. We make these structural distinctions so routinely that they seem self-evident. However, the content of these categories varies from one context to another and may be perceived very differently by the participants. Their boundaries are not self-evident but are contested, even within specific discourses. What could be regarded simply as different aspects of our lives are coded as opposites which represent positive and negative poles. Our understandings of 'home' and 'work' derive from a larger symbolic system, a totality of social and cultural practices including language itself. 'Experience' is always mediated through discursive codes.

The work/home division is given further meaning by the ways

in which other dualisms, public/private, culture/nature, order/disorder and, most importantly, masculine/feminine are mapped onto it. Though home and private life may be romanticised, they are generally held to represent the 'feminine' world of the personal and the emotional, the concrete and the particular, of the domestic and the sexual. The public world of work sets itself up as the opposite of all these things: it is rational, abstract, ordered, concerned with general principles and, of course, masculine. Where the woman rather than the man is in the subject position, these dualisms may be reversed. In the 'mother—son' discourse, for example, it is the secretary who represents order, efficiency and discipline, while the boss/naughty child represents chaos and disorder. It is the boss who succumbs to mood swings and violent emotional outbursts. Continuing this theme, 'home' may represent an ordered and stable haven which contrasts with the anarchy of the business world. Male sexuality appears here as rampant, while women are seen to be 'in control'.

'Home' is distinguished from 'house' by its connotations of intimacy and warmth and by its association with a particular kind of nuclear family structure (Watson, 1986). Those who are not part of a nuclear family have somewhat dubious claims to having or even needing a 'home'. For men, home and work are both opposite and complementary. 'Home' is the domain of 'non-work', where they expect to relax, let their barriers down and be looked after. The distinction is clearcut and there is no difficulty in moving from one to the other. Because men have control of the boundaries they are able cross them if and when they choose. Male bosses, for example, usually have little problem in bringing work home, deciding to work late, going away on business trips or having their wives ring them at the office. Those who spend the least numbers of hours at home actually report the *fewest* mid-career problems (Hunt and Collins, 1983: 99). The office is for them, quite literally, a 'home away from home'.

It can be argued that the dominant discourses are the ones that represent masculine rather than feminine views of the world and that women are for the most part obliged to situate themselves in the object position. Women place themselves rather differently in relation to the dichotomies. Much of their 'work' takes place at 'home'; wives might act as unpaid and unacknowledged secretaries to their husbands as well as taking on domestic responsibilities and 'supplementary' paid work (Crompton, 1986: 125). 'Office wife' encapsulates the ways in which home and work are potentially fused for women. Home is not a respite from work but another workplace. For some women work is actually a respite from home! Home and work set up conflicting demands. Rather than moving easily between the two, women perform a complex juggling act.

They must be careful not to let the two domains be seen to intrude too much on each other. Because this is always in dangers of happening, women have to work quite hard at maintaining a distinction between the two sites. They are careful not to bring work home, or let it impinge in any way, and they will make every effort to create home as a place where (other) people can relax. It is important therefore to explore the relationship between the codes and the ways in which secretaries talk about their experience of the work/home and public/private distinctions.

It is still frequently assumed that women's consciousness is shaped predominantly by domestic and family considerations. Much recent feminist writing has stressed the importance of *work*, and has emphasised the interaction between home and work in constructing subjectivity and identity (Beechey, 1987; Game and Pringle 1983; Sharpe, 1984). Women's reactions to the workplace cannot simply be explained in terms of domestic responsibilities or feminine personality. The other is that work itself is a site on which gender relations are constructed: it cannot be assumed, as it used to be, that gender is created purely within the family. Feldberg and Glenn (1984) have shown the limitations of analyses which presume a work/home division in explaining workers' consciousness. The 'job model' has connected men's work attitudes and behaviour to their conditions and relations of employment, while the 'gender model', invoked only for women, treats their work attitudes and behaviour as a consequence of family experiences. They argue that family situation is important in understanding men's as well as women's reactions, while there is a need to develop a clearer, more precise picture of women's work and to stop falling back on stereotypical explanations based on supposed personality characteristics.

At the same time Feldberg and Glenn play down differences between men and women and emphasise shared responses to the conditions of work, as well as significant divisions such as full-time versus part-time which cut across gender. Though they say that gender stratification at work should be thoroughly studied, gender is reduced to simply one variable among many. They are unable to explain why researchers consistently revert to separate job and gender models even when they have made a conscious effort to do otherwise. Like most industrial sociologists, they take 'consciousness' as unproblematic and ignore the construction of subjectivity. 'Consciousness' is seen to derive directly from experience and refers to the set of aspirations, world views and political analyses that people develop in the process of living their daily lives. The industrial sociology literature assumes a unified subject who in some sense is the master of his actions. Some writers have looked at different levels of consciousness and at the split between concrete experience and abstract values (Mann, 1973; Hunt, 1980; Wacjman, 1983). While the consideration of dual or fragmented consciousness is an advance, it does not go beyond consciousness to the construction of the subject. Wacjman links women's work and domestic situations in an attempt to theorise their contradictory views of the world, but is unable to explain what holds the conscious ideas in place.

The relationship between home and work is not purely a matter of how these two areas combine to construct 'consciousness'. Women's subjectivity is constructed and maintained in the practices and discourses which give meaning to these divisions. Of particular importance here is the sexual and family symbolism which, I have argued, is as central to work as it is to domestic relations. Women are perceived in 'family' roles at work not because work is simply an extension of their domestic roles but because authority in the workplace is also organised around family symbolism. As Black and Coward (1981: 83) put it, 'Women are precisely defined, never general representatives of humanity or all people, but as specifically feminine, and frequently sexual, categories...Being a man is an entitlement not to masculine attributes but to non-gendered subjectivity'. For both sexes fragments of oedipal and pre-oedipal fantasy and desire remain powerful motivating forces though only a fraction of this is allowed into the surface or 'public' levels of consciousness. The 'law of the father', in Juliet Mitchell's terms, is reproduced not just in families but in all social relations. Despite the illusion of being separate, even opposite, spheres, home and work overlap, at both the practical and symbolic levels.

Secretaries' dilemmas

Secretaries are particularly vulnerable to a blurring of boundaries between home and work. In the first place, the tasks overlap. Studies of women clerical workers suggest that women's evaluations of the conditions of their jobs are based on comparison with the conditions of housework as well as of previous jobs (Feldberg and Glenn, 1984: 34). As recently as the 1970s the University of New South Wales was handing out 'Notes on Office Housekeeping' to its training course for secretaries. They were reminded to clean and dust, empty the ash trays regularly, open the windows and adjust the curtains, keep an emergency supply of aspirin, bandaids and so on. 'Don't expect formal recognition of your housekeeping arrangements,' it cautions! As I have indicated in earlier chapters, the work can involve very long hours, while bosses exercise power by deliberately challenging the boundary. While many professional women and men also experience an overlap of work and home, they usually have some control and some choice about how they manage it. Secretaries have little of either. They can be expected to work overtime at short notice and there is no guarantee they will be out of the office punctually at knock-off time. Many had stories about bosses who after procrastinating all day would suddenly start dictating at 10 to 5 and expect letters to be typed and sent that day. Some manage to control their working hours by firmly stating their family responsibilities and leaving the office at a set time regardless of what is going on. Bosses recognise, somewhat reluctantly, the counterclaims of husbands and children, but these are about the only claims they do recognise. It is not surprising therefore that so many top secretaries are single. Many women resolve the contradictions between home and work by taking part-time jobs, but this is not so easy for secretaries or indeed for clerical workers as a group. Most secretarial jobs are still full-time and the overall situation has changed little in the last fifteen years. It is hard to imagine part-time secretaries without a fundamental restructuring of the work. Pacific Industries introduced me to Sue and Helen as 'Stephen's two part-time secretaries', but the women, both of whom had worked there as secretaries before their marriages, see themselves as typists and deny the job is 'secretarial' in any meaningful sense.

Secretaries with small children either leave the paid workforce, become self-employed and subcontract their services, or move into other occupations where they can work part-time. In this Australian secretaries share the British rather than the American pattern. Dex and Shaw have shown that while a high proportion of American women continue in clerical work when they return to work after the birth of their first child (it drops from 38 per cent to 33 per cent), in Britain the proportion drops dramatically, from 34 to 19 per cent. British women, like Australians, move into factory, sales and domestic work where part-time jobs and flexible working hours are more available (Dex and Shaw, 1986: 82−105).

Women classified as 'typists and stenographers' or 'other clerical' workers are far more likely to be working full-time than nurses, shop assistants or cleaners: 85 and 82 per cent compared with 70, of typists and stenographers and 61 per cent of other clerical workers with dependent children worked full-time, compared with only 41 per cent of nurses, 34 per cent of cleaners and 30 per cent of shop assistants. The gap would be substantially greater if the statistics distinguished secretaries from the typing and other clerical groups. Secretaries are less likely to be working casually or part-time than say copy typists or input operators. Word-processor operators can often work six-hour shifts. Secretaries with young children are faced with the choice between continuing to work full-time or moving out of the area. Many postpone this choice by delaying marriage and/or children.

The unit record file of the 1982 Family Survey makes available a number of cross-tabulations which indicate that both secretaries and clerical workers with children were more likely than nurses, shop assistants and cleaners to have deferred their first births for three or more years after getting married. Secretaries over the age of 35 who had children had a shorter childbearing span than other groups. Secretaries with children who stay in the workforce or re-enter it have to be better organised than women in most other jobs (Table 10.2). The figures suggest that because of the full-time nature of secretarial jobs women in their prime child-bearing years are forced to drop out (Table 10.1). For example, 35 per cent of the typing/stenographic workforce was under 25, compared with only 25 per cent of the employed female workforce overall. While one could argue that it is a young workforce biased

Table 10.1   Selected characteristics of women in five jobs, 1982

		Nurses	Other clerical	Steno/ Typists	Shop assts	Cleaners	Total
full-time	N	438	1637	500	594	200	3369
	%	70	82	85	56	35	73
Offspring present:full-time	N	177	529	161	198	146	1211
	%	41	61	63	30	34	50
No offspring present: full-time	N	259	1105	338	394	54	2150
	%	91	92	95	70	41	87
full-time workers: earning $250+	N	308	1334	423	333	71	2469
	%	57	31	31	5.4	5.6	30
Private sector worker	N	439	1637	500	594	200	3369
	%	38	66	72	99	42	68
Aged under 25	N	438	1637	500	594	200	3369
	%	32	41	35	46	9	38
Aged 35 or over	N	438	1637	500	594	200	3369
	%	34	32	39	36	71	36
Had children	N	438	1637	500	594	200	3369
	%	46	39	40	44	92	44
With children deferred 1st child	N	189	586	183	243	168	1369
	%	13	22	24	15	10	18
Age 35+:3 or more children	N	148	525	195	216	142	1226
	%	38	33	32	42	43	36
Age 35+: childbearing span 3+years	N	104	346	128	164	112	854
	%	66	62	62	67	80	66

Source: Adapted from 1982 ABS Families Survey, unit record file

Table 10.2 Women in full-time clerical jobs: selected characteristics by spouse's job and marital status

		No partner	Employer/ manager	Prof with deg	Prof/ Admin (no deg)	Clerical	Sales/ Service	Skilled trades	Unskilled manual	Self emp.	Not working/ other
						Occupation of partner					
fulltime	N	997	35	56	166	132	137	179	219	161	55
	%	93	60	70	75	85	72	74	76	60	80
Offspring present	N	101	17	33	92	52	77	85	110	101	22
	%	84	30	58	63	68	58	52	64	47	68
Earning $250+	N	924	21	39	124	112	99	132	166	96	44
	%	23	57	51	41	44	41	33	33	39	48
With qualif.	N	997	35	56	166	132	137	179	219	161	55
	%	28	46	50	31	30	26	35	25	34	29
Left school 17+	N	997	35	56	166	132	137	179	219	161	55
	%	37	49	54	25	32	25	22	25	28	26
With children: deferred 1st birth	N	134	32	35	103	59	78	83	112	111	32
	%	22	36	23	21	22	23	28	21	17	16
Aged 35+ child- bearing span 3+ years	N	79	19	24	65	35	43	50	62	73	24
	%	62	37	46	62	71	70	60	60	63	83

Source: ABS Families Survey, 1982, unit record file

heavily towards juniors, typists/stenographers also had a higher proportion of their number over 35 than had nurses or shop assistants. Only a third of typing and clerical workers have dependent children, which is lower than nurses (40 per cent) and cleaners (70 per cent).

In my own sample of 107 secretaries only 50, less than half, lived with spouses, while 30 were single and the remainder were separated, divorced, widowed or lived in de facto relationships. Only four had children under five. This is dramatically different from the profile of working women as a whole and substantially different from the lower clerical group. Though the latter were a much younger group (54 per cent were under 25, while the equivalent figure for the secretaries group was 13 per cent), the proportions living with spouses was comparable and one-third (fourteen out of a sample of 42) had children under five (See Table 7.2). Women with young children move out of secretarial work.

Rena, who is secretary to the general manager of a subsidiary of Pacific Industries, is one woman who has stayed, and she is an exception who proves the rule. When I spoke to her she was six months pregnant and had an eighteen-months-old son. She had come back to work when he was nine months not only because they needed the money but because she was 'going up the wall'. Rena would prefer a part-time job but says it is not easy to find an interesting one. After doing a variety of casual word-processing and data entry jobs through Centacom she arrived at Pacific Industries as a temporary and was asked to stay on. She agreed rather hesitantly and has not found the return to full-time work at all easy. She manages because she has half a dozen reliable people to babysit including two sisters and a close girlfriend who has given up work to mind her own children. In addition, 'my mother's great. I can ring up and have a whinge to her any time. She's terrific'. Her husband finishes work two hours earlier than she does and collects their son from the babysitter. Unlike many secretaries she does not have to go through a war of nerves every day about getting away punctually. And since she drives to work her travelling time between home, work and babysitter is manageable.

Rena's boss voices all the usual sentiments about preferring not to have a secretary with young children. Despite this, after a number of bad experiences with secretaries, he is relieved to find someone he can work with and wants her to stay. He says he is prepared to make (unspecified) concessions in order to get her back after her second child is born. Good secretaries are hard to come by in the western suburbs and he has the reputation of being 'dificult'. According to her, 'he tends to take his tensions out on his secretary and...a lot of them took it personally whereas I just tend to shrug it off...He gets critical and picky about little things that don't matter. If he gets on my nerves too much I just say "I'm going for lunch", or "I'll see you in ten minutes" or something. That's how I handle it'. A chain of factors has placed Rena in a senior secretarial position despite having young children. She finds the job interesting and is well aware that she is the best-paid secretary in the building, earning far more than she could as a temp. Her return from maternity leave will will depend both on whether she is able to retain such reliable childcare and whether her boss really does become more flexible.

Subjectivity and class

The first interviews were entirely open-ended. To see whether and how, without prompting, women would apply the dualisms of home/work and private/public, they were asked simply to to describe 'a day in their lives'. The fact that the interviews took place at work might be expected to give a strong cue that it was 'work' they were supposed to talk about, but the responses were actually very mixed. Some began the day with waking up and making breakfast, others with getting on the train, the first cup of coffee at work or the first page onto the typewriter. They almost never got through the whole day and were lucky to make it past lunchtime!

Home and work were discussed in terms of a number of physical sites, including shops, schools, childcare centres as well as the office and the home. The transition between home and work was of particular conern to the the women, who spoke at length about how they got to work and how long it took. Jobs were chosen on the grounds that they were convenient to home, to shops and to transport. Office relocations were a central subject of gossip and rumour, anxiety for some and relief for others.

Women construct home and work differently in different phases of the life cycle. Men do too to some extent (working more overtime, when they have young families, for example) but women's experience is more varied. Sharpe (1984) outlines five normative stages; single without children, married without children, married with young children, married with older children and married with grownup children. To these we might add the experiences of being divorced or widowed, of remarrying and acquiring stepchildren, or of experimenting with alternatives to marriage. The relationship between home and work will vary at

each phase. Young women may be unconcerned with either, constructing themselves through dating, clothes, travel and a wider
social life. If they are secretaries, however, they may devote themselves, however reluctantly, to the demands of work. Rena commented on the shift:

> I was very much career-oriented before but I think once you get married
> and start having children your goals change. Whilst you might want a
> job that's interesting and varied your job isn't your whole life or you
> don't seem to dedicate as much of your efforts into it... You don't live
> for your work... anymore. I was like that... I was quite willing to put in
> long hours and extra effort whereas now you resent that... I don't mind
> working back through the week and things but I wouldn't put in sixteen
> hour days any more... Yes. Like I used to work a Saturday afternoon or
> whatever. I just wouldn't do it now.

Women re-entering the workforce with dependent children
start thinking of themselves as 'a housewife who has a job' and
may consider jobs that were previously beneath them. As the
children get older they increase their working hours, change jobs
or consider retraining and work takes on a different significance.
For Australia (Sharpe does not mention the English experience)
we can add a further phase, as yet unexplained. Women's retirement age remains substantially lower than men's, with only a
small proportion apparently choosing to work past fifty-five. While
some of this is involuntary unemployment, it would also seem that
women do not put themselves full-steam on a work course when
the kids leave home but continue to shift and change their relation
to paid work.

It is not only during changes in the life cycle that women shift
their alignments between home and work. These alignments are
constantly in flux. Marcia, a senior secretary and one who has
been politically active, asked where she drew the biggest lines
around her life, replied:

> There are times when I think it's work and the rest and then there are
> times when I think it's home and the rest. There are times when I
> feel... and I've got to admit it's because I want to, that work takes
> priority over my children, sometimes over my partner and my home and
> my commitments there. Many, many times work has taken priority over
> that, whereas if I were another type of person, one of these other kinds of
> secretaries, I would walk out at five o'clock.

But Marcia has booted out her alcoholic husband and now lives in
a de facto relationship. Her teenage children take it for granted
that she is not there to service them and that household tasks will
be shared. She says her fourteen-year-old son is becoming quite a
reasonable cook! Marcia has a self-confidence and control over

her life that she never had when she was married. At work she has involved herself in equal employment opportunity schemes and specifically in attempting to improve the conditions of secretaries. Her struggles for equality at home and at work are closely linked.

Sally, now in her forties, is a departmental secretary at the Institute. As a working-class girl in Broken Hill she left school at fourteen and a half, did a secretarial course at tech and progressed fairly quickly through the typing pool to become a secretary. In the Broken Hill tradition, she was forced to resign when she married, and later began her own typing business. It enabled her to be at home with the children when they were young, though she says she eventually altered her views on this, 'especially when my daughter told me, many years later, I often wished that you were like ordinary mothers, and weren't at home all the time when I got home from school'! Meanwhile the business did so well that her husband moved in and tried to expand it into printing. This added to existing frictions and eventually the marriage split up. She moved into a flat, enrolled at university and hence found her current job. Since much of her work had involved typing university theses and essays she knew what tertiary education had to offer. There have been a number of different Sallies, constructed by the different meanings attached at different times to work, marriage, motherhood, domestic life and educational and cultural activities.

It will already be apparent that class identities are constructed in these interrelated processes. Marcia, Sally and Rena all come from 'traditional' working-class families. None is unproblematically working-class now although they speak of their backgrounds with pride. For a start, all are senior secretaries and this, I have suggested, is enough to place them firmly in the middle class. Of the three, Rena remains closest to her origins. She lives and works in the western suburbs of Sydney; her office is decidedly shabby, and her boss is a rough diamond who left school himself at fifteen. Rena's husband is a technician and they participate in working-class family and friendship networks. Sally established herself as 'petit-bourgeois' in the old sense, successfully running her own small business for thirteen years. She is now moving towards the 'new middle class' defined not only through her job but by her engagement with the academic world. Of the three, Marcia has the most high-flying job at head office. In her case, getting rid of her husband created the possibility of social mobility.

Class may be loosely based on a set of economic categories and relations, but it has to be actively maintained and reproduced. People situate themselves not only via their place in the labour process or the labour market, but in relation to prevailing discourses on class. A combination of things is important, including social background, occupation, spouse's occupation and background, domestic life and the wider networks and activities that may provide 'cultural capital' and social power. In the course of the interviews with secretarial workers, three 'normative' patterns emerged which involved a 'fit' between these factors and affected their choice of subject matter and general approach. Of course, no one fitted these patterns perfectly and for many these elements were completely out of alignment. This partly explains why their sense of class was weak and why their common experiences as women often overshadowed their class differences.

The first pattern may be described as 'working class'. Most of these women were in what I have described as 'lower secretarial' jobs, typically married to tradesmen, either waged or working for themselves. Asked to describe a day in their lives, they talked more about home and family than they did about their work. Were they constructing the interview as a tea break? While it could be argued that they were treating work as very much subordinate to home, part of the pleasure of the job was actually being able to have these kinds of conversations. For women who chose to use the interview in this way, the conversation flowed easily, and they were not afraid of the microphone.

Hazel's way of balancing home and work is fairly typical of this group. Before her marriage she worked in a variety of sales, factory and then secretarial jobs. After her children were born she moved in and out of the workforce, between caring for them and then a sick mother. She spent eleven years in various clerical jobs at CWJ and is now back there as a casual clerk. As her job is about to be computerised they want her to become the warehouse manager's secretary. It is obvious that she has a knowledge of all sections of the firm, but she finds secretarial work boring and wants to transfer back to the supermarket office. Hazel is adamant that mothers of young children should not work if they do not need to. She is critical of mothers who took their children to playgroup even on their rostered days off, or landed them on the babysitter at six o'clock in the morning. 'So why be a mother, why have children?' Yet work is important to her, among other things as a place in which to construct a feminine identity: 'I love coming to work because you get stuck at home. You don't even see your next door neighbour nine times out of ten...Like when you're stuck at home you don't feel like making the effort to do your hair half the time, or put on a bit of eye makeup. It's different if you go to work.'

Hazel's life is prefigured in the lives of young single women like

Carol (in Chapter 2) and Debbie (in Chapter 6), organised almost entirely around boyfriend and family. Older single women had different strategies at the interview. One of them, now aged 55 and still a stenographer despite having an arts degree, talked about neither her family nor her current job, which she said was boring. Scarcely drawing a breath she described a colourful and adventure-packed life from the time she organised her first strike at fourteen. Her pleasure was in projecting herself as a 'stirrer'. This provided some compensation for the fact that she had not got the jobs to which she felt entitled and for the hinted-at disappointments in her marital and personal life. Her strategy at the interview was to distract attention away from any detailed discussion of her current predicament. Others, especially the younger ones, relapsed into silence. Women in the routine jobs are the most powerless and the least able to articulate their frustrations and discontents. What came across as shyness may well have shielded grievances and frustrations they could not clearly voice (James, 1986: 21). Talk of husbands and children not only filled the space but provided the only real basis for establishing any kind of power in relation to the interviewer.

Many working-class women have achieved some social mobility by taking on senior secretarial jobs and marrying men from sections of the middle class. They talk most easily about family and domestic life and talk, emphasising the support and strength they draw from their families. In some cases they have transcended family difficulties to move into a solidly middle-class position. Marcia has reached the top of the secretarial world and now lives with a senior executive. She is active politically and has a very wide social and political network.

In sharp contrast to the above there was an identifiable 'lower middle-class' pattern. These were typically women working as secretaries to middle managers and married to men at much the same level. They declined to get involved in 'women's talk'. Perhaps because their 'middle-class' status was fragile they needed to draw a firm line between themselves and what they saw as 'working-class' behaviour. Their 'middle-classness' required that they be able to resist intrusions on their 'private' lives, whether these came from their bosses or from the interviewers. These women had a lot of tension about them. They talked in terms of duty, the difficulties of getting everything done, the sheer drag of combining work and domestic responsibilities. They were home-centred in the extreme, and their reason for working was often to help pay off the mortgage. There was not much pleasure in these women's lives, and sadly few talked about any world beyond home/work. Asked about leisure activities one secretary said: 'Well most of the time I am a housewife...It takes me an hour to go home. Then I might do some washing and put the dinner on. My husband comes home about 8 o'clock at night so between 5 and 8, well, I usually do the housework...Come Saturday I am working all day in the house and garden...and then on Sunday, if my husband is not working, then we will go out.' This is from a woman with no children. Others described their main leisure activities as 'cooking something special at the weekend'. It is hardly surprising that there was little interest in politics or feminism— there is no space for them, no wider political or cultural life. Sport, church and music were important to a minority—and been used to create a space for themselves. Single women in this pattern tended to devote themselves to the job and also to have very limited social or cultural lives.

The women who talked most easily about their jobs were the senior secretaries, who were happy to chat about management styles, to define 'good' secretaries and bosses, to describe their job in detail, to discuss what made a relationship work and often to talk quite frankly about past and present bosses. Work seemed more central to the way they constructed themselves. They do not allow their families to 'intrude' into the office because to do so would imply they were not 'serious' workers. They volunteered very little information about their marital status, home situation or personal views, though, they were usually willing to answer questions once the relevance was explained. As far as they were concerned, their home life was not relevant to what they did at work: they assumed a separation.

Ann represents a secure middle-class pattern. Married with teenage sons, she is secretary to a general manager at head office. She describes her strategies in the following terms:

> I like organising things. I do not like sitting and typing, which is why I like the job I have now because I don't do that much typing...It's the first time I've had a job for a long time where I thought I could stay. I would normally change my job every couple of years...I kind of, get bored...But up here it is always changing and I think it will keep me interested.
>
> I don't think about typing at all. I probably think about what I'm going to give the kids for tea or how much longer is this going to be, so I can go home by five o'clock...
>
> I find it's very challenging. A lot of it's in my head...it's not a shorthand/typist/receptionist-type secretarial job. It's above that. You're meant to know something and use your own initiative and organise things and not ask anybody...And I find that if things are difficult and I've got a lot on, I will take it home and I'll wake up at two o'clock in the morning and I will think what am I going to do about that? Then in the morning it's all right.
>
> My job pays basically for the kids' school fees...I have a cleaner, my treat.

Ann presents her job in conventional terms as providing only a secondary income. And yet it is this job that secures the family's upper middle-class position: they are able to employ a cleaner and send the children to private schools. She herself works very hard in the domestic sphere yet she talks the language of 'challenge' rather than in 'duty'. The two spheres run into each other, but because she is a good organiser she can think of many things at a time. She enjoys her family and also requires a job that is stimulating and demanding or she gets bored. Her work identity is in no sense an extension of her role as wife and mother.

The securely middle-class women used their marriages as the basis for wider social networks. They spoke more of pleasure, both in their work and in other parts of their lives. Things like home ownership were taken for granted and more of their incomes went on 'luxuries'. Building a swimming pool or a tennis court, sending the children to private schools, taking opera and concert subscriptions, employing 'help' in the house are the things that mark out their class position. They entertained more, participated in cultural activities, travelled more often and took regular holidays. Frequently they were undertaking some form of higher education, whether it was a university degree or professional qualification. In short they, and others like them, were constructing a position of social power through processes of mutual recognition. In so far as two substantial salaries are a desirable basis for building such a class position, single secretaries are at a disadvantage. But many achieve it through acquiring 'cultural capital' and establishing wide social networks.

Public and private

The terms public and private refer to areas of social life and social space that are perceived to be separate and even mutually exclusive. Historically the 'public' referred not to work at all but to civic, political life, a world beyond work and the realm of necessity. In this sense very few women or men have much of a public life outside the act of voting. Under capitalism 'work' became separated from the domestic sphere and moved into the public domain, while the domestic became the specialised domain of emotionality and self-expression (Zaretsky, 1976).

'Public' consistently refers to the realm of order and reason, with the private representing disorder, desire, emotion. Annette Kuhn (1984) identifies three referents of 'private': a geographical notion of private space—the home against the street; an association of privacy with property and ownership—private as against state ownership; and an analogy of privacy with individuality or selfhood, as in entitlement to one's own opinions. Privacy is also

227

applied to the body with notions of inner and outer, of bodily integrity and territoriality; and to consciousness with notions of outer (public) and inner (private) selves.

As we might expect there is a degree of correspondence between public and work and between private and home. On closer observation this breaks down. The public/private distinction cuts right across the home/work distinction and is generated everywhere, in the minutiae of everyday life as well as in constructing the larger divisions. Might it be linked with a subjectivity that is fragmented into conscious/unconscious? There are places where rigid barriers need to be maintained and others where the whole personality may flow. Goffman (1971) referred to these as 'backstage' areas where the public performance could be dropped.

Home for example, has its public and private spaces, so does work, and so does 'the individual'. The sitting room is more public than the kitchen, which in turn is more public than the bedroom or the toilet. (Different notions of public/private are evident here, since the bedroom as a space has restricted public access, while the toilet has limited public access but is a place where you can briefly shut yourself off and be separate from other individuals.) At work the toilets are a private women's space in two senses. They are the place where women retire to beautify themselves and also where gossip and confidences are exchanged that are not for the ears of men. A pool supervisor comments: 'Naturally on Monday morning in the toilet, always in the toilet, if you go into the toilet you can hear the whole gossip about what this lady and man did, or what two men or two women did, on the weekend...Everyone does gossip.' A woman manager, who had attempted to take up the cudgels on behalf of secretaries, says resignedly: 'What women will say to each other in the toilet is rather different to what they will say publicly.'

Women will complain to each other about working conditions but will not necessarily be prepared to repeat the complaints 'publicly', meaning place them in front of men or managers in such a way that they may be acted upon. Women think of themselves as being 'private' when there are no men present. This is when they can drop their guard. The more fluid boundaries between women create the preconditions for what gets called 'bitching'. The intervention of the symbolic order, in the form of men, is seen to break this up. When men are present women feel they have to maintain a boundary or risk sexual harassment. A personnel assistant said of her relationships specifically with men: 'I like to keep my work strictly work and if anything else gets discussed, it might be, "did you have a good weekend?" or "what did you do on the weekend?" and I find that's as far really as I'd like to go. Anything else I feel as though they're infringing on my intimate zone, my personal zone...I think it's men putting themselves more on women than secretaries putting themselves on the manager.' For men public/private has different meanings. In the company of other men they may be able to say things they would not say in front of women; but they need to erect a public facade, and defend their own boundaries. With women they can afford to be more intimate and are thus 'private' in quite a different sense.

The 'private' secretary is the one who 'belongs' to one boss. The notion of ownership is operative here. She is distinguished from the secretarial workers who are public property, who work in a pool or for more than one manager. Women may see it the other way round entirely. They may experience the typing pool as private in the sense that it is a women's space, in which they are shielded from the direct control of men. The 'private' secretary perceives herself as being on 'public' display, or accessible to 'the public', and individually more vulnerable because she is isolated from the group. Even if she has a room of her own it is rarely respected as private space. People can walk through it more easily than they can the typing pool. For women the main division may well be between the (private) women's culture and the (public) heterosexual culture. Both have their attractions and their drawbacks. Each crosses both the home/work and public/private divisions.

It has been argued that every patriarchal society has made some kind of distinction between the public and the domestic or private and restricted women to the latter (Rosaldo, 1974). What then should be done about it? Is is sufficient to insist on women's entry into the public sphere on equal terms with men, with the private simultaneously revalued and domestic work shared between men and women? What would it mean to break down the distinctions? Elshtein (1981) warns that without a maintaining a domain of the private, beyond state regulation, we are on the way to fascism. Feminists do not necessarily want to break down all distinctions between personal and public life but they have insisted that the two need not be opposites, and that 'the personal (too) is political'. They have challenged the idea that politics in the public arena can be constituted without reference to the quality of personal relations and questioned the assumption that reason and emotion are in contradiction (Siltanen and Stanworth, 1984).

Working women have not been prepared to break down the divisions between the public and the private. They frequently need to draw the boundaries very firmly in order to protect themselves and yet in doing so they reproduce the sexual division of labour both at home and work (Game and Pringle, 1984). No one is at all clear what is involved in transforming the existing categories. It will require further work on the deconstruction of the existing codes and the creation of alternative codes. Since reality cannot be changed merely through creating language or coining new discourses at the drop of a hat, it will be a long process. Challenge to the codes will go along with further scrutiny of 'experience' and struggles to change existing institutions and practices. While it is not enough to take experience at face value, the gap between women's experience and current cultural codes is an important starting point.

·11· Bitching: relations between women in the office

> I must tell you about this because I think it is a
> terrible thing to happen on a Ladies Night out as
> they refer to it. It was during Christmas and I
> thought to myself...just as well I wasn't there you
> know...because they were tearing different people
> to pieces. You know, as to their behaviour, the way
> you hold yourself in company, your drinking
> capacity and...you know...I think it is a terrible
> thing. And especially for the young—they don't
> realise that you are being judged...There is a lot of
> fault-finders here and they are always ready to talk
> about somebody else.
>
> *SECRETARY AT MALVERN*

> I'm like Mum, I can't stand bitchiness and men talk
> to you sensible...Women bitch because one is
> skinny and one is fat and you want her body and she
> wants yours. Men aren't like that. They are just
> happy with what they've got where women are really
> picky...I would say it would be more the younger
> ones...I think that when you get older you have
> your fiancees and you get married and you settle
> down a bit more...When you're young you're never
> satisfied...always jealous because she has got the
> bloke that you want and things like that. It's pretty
> stupid.
>
> *CLERK AT CWJ*

Secretaries are supposed to be 'above' bitching. Though all women
are 'at risk', it is regarded as an essentially working-class activity,
something that goes on in the typing pool rather than the board-
room. Where a group of women in, say, a typing pool may enjoy a
certain group solidarity in bitching about outsiders, secretaries
must be more circumspect. Yet whether a particular interaction is
classified as bitching is often a highly subjective matter. 'Bitching'
is not a self-evident empirical category but a social and discursive

construction. What I shall call the 'discourse of bitching' is important in marking out both class and gender relations. It distinguishes, first, between masculinity and femininity and second, between different types of femininity. Both the 'middle-classness' and the 'femininity' of secretaries depends on their maintaining a detachment from office bitching. The division between 'higher' and 'lower' secretarial workers is not just a difference in pay and conditions but is culturally constituted. The latter group are perceived to indulge in an activity called 'bitching', while the former are not. However, secretaries do not simply stand above bitching. They too are implicated in its social relations for, as women, they are always 'at risk' of being included in the label.

There is considerable confusion about what bitching is. The distinction between 'bitching' and friendly conversation, gossip, joking, rumour, flirtation, friendship and politics is somewhat arbitrary. It has less to do with actual differences in behaviour than with the ways in which behaviour is labelled. In talking about 'bitches' at least three levels are conflated: who is being bitched about, who is labelled as doing the bitching and who, if anybody, 'really' does the bitching. Working-class women are presumed to be simultaneously the subjects and the objects of bitching. When this is analysed it becomes clear first, that anyone may be bitched about, and second, that anyone may bitch. The question is not 'why do women bitch' but why is the behaviour of some groups of women defined and labelled in this way, with unpleasant consequences for the women concerned and, it may be argued, for all women. Rather than believing in the existence of a despised minority of 'bitches' we may acknowledge bitching as a pleasurable, and in some senses valuable, activity in which most people participate.

There are two apparently contradictory approaches to the subject of women's relationships with each other. One version has it that women do not 'bond' in the way men do (Tiger, 1969) and that their friendships are subordinated to a life organised around the requirements of family relationships. Women's friendships are regarded as fairly instrumental, providing support when needed and otherwise pushed aside in favour of husbands and children. Women are assumed to have limited social relations outside the family. Their networks are small, the number of their friendships limited. It is further assumed that close friendships between women only work on a one-to-one level; women do not handle larger groups and if you put them in groups of three or more bitching will inevitably take over because their conversation is so trivial. A politician's secretary expressed some of this: 'Women as a group bore me rigid. One-to-one they're terrific. Women's lunches are just ghastly. Women have nothing to talk about in a group.' Large groups are seen as the preserve of men, or run by men, and women take it for granted that if men are present they will 'naturally' be the leaders.

Others have argued that it is not women but men who are incapable of friendship. They stress the essential solidarity between women, the importance of women's friendship and mutual support, the value of physical and emotional space away from men. In this view men are emotional cripples incapable of communicating with each other, while women have passionate and intense friendships. It is argued that men have to treat these friendships as invisible or they would find them too threatening to deal with. Feminism has celebrated women's friendship and seen therein the hope of radical change in gender relations. In quite lyrical language, Adrienne Rich talks about 'lesbian continuum' to include a range of woman-identified experience and to 'embrace many forms of primary intensity between and among women, including the sharing of a rich inner life, the bonding against male tyranny, the giving and receiving of practical and political support' (1983: 192).

Rich uses *lesbian* here in a new way to consider not sexual behaviour or preference but to link a variety of women's experiences and strong emotional bonds. Lesbian continuum may include mother−daughter relations, the relations of childhood, the girl culture that constructs adolescent femininity, and the relations between adult women. Creating new meanings for 'lesbian' is part of an attempt to revalue women's space and to encourage women to take pride in what the heterosexual world has treated with contempt. For Rich women's experiences with each other are 'a potential springhead of female power', a base from which to change the social relations of gender.

A discussion of bitching opens up questions about the complex relations of mutuality and hostility between women. Bitching may be a sign of frustration; but, in its attempts to analyse personalities and situations, it may also be an expression of caring for other women and a desire to see an improvement in their conditions. It is not clearly separable from listening to a friend's troubles, sharing her outpourings of anger and disappointment, or making her feel better by putting down those who appear to have caused the hurt. Yet the price of this support is shared victimhood. The problem with bitching is that it can reinforce self-pity and powerlessness. But it also has its pleasures and advantages. Is it simply to be suppressed, along with sexuality in the workplace, or might it be a basis for the 'springhead of female power' that Rich hopes for?

The bitching discourse

'Bitch' has been applied opprobriously to women since at least the fifteenth century. It has traditionally meant a 'lewd or immoral' woman or a 'malicious, spiteful and domineering' one (Websters, 1965). The more recent use of 'bitching' as a verb and an activity has American origins but was well established in Australia by the 1960s when it largely replaced euphemisms like 'catty'. There is a 'discourse' on bitching which will be instantly recognisable to most people and was reproduced in every workplace and college that we visited. It is reproduced most strongly by women. Men either ignore bitching or make a joke of it whereas women try to analyse it. All the commments in this chapter are from women. Bitching refers to making spiteful, malicious or put-down remarks over what are perceived to be essentially trivial issues. Women are seen as constantly 'picking' on each other as a way of assessing or asserting their status and reputation:

> Look, I'm not saying that I am an angel and I don't talk about other people. Everyone does I reckon. They like to know everyone else's business. . . If you came in in something different, or if you don't tend to wear a uniform every day and just wear your normal clothes or something, they will then say, oh, she must have a good wardrobe. . . and this and that and all the rest of it. . . Now someone might come in in a hot pink dress and then everyone will have something to say about it. . . that it is not dignified or something like that.

While women *complain* about men, they do not usually refer to them in as personal or sexual a way and will often make excuses for them. It is other women who are regarded as the main subject matter, and criticisms are typically about clothes and manner, laziness or uncooperativeness, lateness or trying to gain favours through the use of sexuality:

> This girl out here has only just learnt shorthand and she has been here ten years. But she is the sort of girl who is very possessive of her boss. Like if I took a cup of tea into him, she would nearly pour it over you, one of those sort of girls.

> I resigned last August because they gave me another boss. I had four bosses and there was one girl sitting there with one boss doing her nails all day. And I was eleven years older than her. It is not that, but it just wasn't on. And I though, that is it, and I wrote out my resignation and that was it.

'Doing her nails' is a code for a series of behaviours which have more to do with competition for male approval, and genuine resentment about a situation where reward structures are not based on skill.

As the choice of term implies, bitching is women's business. It is no more possible to label men bitches than it is to label them sluts or tarts—though, of course, gay men have appropriated all three terms. It may be acknowledged that 'men bitch too', and we do not have to look very far to find men indulging in manipulation, back-stabbing, whingeing and gossiping. But the term is not easily applied to them. This disguises the extent to which men do bitch and, perhaps more significantly, the extent to which they are bitched about. The apparent absence of men from the bitching discourse facilitates the presentation of masculinity as rational, abstract and autonomous; women by contrast are looked into the petty and the concrete.

While individual women may bitch it is thought to be near inevitable when women get together in a group: what else would they have to do? The supervisor of a word-processing pool sees bitching as a major problem in all-female work areas:

> You have an average of 25 girls in each section. And when you get 25 girls in one section then you just get one big bitch session. You have your nitty grittys, you have one crowd that sticks with this crowd, and this crowd sticks with this crowd and they just meet in the middle and it is just explosion city.
> *And why does that happen?*
> Because girls are the biggest bitches out. They have got nothing to occupy their minds. If they had a few fellows in there, not just to perv on or whatever, but to break the monotony of talking about what they did, they cleaned the kitchen sink or hung the curtains or fed the baby, the usual things that women talk about and instead they could talk about football or cricket or what ever the male does . . .

This is echoed by a woman clerk:

> Well there are about twenty something of us in this stock control office—eight males and the rest females. But if it was just 22 females, it would be hell I reckon.
> *Why?*
> Because females are catty, and we all go on about this and that I suppose. They like to know everyone else's business . . .

In their earliest weeks at college the secretarial studies students mouthed the axiom that women together are catty and bitchy and said they would prefer to work in a mixed group. At the same time they said they preferred being in a single-sex class away from boys and expected to have close female friendships of the sort that last a lifetime. They said it was girlfriends who gave continuity to their lives: it is boyfriends rather than girlfriends who come and go. When they stressed the importance of making friends at work it was *female* friends they had in mind. Girl culture is valued as a place of safety and respite from the heterosexual arena. It is also the place where they prepare for the next round, by listening to each other's problems and by helping as well as competing in all the activities that construct their self-images. Yet along with the solidarity bitching activity was acknowledged. There was no time to question them about this in any detail. We simply asked them whether they thought girls bitched in the context of the college, and if so what about. Some admitted to bitching about groups that they thought inferior, as in the following exchange with two students from a small private college:

> I wouldn't go to a girls' school.
> No. There's too much bitching.
> There's a fair bit of bitching going on around here too. Girls come in and . . . (*much giggling*) . . . they're not up to our standard. It's as if we are back in sixth class. So we hassle them.
> Its horrible!
> *Is this the girls who come in to do the six week course?*
> Some of them. We don't mean to be horrible. We should be out of that stage by now . . . so we've been told by Miss Ball. We're naughty!
> *So why do you do it?*
> 'Cause the other girls do it. To keep up with the other girls.

The favourite subject of bitching within the colleges is apt to be the woman teachers, who are in some degree mother substitutes. Bitching enables the girls to pull away and establish their separateness. Just as importantly, it maintains their reputation in the eyes of the peer group and, by focusing on the outsider helps to establish group cohesion and some kind of safety. Male teachers are never the subject of bitching.

While all women are capable of bitching behaviour, it is thought to be most common among women who do not have a man or who are considered unattractive to men. Spinsters, both young and old, are singled out, as are women who are divorced, separated or known to have marital problems or unstable love lives. All are assumed to be jealous of their more 'conventional' sisters and therefore out to destroy them. Of couse bitching makes them even more contemptible and unattractive:

> Our share department up to about six months ago had six ladies in it and they all retired within about twelve months. None of them were married and they have been doing the same jobs for between 35 and 40 years. They all hated each other, absolutely . . . but they wouldn't leave . . . I think that they had really lonely home lives, that this was their family . . . And that department was definitely ridiculed always because there were all these ladies and they weren't married and they hated everybody and everybody hated them, and they just kept to themselves and that was it.

Bitching is tied to not having a visible sexual relation with a man—the presence of a man acts as a safeguard. Women bitch because of what they lack; groups of men do not need to bitch because men are regarded as complete in themselves. So it is constantly reinforced that women *need* men to save them from drowning in this sea of female nastiness. It is men who brighten up women's day at work. Women alone together are seen as trivial, incompetent, directionless, snivelling, pathetic.

> *Do you like working with other women?*
> No. Not really. No. Two or three is just okay. Any more than that and it does cause problems. There is a personality clash...I think you always get personality clashes with a lot of women working together. Always. (typist)

It is assumed that men and women are different by *nature* and that this explains women's bitching.

> Yes, women are bitchy. Maybe it's just quite hard work. Yes, they tittle-tattle. Yes, I think women as a rule do. I think even small girls do...You watch small children and watch girls. They always sort of prance around with an 'I'm better than you' attitude, whereas boys will sort of play better, or they have a fight and forget about it. Whereas girls always seem to have a slightly bitchy attitude. Even when they are small. (secretary)

> I think it's there to start with. Maybe work could bring it up. When you get a lot of girls together, bitchiness is found. But then men can be just as bad. I don't think it is actually all women; you can get very bitchy men as well, who you have to get on with, who like to be slightly better or like to be seen to be slightly better than somebody else. Which is where you might get somebody's secretary who sits and twiddles her thumbs because he likes to have a secretary there—which is really, I suppose, the ultimate in oneupmanship. (secretary)

Bitching is attributed to women for what are assumed to be inbuilt physical and psychological reasons. They are believed to be more subject to their bodies, particularly to the monthly cycle, as well as being moody and over-emotional.

> ...I think it's to do with their own personality. It is nothing to do with the work so much, I don't think. It is just that they, a lot of women are very, very moody people. I've worked with a lot of girls now, different sections and that, and sometimes in the corridors they will answer you and sometimes they will just walk by you, as if you are not even there...Some are only like it at some times of the month...And with the men, I've always found the men great to work with. Never had any trouble...They are the same all the time. It is very rare that you find a man that is bitchy or anything like that. (personnel officer)

Women are stereotypically jealous, deceitful and obsessed with finding fault:

> (*Why do you think women bitch?*)
> Jealousy. That is the only thing that I can put it down to. Jealousy or trying to air their authority.
> *Jealous of what exactly?*
> I can't put my finger on what it would be, but it is either that or trying to air their authority.
> *Are friendships important to you at all at work?*
> Yes, because if there isn't friendship then there isn't any point in being there at all because there is just bitching behind the back all the time.
> *Do you see anyone from work outside the workplace?*
> No. Once I leave here then I put my work behind me...I think it is better because if something happens than it could ruin the work situation. I think it is better to leave the work friends at work. (word processor operator)

She points to another component of the discourse, that women resent other women exercising authority over them:

> There was one girl in there, she absolutely hated me because she was going to be made supervisor and she wanted to boss me around and she couldn't because she didn't have any authority over me. So I just used to retaliate with her and do the opposite, and that just made her more aggravated, but I enjoyed it because she was a real bitch...She just likes to throw her authority around because she is the only one in there now, and whoever comes in she is their boss then, and she just likes to throw that around.

It is unlikely that this would be said about a man in authority even if he were disliked.

It is part of the 'bitching discourse' that women resent any woman who treats work in a 'male' way and seeks to move up the ladder. Junior secretaries resent the authority and the favours that those more senior may derive from their (male) bosses. Given the importance of male approval, they may also be resentful that they are not in a position to use their sexuality in open competition. Age or experience may be cited as a more legitimate basis for authority:

> They resent you having power over them because your boss is a higher-status boss than their boss...That derived power and status that you get from who you work for...Down the bottom you very often have to work a hell of a lot harder. A very difficult issue when you are a junior secretary is that you might be working for a number of people and that is very hard. Very hard because they all want work at the same time. And for a young kid to have to try and juggle that is a very hard situation. (secretary)

Well, there were two that used to pull their rank; one of them was
secretary to the chairman and the other was involved in doing copy for
promotions...and then there was the rest of the office that dealt with
hotel bookings and they were sorts of different grades. There were more
experienced women who knew all about the hotels and then there was
the next ones who knew the basics and then there were the trainees.
Everyday without fail, someone would end up in tears and then one day I
ended up in tears and I just used to go home and take it out on the girls
that I lived with... (secretary)

It is a commonplace that senior secretaries do nothing and those
lower down in the hierarchy have to do all the work. Sometimes
there is truth in this, for pay and status are usually based not on
job content but on the status of the boss. At Darling, it will be
recalled, the managing director's secretary used her position as
the most senior secretary to veto arrangements made by the rest
of the group and refused to muck in and help. The bitching
discourse enables complaints about this to be easily dismissed by
management. If they can be dismissed as 'just' bitching, then no
action needs to be taken.

Brief workplace interviews are not the ideal way of finding out
about the content of bitching. People are usually too embarrassed
to describe examples in any detail. Participant observation would
be the more effective way of collecting this kind of information
but would place severe limits on the number of examples one
could collect. On the other hand the interviewers were often the
recipients of what could be labelled 'bitching'. Some subjects positioned us as a 'safe' audience, our role being to listen sympath-
etically while they raged about a series of things including salary
structure, working conditions, bosses or supervisors and about
other women. What they were asking was that we hear and sympathise with them in their trials and tribulations, not that we do
anything to change the situation.

Where women's behaviour is labelled 'bitching', quite similar
behaviour in men may be regarded as joking or fooling around
and positively evaluated. (Both sexes gossip, though this too is
gender-differentiated—men gossip about 'important' things
whereas women are 'nosey'.) Men's jokes are frequently based on
putting down women or harassing them, but the slide is not
acknowledged. They are seen as creating pleasure in the workplace. A woman clerk commented: 'We joke a lot, especially if
there are men down there. We joke a lot with them, about their
wives, and they might say something or other and we all kind of
joke. They pull the mickey out of a lot of people down there. But
nearly all of us can take it. It is just like a big joke.' If women 'pull
the mickey out of people' they come dangerously close to bitching,

but if men do it it is joking. Women are largely excluded from joking, at least in mixed company. If a woman says anything considered risqué or if she is too tolerant of dirty jokes, she may become a target for sexual harassment. Women tread a fine line between going along with a joke and being accused of being humourless if they protest too early. Perhaps in the circumstances it is safer, and more pleasurable, to bitch. As one secretary said: 'I think we all enjoy that. I think that's just being human...Anybody's fair game I think. We even bitch about each other to each other...but I think that's just a game you play...I think I'd be a prime target. It doesn't worry me...It's just a game.' She understands though how easily it can slide over into the 'nasty' category and needs to reassure herself that it's 'only a game'.

As we saw in Chapter 3, women bosses are a subject of relentless bitching by secretarial workers as well as being represented as 'bitchy' themselves. The mother—daughter script is much in evidence here. Secretaries may be jealous, consciously or otherwise, of what the other woman has achieved; or they may set higher standards for women and then be disappointed when they do not live up to them. Bosses may also be ambivalent about merging and anxious about their separateness. Shirley, who fitted the dragon stereotype more closely than most secretaries we interviewed, said that women 'either put you down or see you as a competitor. Men are much more appreciative'.

While the emphasis in the discourse is on women's natures or personalities there is some recognition of bitching as a response to concrete working conditions, and the interest therein a part of women's culture:

> You get to a point in your job where having a whinge or a bitch is like a symptom. Where they've perhaps been in a job for three or four years doing the same sort of thing, day in, day out, they get sick of it but the workplace is such that they don't want to leave their jobs, they don't want to lose the security but they're not happy so they start bitching to each other and it's their way to let off steam...I hear a lot of complaints about money. They're not paid enough. Their employers expect a pound of flesh but they're not willing to give anything back, but I've found you get a lot more results if you talk to your boss...A lot of the girls whinge and whinge and whinge but they won't speak to the person they work for. He wouldn't know if they were happy, sad or what. And that's a lot of the problem. A lot of bosses don't care.

It is a common complaint that women will whinge to each other but that if one of their number takes up the complaint with management they will suddenly find they have no support. 'People will say, well, if you don't like that, you be the spokesperson and we will back you up. And how many times do you get the backing?

So you have made a fool of yourself and then they will all sit back and not say anything. That is what frustrates me.' There is both a fear of change and a belief that change is, anyway, impossible. Bitching can also derive directly from the divide-and-rule strategies of management: 'There is a little bit of jealousy here and there...But not a real lot...Each Friday we have a staff meeting and you get excellent achievement badges, like if you have really worked or done something out of the ordinary...it does create a bit of animosity around the place...It really is a team effort, because everybody pitches in and helps' (clerk). When there is no clear chain of authority or any kind of collective decision-making, tension becomes inevitable:

> I used to sit at the desk and it was like a nerve game...If you thought you had answered three phone calls and they hadn't answered one, you would sit there and wait and wait and wait until someone answered the phone finally. And one day I had had enough...And when I came back onto the floor after doing something else she was standing talking to someone actually about me and she had her back to me and couldn't see me coming and the other person could and didn't get a chance to stop her. And I just made the remark, caught you that time, Frances! (secretary)

Bitching occurs in all-women workplaces as well as in pockets in mixed organisations. It operates in collectives as strongly as it does in hierarchies, in some cases more so, as the women may be more ambitious and find greater difficulty in reconciling their goals with the welfare of the group. Success itself may create difficulties for women who are more used to being supportive to each other in adversity. It is nevertheless possible to identify workplaces that are notorious for bitching and others where it is virtually non-existent. The large all-female areas of offices are held to be the main 'sites' of bitching (either at the desks or in the toilet). These are the areas of low-status, monotonous work looked down upon by everyone else. Typing pools, data entry sections, finance and accounting departments are the most frequently mentioned. Bitching may fairly readily be related here to low self-esteem and the feelings of marginalisation that that reproduces. Bitching may be the only way these women can deal with feelings of inferiority and make themselves feel better.

Bitching and friendship

Given all the foregoing it is perhaps surprising that women find friendship with other women such an important part of their working environment. Invariably they say they do, although the meaning of friendship is left undefined. Friendship may have rather different meanings for middle- and working-class people. For the former, friends are people you enjoy spending time with, without reciprocal obligation. For the latter, friends are people you trust, not necessarily people you like.

Neither definition conveys quite what it is that women describe as 'friendship' at work. Single women socialise with workmates more than the married women, but they too say that their 'main' friendship networks are constituted outside work. 'Friends' are mostly made at school, or via sporting or leisure activities. Married women rarely socialise with each other outside work or visit each others' homes unless their husbands also get on and they can spend time together as couples. For the most part the relationship begins and ends at work, or on the journey to and from work. The main exception is if they have come to be working together as a result of being friends, where, for example, one woman has found a job for her friend in the same office. If they live near each other or have children the same age they may share transport or do things jointly around the children. In suburban offices young girls often do babysitting for the other women. But these arrangements are fairly minimal. Jane distinguishes between 'the friends you have lunch with at work' and 'family friends—the people you see at weekends'. She is married to a senior business executive and they do most of their socialising with other similar couples. She concedes that work friendships would fizzle out quickly if she changed jobs. Though women were generally keen to stress to us the importance of socialising at work their reality suggests otherwise. Thus Chris, a secretary working in personnel, says: 'I think it's important to have friends at work. I mean most of your living life is spent here...I think it is important to socialise, even in work hours...to have a few sort of casual words to people and not to be frowned upon all the time.' She slips from 'friendship' to 'socialising' to 'a few casual words'. For most women socialising amounts to little more than ritual birthday and Christmas lunches and the occasional girls' nights out. After-work drinks and weekend activities are strictly for the young and un-married. Solitary lunches are typical, with women using the time to shop or window-shop or just to get away from work. An obvi-ous point is that they did not have the money to spend on regular lunchtime socialising. It was more likely to happen in offices where lunch was supplied or subsidised or in suburban locations where the shops were some distance away and lunch was brought from home.

Morning tea, however, is symbolically important as the point in the day when everyone downs tools for a gossip and chat. 'Cafe-bar' and the possibility of making continuous cups of tea or coffee have not destroyed what may be a peculiarly Australian institution. In some places (at Jessie Street for example) battles have been fought for the right to close the office so that everyone may be present. Secretaries frequently bring in treats to share at morning tea, particularly if it is someone's birthday. Quite often these are all-women occasions, with 'the secretaries' either having their own space or making it clear that 'outsiders' are unwelcome unless specifically invited. In some places it had become a convention that the men and the women go to tea at different times. Missing morning tea may be seen as highly deviant behaviour in secretaries, an indication that you do not fit in or that you consider yourself as 'above' the rest of the group.

'Camaraderie' may come closer to describing these relationships than 'friendship'. Yet the two have more in common than we might expect. If women's identities are formed in merged attachments they continue to create and maintain a sense of self through connecting with others rather than (the more typical male pattern) establishing difference from them. This happens not only in close friendships but in the most casual encounters. Psychologists Orbach and Eichenbaum (1987) analyse the ways in which a woman is able instantly to identify with another woman's feelings or predicament and in a sense 'become' that woman. The pleasure of this kind of identification does not require 'deep' friendship: it may be completely banal. This desire to experience self through connection, to be part of a 'flow', may explain the pleasure in endless chatter about husbands and children which informs so much of women's talk at work. When they go home they simply turn off the flow: 'I don't think that people actually interact on a social level. They don't really share their lives. They don't see each other outside work. They just gabble on about the husband and kids, like what they did at the weekend. I know more about, what's his name, Warwick and Finola, almost down to the brand of toothpaste they use...' (secretary) Not all women want this kind of merging. It may have no relation to their current concerns and may signify to them that they are not 'allowed' to have broader interests. Lurking in the background may be aspects of the mother–daughter relationship they do not like, in particular the idea that acceptance by another woman was at the price of the denial of their own needs and initiatives. There is not much room here for difference or individuality. Women without husbands or children cannot easily talk about themselves and may feel obliged to create a cover. One or two women resolutely talked about their dogs and cats while others skipped the occasion entirely. The identification required may mean the suppression of any hostile or ambivalent feelings being expressed and prevent any genuine empathy from developing. Feelings of envy or competitiveness are perceived as so threatening that they may be internalised as self-hatred. In turn they may be projected outwards as a bitchy remark or a put-down, as the only way of freeing oneself from them. This may also have the effect of solid-ifying the group against the outsider. Keeping others out and being able to put them down is a safe mechanism for the group's negative feelings. It is not difficult to see how groups of women could swing quite rapidly from the cosiness of morning-tea gossip to bitching when the identification process has jarred in some way.

More psychoanalytically inclined feminists than Rich have argued that, far from being a challenge to 'compulsory hetero-sexuality', women's friendships are complementary to it. Women not only compete for men but support each other in their re-lationships with them and help each through the bad patches. These two aspects of women's friendship are interconnected. Chodorow (1978) suggests that little girls turn to the father not because he is inherently superior but because he represents dif-ference both from themselves and their mothers; women may 'escape' into heterosexuality to individuate themselves from other women. For Orbach and Eichenbaum the 'developmental and social processes that are at the heart of women's easy connections are the very same processes that are at the heart of their difficulties with one another (1987: 43). They talk about the 'bittersweet' quality of relations between women where merged attachments coexist with intense feelings of envy, competition and anger. Our memory of our mothers may, as Campioni (1988: 15) suggests, be a memory of being allowed to be a separate being only at the price of love and support. We had to deny our mothers in our at-tempt to become our own selves. The hatred and anger often directed at the mother represents our feeling that we lack a love that both recognised us as capable beings, yet acknowledged our need for nurturance and support. A number of feminist writers (e.g. Flax, 1978) have described the search for equality in women's relationships in terms of the fine balance between autonomy/ independence and merging/dependency. We want to feel both separate and connected. But the emphasis on nurturance may suppress the possibility of dealing amicably with disagreement or difference and start to be experienced as smothering; and the other's search for autonomy may be treated as rejection. Rather than identifying certain activities as 'bitching' and then moralising about them, it may be possible to take the negative feelings that are expressed and be more accepting of them. Orbach and Eichenbaum suggest that envy and competitiveness should be seen as signposts to other feelings. Seen another way, envy could be interpreted as rebellion against deprivation, competition as

'energy towards life, towards self-actualisation, towards differentiation and the right to be one's own person' (1987: 109). They
argue that women need to break free of the old merged attachments and forge new 'separated' attachments. This will involve
being honest with each other about their true feelings and transforming bitching into action for change.

Gender and class

Secretaries have to negotiate not only the heterosexual culture of
the office but relationships with women. In most offices they are
expected to work quite closely with other women. Even when they
work exclusively for one boss they are likely to be in close proximity
to other secretaries and it is important to the smooth functioning
of the organisation overall that the women get on. Secretaries
usually rely on reciprocity and cooperation to get their work
done. This may include answering each others' phones, taking on
each others' typing overloads, sharing equipment and communal
tasks such as filing, photocopying or ordering stationery, syn-
chronising their use of the printer and generally covering for
each other. Often they have evolved complex and subtle work
rhythms, which can easily break down if someone does not pull
their weight or defines their job too narrowly. Jane, as secretary to
the general manager, has informal responsibility for ensuring that
these arrangements work smoothly. She comments: 'A girl we had
before the one we have now, she wasn't very helpful. She would
do it if we asked but she never offered...You sort of didn't give
her the work...because she wasn't that good anyway...But Kay's
really good and you can trust her and it helps a lot.' Personnel
officers are often more concerned to 'match' secretaries with other
secretaries than with bosses. Frictions and tensions can develop as
easily here as in the typing pool.

Secretaries' status as 'middle-class' requires that they refrain
from bitching. Yet this class status is fragile because they can,
much more easily than middle-class men, be drawn into the culture
of bitching. As I have argued in the preceding chapters, women's
class identity is more tenuous than men's. Secretaries are more
likely to be associated with 'bitching' if they work in suburban or
regional offices, particularly of companies like Malvern which
have a strongly macho and working-class image. At Malvern,
many of the secretaries were married to working-class men and
their participation in the culture of bitching pushed them towards
a working-class rather than middle-class identity. On the other
hand, 'middle-class' women returning to the workforce in more
routine jobs than the ones they had left, may find the bitching

behaviour of their new colleagues quite intimidating and resist taking part in it.

In general, secretaries have to present themselves as 'above' bitching and gossip and to be discreet in what they say. No boss wants a secretary with a reputation for bitching. Secretaries have to find other ways of relieving tension. Rather than bad-mouthing people in the office they may behave in a haughty way or freeze out individuals that they do not like. This may earn them the reputation of 'dragons' rather than bitches. Or they may make absolutely poisonous remarks about colleagues but will be careful to ensure these do not feed into the gossip network. Perhaps they will be made discreetly to a close woman confidante over lunch, well away from the rest of the office. This will have the effect not only of letting off steam but of drawing the two women closer, confirming their friendship and their superiority to others they work with. It will only be labelled bitching if the accusations become public—if the women are overheard or fall out with each other.

Bitching cannot be analysed simply in terms of personality. The psychological explanations provide insight into its mechanisms but the merging, the intimacy and the disappointments do not occur in a vacuum but in a broader context of patriarchal relations. Women have little direct access to power and have to achieve their ends indirectly. Bitching is an element of this, an admission of powerlessness and ambivalence. Men, having greater access to public power, can afford more direct conflict. Instead of bitching they can openly say what they think, fight with each other and then patch it up. They do not endanger their sense of self whereas women will feel personally attacked and may not talk to each other for a long time. One secretary noted the contrast in the following terms:

> I attend this Operations meeting every Monday morning...I'm the only woman there and there are nine men...and they will swear at each other and yell...They make nasty remarks, often very personal...'You bloody don't know what you're talking about you stupid, whatever'...and 'You wouldn't know if your arse was on fire'...I've seen men get really hostile towards each other, and they obviously don't like each other, right? And they'll walk out the door and say, coming down the pub, mate, for a drink? And I think, what! And I've come to realise that they don't take anything personally...Women can't do it...At the senior secretaries' meeting...we had lots of problems...and got a lot less done than we really should have, because people were so concerned with upsetting another in the group by disagreeing...They'd come and say to me, gee, fancy saying that to Gwen. I really agree with what you said. And I'd say, why didn't you say so in the meeting? Oh no, she'll get upset if I say that to her...

Women's experience of bitching is linked to the mother—daughter relationship with its merging and hostility. While the girl may want to move away from identification with the mother it is the presence of the father which symbolically enforces the separation. The constant refrain of the adult women that having men around stops bitching echoes the childhood situation. This may explain why bitching is most common in groups of women who are largely separate from men. As women move up the ladder they usually come more directly under the authority of men and 'bitching' is diverted into private conversations or gossip. They can then locate themselves 'above' bitching and look back to see it operating among women lower down the scale.

Bitching is the adult extension of the adolescent girls' discourse on 'sluts' and 'tarts' and performs similar functions in keeping women in line. For girls and women the defence of their reputations is crucial to their standing with both sexes. Tarts have tarnished reputations, are located outside the 'respectable' world and are regarded as unacceptable as wives and mothers. The language of sluts and tarts is used by girls of all social classes (Lees, 1986). But the insult, of course, has class connotations. To say that someone is a tart is to say that she is déclassé. A 'slut' or 'tart' is supposed to refer to a girl who sleeps around promiscuously, but the insult may have no relation to actual sexual behaviour. It can be applied to a girl who dresses, talks or behaves in a way that is defined as 'cheap'. This constant slide means that any girl may be designated a slut.

A bitch is not directly analagous to a tart but the processes of identification are similar. It is possible for a woman (or for that matter a man) to be bitched about without the accusations 'sticking'. A woman can get a bad reputation either by being bitched about or by bitching herself. In some ways the latter is the more dangerous, for it is the activity of bitching rather than the reputed behaviour that is at stake. Women frequently accuse each other not only of being bitches but of 'bitching'. Those who apply the label do so to distance themselves from it, perhaps to project parts of themselves that they dislike onto others or to build solidarity with the 'in' group (Lees, 1986). Whatever nasty remarks they might have made about people, most of the women interviewed were careful to deny their own participation: bitching was something that others did. Just as adolescent girls can be labelled sluts or tramps without actually engaging in promiscuous sexual behaviour, so adult women can be labelled 'bitchy' for being assertive or aggressive or merely for being unmarried or unhappy. The label of 'bitch' is ultimately important in terms of a woman's standing with men; and it is men who, in the last resort, arbitrate and adjudicate bitching behaviour. They are able to pronounce, from the 'outside', on whether a woman is in fact being bitchy or humorous or has a just complaint.

The question 'why do women bitch?' is no more helpful than the question 'why are women sluts?' It must be rephrased to take into account the labelling process. The fear of being labelled a bitch (in either sense) serves to channel women into consistently expressing a preference for men, despising women's company and treating women friends as secondary. If any women can be labelled a bitch, the best defence is to get in quickly and accuse someone else of bitching. In this way all one's own feelings of envy or frustration can be projected elsewhere. Differentiating the bitches from yourself may be a useful way of protecting your own reputation. The danger of course is that in doing this you too will be labelled a bitch. At very least you will be colluding in the bitching discourse.

The bitching discourse is important in the maintenance of men's power. Men get a vicarious pleasure out of women's bitching and delight in repeating, and laughing about, what women have said about each other. Women's bitching often constitutes for them an important source of information and gossip. Because of their structural position they do not have to worry about maintaining their sexual reputations and their purity. Because women have to make themselves acceptable to men they must watch out for their reputations. Accusations of bitching break up the potential oppositional solidarity of women. And they represent women as being out of control and *needing* men around to keep them in order. This not only reinforces but constructs a male-dominated pattern of heterosexuality in which women express contempt for each other, a preference for men over other women, for male bosses and for mixed workplaces. Despite the emphasis that women place on the importance of female friendships at work they are constructed as routinely preferring the company of men.

The particular forms that bitching takes arise from women's powerlessness, their lesser space to manoeuvre, their difficulties in asserting themselves directly, and the numerous things that men do to divide and conquer. We can note the relevance of female personality construction, the relational self and the kinds of mergings and overlaps that can cause tension. We can look at the actual working conditions and the divide-and-rule strategies that can cause dissatisfaction. We can look at the lack of legitimacy in women exercising power. But tying all these things together is the way in which women's preferences are systematically directed towards men and away from women. The mere presence of men is held out as a source of pleasure for women while their dominance is said to make them safe from that bitchy all-female world. Where women's authority grates, men's authority is accepted as rightful and desirable. It follows that women focus on pleasing men and derive pleasure out of the male approval. In our kind of patriarchal culture, women's main priority is how to achieve success as 'heterosexual woman'. This requires that she prefer men, not just in bed but in every situation. While lip-service is paid to female friendship in this structure, it is fundamentally subordinate.

The marginalising of women's groups inevitably defuses political action. Adrienne Rich is surely right in looking to a revaluation of women's culture as a basis of change. It is not, however, a choice between 'women's culture' and 'compulsory heterosexuality'. Women's culture is not in any obvious sense an area of liberation from the evils of patriarchy, and heterosexuality may take different forms. Both spheres need to be transformed. An important part of this will be the transformation of bitching from an expression of passivity and resentment to women's assertion of power and control over the conditions of their lives.

·12· Secretaries and feminist politics

> I believe in equal rights, equal pay, equal career. I think that that is fair...But I still like people to open the door for me...

> I think a lot of it's a lot of rubbish...I quite like being a woman...I believe in equal opportunity but not to the extent where people go to extremes... People don't like extremists...whereas if you are more moderate they say, oh, perhaps she has a point.

> When I was about four, a friend of my father's asked, what do you want to be when you grow up? And I said, a man!

What does feminism represent for secretaries? The most vivid and recurring image of 'feminists' put forward was 'those women who march on Anzac Day'. This came up throughout the year, not only in April—May when the subject was topical. It refers to those groups of women who have, since the early 1980s, sought to march on behalf of 'Women of All Countries, Raped in All Wars'. The fact that it was mentioned so often indicates that the women's action had had a profound impact. All who referred to this image did so to distance themselves from it, for it troubled them. They found the implicit accusations of rape embarrassing and the 'confrontationist' tactics distasteful, even shameful. The 'ratbags' who participated represented everything that these women did not want to be; in particular they had 'gone too far' and incurred male wrath. Perhaps the most common image of feminists was of the 'overalls brigade', women who have rejected femininity and do not care about their appearance, who have BO and hairy armpits. That feminism is associated with 'bra burning' and 'boiler suits' is evidence of the power of media representations. The lesbian secretaries, with one or two exceptions, shared this view and dissociated themselves from feminism. Feminists are seen as unattractive women who cannot get a man and become bitter, women who hate men and yet who strive to be like them, who are strident and unwomanly and who 'go about things the wrong way'. It did not consciously occur to any of the group who described feminism in this way that the interviewers might be connected with 'this kind of feminism', might themselves have marched on Anzac Day!

This seems to fit in with the stereotype of secretaries as obsessed with femininity and with pleasing men, hence essentially conservative and hostile to feminism. Yet this is far from the case. While secretaries mostly speak from a position 'outside' the women's movement they are not unsympathetic to all feminist demands. Much that was 'radical' in the 1970s is now accepted as everyday commonsense. Secretaries pay at least lip service to equality in the workplace, including equal pay, access to career structures and improved fringe benefits, and they reject the more servile implications of 'office wife'. At every secretarial college there is at least some engagement with feminist ideas.

Most secretaries dissociate themselves from a distinctive feminist politics. Though they talk about 'equality' they do not have any strong commitment even to the legislative processes which might bring it about. Many felt strongly about equal pay...but thought they already had it! When they felt they were badly paid it was by comparison with what other women, or secretaries in other places, were getting, not with what men earned either in trades or comparable occupations in clerical and administrative areas. By far the largest group held that feminism was 'all right' as long as it was pursued in a soft and gentle, cooperative, gradualist and feminine fashion. These women pay lip-service to equal rights and opportunities but have no interest in exercising them.

For the most part the interviewers were perceived not as 'feminists' but as 'sociologists', writers or independent researchers. If we were linked with feminism at all it was with a second image that came forward. This was of a kind of 'liberal' feminism perceived as the worldview of women with career ambitions, who had made it into management. Feminism of this sort was associated with 'bosses'. Secretaries in the private sector were not overtly hostile to 'liberal' feminism but it had little personal relevance. Equal employment opportunity and affirmative action were for other women, not for them: 'Equal employment, I think that's great. It's good that it is there for the women who want it.' They constructed themselves as not having any career ambitions and as putting their families first: 'I've got two sons and a husband. I'm quite happy to be a secretary and my family come first. If I was single or divorced or I needed to work I might have a different view.' Their knowledge of affirmative action was limited. Yet many worked for government departments which had been involved in EEO programs since 1980, or for companies that had participated in the AA pilot scheme that was in operation before the federal legislation came into effect in 1987. The latter often accepted the management line that equality should come about 'in a natural way' rather than being 'forced' on them, ignoring the fact that, until threatened with legislation, few companies had initiated any changes in the direction of 'equality'. Secretaries in the public service are either ill-informed, or highly cynical. The following exchange took place with a woman who was otherwise interested in her working environment:

> *What do you think about Affirmative Action?*
> What's that?
> *Well, what about EEO?*
> I think they carry on too much.

To be a feminist is to give up any right to be treated with courtesy or gallantry by men and to lose their respect for your womanly qualities. Women repeatedly distanced themselves from feminism on the grounds that they like having men holding doors open and otherwise pampering them. As with tea- and coffee-making this has immense symbolic importance and is used by men to construct power relations. Women in lower positions are particularly vulnerable. Robert, a computer operator, claimed he had held the door open for a woman one day and she refused to go out. He commented, 'that's ridiculous, that's taking it too far'. While he spoke jokingly there was something menacing in his tone. Whatever happened in the interaction we can be sure that his holding the door open was in this case not a simple act of courtesy but an assertion of masculine prerogatives. Women have little choice but to 'like' such actions. Though they may be no more an expression of male admiration than is a wolf whistle, to interpret them in any way is to invite male hostility. There is an enormous fear of being perceived to be 'anti-male'.

Most secretaries were not prepared to involve themselves in workplace politics. A union official (and ex-secretary) observed: 'Secretarial work can be a beautiful safe haven...like being a dependent wife. You can sit there and whinge how dreadful and hard life has been to you...The one thing the women's movement has done has been to remove these excuses and a hell of a lot of women don't want to know about it...because it's giving them the responsibility for their situation which they'd rather not have. They'd rather blame men for it...'

In government departments, unions and tertiary institutions where feminism had been more widely debated, it had stronger support. The Workers' Association interviews were set up after four women answered our advertisements seeking feminist secretaries. Feminism had been a subject of such fierce political debate among officials of their union that they could scarcely avoid taking up some kind of position on it. Was this another example of secretaries echoing the concerns of their bosses? Or do union jobs attract those who are already politically committed? Secretaries who work for unions are divided between those who already have a feminist or socialist politics and those who respond as they would in any other workplace. The latter group often saw feminism as something that their bosses carried on about. Secretaries were aware that pro rata their working conditions were not as good as those of professional women; they did not have the same access to superannuation, maternity and holiday leave, promotion prospects. They often viewed the professional women as concerned only to better their own conditions; where attempts had been made to involve secretaries, for example, through 'assertiveness training' sessions, they felt patronised. Their ambivalence about feminism linked in with an ambivalence about women bosses. They often thought to feminists/women bosses as unsympathetic to the problems of 'ordinary' women and as wanting to make them reverse their priorities and to rip them away from their families.

Quite a large minority of secretaries had never heard of feminism or confused it with 'femininity':

> Do you mean am I classed as being feminine or what? How I see it is wearing nice clothes and looking nice all the time...I don't believe in women's lib...burning bras and all that stuff.
> I would refer to myself as a lady. I think I'm feminine in that I have all the female characteristics...Are you talking about women's lib?! I don't have much time for women's lib. I think people should be individual and not react to trends.

Others had simply never thought about feminism and had no feelings one way or another. To them it was irrelevant. Many connected feminism with a particular generation and era: 'I think feminists and secretaries have a lot in common...but then again, I'm probably the age group.' (age 37) For younger women particularly, 'feminism' is the ideology of the over thirty-fives! Even for those who identify with its aims, the term 'feminist' has become a little passé in the 1980s. Just as earlier generations caricatured the suffragettes as frustrated old spinsters obsessed with the vote, the tide is again turning. Contemporary feminists are also in danger of relegation to a past era by younger women who take for granted the gains of the seventies and do not realise that they had to be fought for.

Feminist secretaries?

After advertising specifically for 'feminist' secretaries to come forward a number volunteered to be interviewed. These, together with the self-identified workplace activists, created an identifiable group of about 30 women who were feminist in a stronger sense than being 'for' equal rights and equal pay. All were over 30 and all were or had been senior secretaries carrying a heavy administrative responsibility. Several had moved out of secretarial work altogether and into finance, administration or personnel. They were a disparate group, extremely varied in their aspirations and their political views. While most support the Labor Party a sizeable minority vote Liberal and a number have no interest at all in party politics. Few had been in the 'women's movement' in an institutional sense though they had some identification with it. A handful had been in the Women's Electoral Lobby, drawn more by the childcare issue and the setting up of playgroups than by industrial strategy. As the children got older, and childcare waned as a personal issue, they had drifted away, being 'too busy doing other things' like re-establishing themselves in the workforce.

Those who had been involved in strikes and industrial campaigns had worked through the unions. The majority of the feminist group dissociated themselves from organisations like IPSA and the Secretaries' Forum which they saw as too timid: 'You should go and have a look at some of them. I once made some flippant remark...to this friend of mine that we should take it over and make it worthwhile. Everyone was too busy and we didn't do it but I was only half-joking and I had half-meant it...Anyway, I got this newsletter...and I used to read this thing and, oh God, it was terrible.' They were also critical of the unions, not only of the Federated Clerks but the public sector ones too. Nevertheless they thought the unions offer more opportunity for radical change than did the secretaries' organisations.

While 'feminism' meant a variety of things to these women they had a lot in common. Most strikingly they had an irreverent sense of humour which they used to completely cut through the existing power relations: 'You'd have been doing a more useful job mincing sausages than typing what he said,' said one women of an ex-boss. Though it hurt them to be labelled as 'dragons' or 'anti-men', they had confronted their own fears of such labels and were willing to confront men and speak up for their rights. They had a strong sense of their own worth and of the injustices suffered by secretaries. All were capable of seeing beyond their own immediate predicament to engage with the future of secretarial work as a whole. They are angry about the ways it is trivialised, via images of the secretary on the boss's knee and so on; about the lack of professional recognition; the failure to use or value their skills; being landed with menial tasks as well as a score of personal services which keep them from doing higher-level work; the difficulties of transferring from secretarial to related occupations;

the insulting way they are often treated by bosses who do not recognise what they do or respect their opinions and who may put them down in front of other people.

As a group they were aware that, in other circumstances they could have done 'more' than secretarial work. They had stories of being taken away from school too early, having to look after sick parents or younger siblings, of being unable to afford to go to university or having parents who felt that higher education was a waste of time for girls. Some went to university and dropped out, or married and gave up professional career prospects. Often they have 'knocked around' in a variety of other jobs and been involved in union activities and workplace disputes. One had been a ball-room dancing teacher and participated in the last authentic lock-out in New South Wales. She started as a secretary when she went to work for the solicitor who took their case! While the class backgrounds of these 30 women vary, a high proportion is from the working class.

It might be tempting to 'discover' an indigenous 'working-class feminism', but the situation is more complex. These secretaries are no longer working-class. Their feminist or socialist convictions have developed as part of a more general assertiveness which has enabled them to move into responsible positions and to an extent transform their own working relationships. Even those who still identify as working-class have moved some distance from their class origins. Yet their class background enables them to cut through the pretensions attached to secretarial positions: they are not impressed with the status of being 'someone's secretary'. One woman who had just retired after a long career refused ever to be called a secretary because she could not bear its servile connotations. Even working for a union she had difficulty with secretaries' lifestyles: 'to work on the fourth floor you'd have had to be revirginated and have a blue rinse!' Though she occupied senior positions she always insisted on being called a typist. Pam, who also now works for a union, says:

> You were classed as being in a bracket with management even though you weren't being paid like management...There was a class distinction even down to who got the percolated coffee and who had to pay for it...And you were expected to work the same hours as say the managing director but you were on these shit wages...I would see all these people who had company cars and hopes of promotion...and there was I in a dead-end job and expected to feel grateful. It was put over to you all the time that you were in this top position but it was dreadful.

These women make a realistic assessment of what secretarial work is and could be. They neither denigrate it nor idealise it. They may concede that much of it is boring and monotonous while they are well aware of the skills that are involved and the ways in which these skills are systematically undervalued. At times they are scathing about secretarial work, curse the day they became secretaries and share their plans of 'getting out'. I asked Sheila whether she had had a childhood vision of becoming a secretary: 'No, no. Oh, God no! Who wants to be a secretary? You are just part of the furniture basically and that is the way you get treated...All women experience that sort of thing...It is a matter of degree...well, no, in the case of secretaries there is a qualitative difference.' She recalled as typical an experience with the managing director of a company very similar to Malvern. She would finish his work quickly and then read a book or do crosswords: 'They realise that you are intelligent but they are afraid to give you high-calibre work. What they want you to do is low-calibre work just to fill if the time, to look busy...it makes them look bad if you are sitting around doing nothing...So when a little kid in the general office left, I got to pick up the work. This could involve things as demeaning as counting screws into bags.'

Sheila had been taken away from school three months before the HSC, something for which she never forgave her parents. She would not recommend to any eighteen-year-old that they become a secretary, unless they go to somewhere like Canberra CAE and get a secretaries' degree which would entitle them to some respect. What satisfies her about her current job is that she does have the opportunity to do more. She knows everything that is going on, supervises a large clerical staff and actually enjoys the continuing power struggles she has with her boss. She described with relish how she had forced him to break precedent and ensure she attended the chairman's lunches:

> At first he said, oh no, it wouldn't be appropriate for a woman to go. I said, why not, I don't eat my peas with a knife...I said, I am not going to let you blame those poor innocent gentlemen this time round. You are going to take responsibility for it. Then he does his block...and says, 'I find your expectation that you should go totally incredible'...So I end up being blamed for being discriminated against! To do him credit he would probably prefer me not to be there because somebody might not like it...It takes him a while to work up the courage...but I am going to the meetings now. I don't think there are any of the other partners would have done the same thing for their secretary, but he eventually does. A very complex man!

While still classed as a secretary, Sheila now does essentially administrative work. Others have moved right out of the secretarial category or are attempting to do so. Many are completing degrees or professional diplomas. They speak of lower secretarial work as boring and monotonous, of the master—slave relationship that is still at the core of relationships with bosses, of the humiliations of being treated as dumb or expected to perform menial services. And yet they do not put down secretaries or secretarial work. Despite their stories of frustration and disappointment, they take pride in their work and find pleasure and satisfaction in it as well. Where they feel contempt, it is for the treatment secretaries receive. They believe that secretarial work needs to be revalued and its links with other occupations fully acknowledged. As they see it the problem is not in the work but in the power relations that structure it. They frequently say they would not choose secretarial work again; or that they moved into it only because other possibilities had not worked out; or that they want to get out. These are entirely personal strategies but they may, ironically, be what transforms secretarial work most. As with nursing, the exodus of senior staff is creating a crisis. In the private sector at least, management has been forced to offer higher rates of pay to keep top secretaries.

Jan believes that secretaries are now in a better position to speak up: 'The bosses won't like that so they will try and get the other sort of secretary...Women will try and leave as more opportunities open up elsewhere...and when the little boss doesn't have his little handmaiden sitting outside the door...then that will force them to rethink the whole role of secretaries...because the feminists will be saying, it's your own fault boys, look at the way you have been treating us!' What characterised the feminist secretaries was a willingness to speak out, both on their own behalf and on behalf of other women, often risking their jobs. As Jan said: 'I am a super-efficient secretary but I have got sacked on a number of occasions because of my mouth.' She found it frustrating that other secretaries would not speak up for themselves: 'They will say it to another secretary...but that is different because that is 'in house' as it were...in the 'family' and speaking to an audience that you are probably going to get a sympathetic hearing from anyway.'

In a patriarchal society it is inevitable that women will seek men's approval and fear their disapproval or hostility. It is not surprising that women can so readily be brought into line by the accusation of 'man-hating'. Those who identify as feminists have managed to overcome a lot of these fears, to 'demystify' men's power and become willing to challenge men. Often this is a long slow process in which their work and other experience interact. Jan delights in her personal and financial independence: 'What I'm saying is you can be your own person, you don't have to laugh at all the stupid jokes and play that role that men like you to play very often..., Basically they still want to be 'Lords of the Earth', which they are and they know it. And no group in the history of this world has ever given up power without a fight.' The questioning, the efforts at transformation that were there at work were also central to their personal lives. While a number of this group had been married for a long time none had what could be labelled a 'traditional' marriage. All believed strongly in equality in the home and those who remained married had successfully negotiated some space in the relationship. While families were important they were not everything. Sylvia, married for twenty-five years, says that her husband is by no means her closest friend:

> It is an awful thing to say isn't it! We share a house, we share a
> friendship very pleasantly. And I have a great loyalty because I made my
> marriage vows. I am one of those who believe you should stick with it no
> matter what...I am very fond of him but I don't feel very close to him
> because we are mentally on different wavelengths...I am doing an
> external degree...and there is no way that I could bounce ideas off
> him...I have a niece who is very close to me...and she and I have had
> some deep and meaningfuls...

Those who had been through divorce identified the decision to leave a bad marriage as a time of personal growth. In kicking out husbands who were violent, manipulative, alcoholic, moody, selfish or simply took their male prerogatives for granted they had gained enormous confidence and self-respect. Often they remarried or established de facto relationships that were on an entirely different footing from their marriages. Where they had children they had encouraged them to be independent and to contribute to the domestic tasks. Some women had opted to live alone or to focus on non-family relationships, friends over lovers. Clare, a divorcee with two children, enjoys the fact that she can make decisions without having to discuss it with a husband, a father:

> I can decide I don't want to cook and I'm not forced to cook because
> there's a man there who wants to eat.
> *Is that what husbands do?*
> That's my experience.
> *Explicit or implicit, he's there and he's got to be fed?*
> The problem is meat and vegetables!

Betty Friedan (1983) has accused the women's movement of replacing the 'feminine mystique' of the housewife with a new 'feminist' mystique of the 'Superwoman' who excels, apparently effortlessly, in every area of her life. Yet these women have, to a considerable extent, broken out of the vicious circle of home and work and of the struggle to balance the two. They understand the impossibility of undertaking two or more full-time roles and were initiating a restructuring that would enable them to participate fully in the worlds of home and work, public and private life, without being overwhelmed by them. This involved redefining each of these areas and their relation to each other.

Friedan is right in claiming that women cannot be categorised into pro-family versus feminist. The working-class feminists in particular had outwardly conventional personal lives and moral values. 'Family' does not automatically represent conservatism or the 'traditional' values of the New Right. A secure domestic life often provides a source of self-esteem and a power base for doing other things. Yet Friedan overlooks the struggles that have gone on within families to achieve this; she glides over men's power as if it no longer existed. Even 'middle-class' feminists have never been opposed, in a blanket way, to all 'family' relationships; what they have opposed is the uniform imposition of a certain normative form of the family onto everyone. The opening up of alternative possibilities is important not only for its own sake but as creating the basis on which family relationships themselves could be re-shaped and transformed. It is difficult to confront a domineering husband if you cannot imagine that any other kind of living arrangement is possible or socially acceptable.

If the 'feminist' secretaries had renegotiated their relationships with men, both at work and at home, they also spoke warmly of other women and of the strength of their female relationships. They were positive about working with women and reported some good experiences with women bosses. If at times they were disappointed in women it was because they had high expectations. They valued the personal quality of women's relations which, though it could lead to bitching, also gave groups of women enormous rapport and enabled them to work closely together in conditions that men would not tolerate: 'When women have got something interesting to do and they work together as a team...I don't think there is any bitching...Women work very well in crowded areas where men won't.'

What distinguishes the group of self-defined feminists is an ability to think about their work situations in a broader way than purely in terms of their own interests or those of their own immediate group. They want to see secretarial work properly valued but are divided on how to achieve this. Two things they do seem to have in common are a degree of cynicism about new technology and a sense that AA and EEO policies alone will do little to benefit themselves or other secretaries. Some proudly call themselves 'Luddites' and see no good at all in the new technology, which they are convinced has contributed to a worsening of working conditions. Others are more sanguine that new technology may transform secretarial work and create bridges to other occupations. However, they do not treat this as inevitable. They are well aware that, given the prevailing power relations, secretaries could again be disadvantaged. They point to the worsening conditions for junior secretaries, to increases in the pressure of work and the emergence of problems like RSI and other health hazards.

It is to the revaluing of secretarial skills that they give the highest priority. But how is this to be achieved? The old assumptions about what counts as 'skill' go very deep and are difficult to challenge. Jan was involved in an equal pay case brought by the PSA on behalf of secretaries at the University of New South Wales in the late 1970s:

> Well, we lost. We didn't have the greatest judge in the world. He was a bit old and knackered, a wonder boy for the oil industry but he is a Catholic man in his middle fifties with seven children! And his wife doesn't work. So we were behind the eightball right there...He said that the union didn't prove that women were discriminated against by reason of being women... And the union didn't do such basic things as show the sorts of parameters that have been used for the evaluation of this particular skill...or produce witnesses...Both the union and the employer just assumed that typing was a low-skill job and shorthand wasn't much better...No evidence was produced as to the length of time it takes to become a competent typist in say, the School of Physics...A man was conducting the case so it was just engrained that it is women's work and therefore it is low-status.

Jan is well aware of the ways in which secretaries' work has been systematically undervalued by industrial tribunals compared with comparable male work such as printing. As for answering the telephone and making judgements about what to do with calls, 'I would be prepared to bet every cent that I would like to own for the rest of my life that nobody has ever considered for an instant how that particular task should be valued and that it is a very, very important part of the work.' For ten years she has been arguing the importance of a proper evaluation of skills and now looks to 'comparable worth' as a way of measuring job content and assessing 'equal value'.

It is a contentious issue whether 'comparable worth' is, in the Australian context, the best way to achieve wages justice. In 1985 the ACTU ran a test case on behalf of the nursing unions and it was rejected by the federal Arbitration Commission. Among other things comparable worth was seen as un-Australian, a threat to the arbitration system and 'a move towards deregulation of the labour market in the American free enterprise manner' (Ryan, 1988: 12). Should feminists, then, continue to push for comparable worth or operate within existing methods of measuring 'work value'?

Australian minimum wages are fixed by the state and federal arbitration courts which make awards on the basis of submissions put forward by unions, employers and government. The ACTU brings national wage cases on behalf of all workers and individual unions can make further submissions on the basis of changes in 'work value' or increased productivity. In 1983 the Labor government and the ACTU reached an Accord by which they agreed to limit wages growth. Women and their needs were largely left out of this deal (Pringle and Game, 1983). The Arbitration Commission will not consider claims for wage increases which fall outside the strict guidelines set by the Accord and the nurses' case was ruled out of order on these grounds.

Some argue that the ACTU did not do its homework properly and that the 'comparable worth' principle was not properly tested. It had not even firmly established with which groups the nurses would be compared, though ambulance drivers had been proposed. Since the commission did at least reaffirm its 1972 principle of equal pay for work of equal value, others claim that the way is clear for unions to run 'work value' cases (O'Donnell and Hall, 1988; Ryan, 1988). But both 'work value' and 'comparable worth' are constrained by the guidelines which prohibit increases with a major labour cost impact and forbid flow-ons to related groups. The ACTU and most unions are reluctant to upset the applecart by challenging the Accord in this way. Though there are 'anomalies' clauses, the granting of equal pay is apparently too big an 'anomaly' to be faced, either by government or unions.

In any case who would put forward such an argument on behalf of secretaries? The nurses are highly politicised, and despite inter-union squabbles they are at least unionised, with access to research and resources and the means of creating a favourable public opinion. Outside the public sector, secretaries are isolated, mostly non-unionised and with little sense of any collective purpose. Where there has been collective action it has been based on particular workplaces. Generally it has involved specific issues and has often been shortlived or dependent on the efforts of a very small number of highly committed women to sustain it. The AUNTIE network at Darling was of this kind.

The scepticism about affirmative action was a surprise. One might have expected that senior secretaries, poised to move into management, as many of the women in this group were, might have been more enthusiastic about its potential. For them AA emphasises formal workplace structures and takes no account of the relationships and discourses in which secretaries are situated. Where they have used it it has been to attempt to improve the recognition of secretaries' skills rather than to move secretaries into management. Secretaries at Darling had managed to use the company's participation in the AA pilot study to push for regrading on the basis of skill—with limited success. They had few expectations that AA would enable secretaries to move sideways into administrative or technical positions. On the contrary they were well aware that the company could pay lip-service to change while ensuring that any change was balanced by countervailing tendencies. Pressures to re-evaluate secretaries' skills and give them more responsibility were countered by pressures to cut staff and have secretaries absorb more routine tasks.

If the group were sceptical that affirmative action would bring about fundamental changes or improve conditions for any women, they felt that secretaries were least likely to benefit. It is because of the stereotypes, and because secretarial work is labelled as trivial or servile, that it is so difficult to move out of the mould. Pam says: 'Once you are labelled as being a secretary you have less chance than a filing clerk of getting on... That word 'secretary' has a stamp of typing and shorthand. It is like being a process worker.' Rita identifies the problem as 'the whole connotation of a secretary as some kind of blonde, big-busted wiggly-waggly, who paints her nails and plucks her eyebrows and is a mindless idiot... If you ever see 'secretary' mentioned it is always in a derogatory sense.' The feminist secretaries identify sexuality in the workplace as crucial to the operations of power. They are aware that it is so pervasive as to be invisible. Thus Jackie comments: 'I think most of them feel like the girl who works for us... One day we were talking about sexual harassment and she said, "I've never been sexually harassed". And I said, "Yes you have. It's just that you're so used to it... you don't even notice it... you just consider that normal. You've never been treated any other way except as a sex object to the opposite sex so you don't even think about it." And she doesn't.'

While all the women were relieved that sexual harassment has been named and turned into a political issue, they had less to say about sexuality and pleasure. The strand of feminist thought that has fed into AA programs treats sex in the workplace as sex outside its 'proper' place. In seeking to banish sex from work it denies or ignores the operations of pleasure and power. AA may be viewed at one level as reinforcing the idea that women are 'out of place' at work, except in specifically sexualised roles such as secretary. The price of 'equal opportunity' at some deep unconscious level is the denial of femininity. Secretaries are caught between being aware that it is their sexualisation that in some sense keeps them subordinate, and also finding power and pleasure in their sexuality. These women had a great deal of charm and, in their relationships with their bosses, and others in the office, were likely to be engaged and energetic rather than withdrawn or detached.

Because secretaries are more sexually defined than most other women workers they are also well placed to see the contradiction. They do not wish simply to deny their sexuality or their femininity. It is not surprising that some use their sexuality aggressively to get what they want, for this is the strategy that is most available to them. The difficulty for feminists is that discourses on sexuality permit them only two options: they can be 'pro' sex on men's terms or they must be against it in any form. The libertarian strand within feminism is easily sidetracked towards the first (Rubin, 1984; Segal, 1987), while feminists who have made more fundamental criticisms of heterosexual relations have come to be perceived as 'anti-sex'. The possibility of a radical transformation of sexuality is excluded. Feminists are presumed to be concerned with 'degendering' social relations including work relations; and they are expected to frown on sexual interactions at work, policing the boundaries of the acceptable through definitions of 'sexual harassment' and speaking out against sexual objectification. In fact this draws on an outdated argument that women are disadvantaged by their differences from men and the solution is to abolish or minimise these differences. More recent feminist literature has had a more positive view of 'difference', seeing therein strengths as well as weaknesses. Radical feminist writers have celebrated difference and recommended that women build on these differences rather than attempt to reduce them. These has been much discussion of the ways in which 'women' and 'female sexuality' cannot appear in discourse at all except as a negative; it is barely possible to 'speak' of women's sexuality at all except in terms controlled by men.

What would it mean to name a sexuality that was outside male control? For women to experience themselves as subjects rather than objects in discourses about sexuality? While these questions have been raised poetically and rhetorically, they have not yet been applied to concrete situations, least of all work. What *could* it mean for secretaries to assert their sexuality in a way that challenged men's authority? Is it possible to transform sexual relations without abolishing pleasure? Is it possible for a feminist to take a position that is not anti-sex?

The popular press persist in dealing with sexuality in terms of the old cliches and are unable even to raise such questions. To them any reference to sexuality must be reduced to the level of a schoolboy grope. An earlier attempt of ours to discuss sexuality at work was treated with complete incomprehension and saved for a wet Monday morning when it received the front-page headlines: 'Shock for feminists: secretaries like (male) bosses who flirt' (*SMH* 7 April, 1986). The writer had somehow gleaned that secretaries enjoy sitting on the boss's knee and derive pleasure from sexual harassment! The point that was being made was that since sexuality has been formed in patriarchal relationships it is important to start from an acceptance of where women are now. Rather than simply denying existing pleasures, desires or fantasies and driving sex from the workplace (thus, I would argue reinforcing men's power) it may be possible to move beyond the current patterning of relationships and to transform pleasure and power.

The strategy of the Olympia montage (see Chapter 4), with its gaudy celebration of secretaries as wives, mothers, whores and slaves, was to parody existing sexual meanings of secretary and thus to move out of or beyond existing discourses. Does parody force people to construct new meanings? Or does it inevitably reaffirm the values that it is ridiculing? Those who were involved in the project regarded it as subversive as well as pleasurable. Were they fooling themselves? They could not of course control the context in which it was viewed or the meanings given it by others. Whether they 'succeeded' is doubtful. It was a very interesting try which shows up how risky it is to attempt to intervene in prevailing discourses on sexuality.

Feminism and resistance

The views represented above are, in a sense, the 'standpoint' of this book. It is feminist secretaries with whom I most easily identify and sympathise. I could so easily have been one of them. And yet I am not one of them. As Bev James points out, it can be too readily assumed that a woman doing research involving women will have much in common with them, when in fact the research is shaped as much by the differences as by the similarities (James, 1986). Whether I, or my group of 'feminist secretaries', can or should speak for secretaries 'as a whole' is problematic. In this 'post-modern' age it is no longer fashionable to speak of 'identity' politics. The feminist 'standpoint' theorists have argued that because men are in the master's position vis-à-vis women, they have systematically distorted women's experience. Women as an oppressed group are well placed not only to criticise the masters' view of reality but also to create a more 'adequate' version of reality (Harding, 1986). Often implicit in such accounts is a notion of some 'core identity' as women. Yet such accounts may also contribute to the post-modern critique of universalising theories which assume it is either possible or desirable to produce one coherent account of 'reality'. These theories make us aware that the 'unified self' is a fiction, thus problematising, not only the concept of 'man' but of 'woman'. What then can it mean to write about secretaries from the standpoint of 'women' or 'feminism'?

It seems to me that a feminist standpoint does enable us to

grasp aspects of the workings of bureaucracy and rationality that remain submerged in masculinist accounts of power relations and authority structures. This is extremely important for secretaries for it draws attention to the ways in which sexuality is central rather than marginal to the workplace, the ways in which women are excluded from the dominant discourses or placed in an object position, and the extent to which they have to structure and interpret experience according to men's conceptual schemas. It does not follow from this that a feminist standpoint has all the answers, for there are many different versions of 'reality'. Fortunately it is not necessary for secretaries to develop a full-on 'feminist consciousness' or a unified identity before resistance becomes possible. On the contrary, there are times when 'feminist consciousness' as it is currently constituted actually restricts the possibilities of resistance. The demand for gender-neutrality, for example, has been important in a number of areas; pursued to its limits, degendering cuts feminists off from resistances which assume women's difference. Where gender-neutrality masks a form of male domination based on 'bureaucratic rationality', resistance must be based on the demand that women's gender and sexuality be fully and equally recognised. This requires strategies that embrace sexuality, whether in the workplace or in 'grooming and deportment' classes, and seek to transform it.

It is not only those identified as 'feminists' who have been involved in processes of resistance. Any assertion of power is accompanied by some element of resistance, however small. The question then becomes, under what circumstances do individual resistances snowball and become part of a larger strategy? And does resistance mean the renunciation of current pleasures? People should not be expected to give up one set of pleasures without receiving others in their place. Resistance is more likely to be effective if it is enjoyed that if it is carried out with gritted teeth. For if power and its exercise may be experienced as pleasurable, the same is true of resistance. Consider the following exchange between two secretaries:

> I once put salt in one boss's coffee.
> *What happened?*
> He was absolutely furious and I said that I had made a mistake, that it looked like sugar to me!
> *Who is the person who poisoned the boss with the Ajax?*
> I can't remember that story.
> *You told me that some girl kept putting Ajax in her boss's coffee.*

Another secretary described a similar strategy:

> *Did you refuse to make him cups of tea?*
> No, I didn't. But he didn't like the way that I made it! I used to load up

the sugar or take out the sugar accordingly when I was really mad with him...Shall we say his wife did everything that he wanted, when he wanted, and I used to rebel a little bit...because he was just so rude.

In all cases the boss eventually gave up asking for coffee! Not only were these strategies more effective than straight-out opposition but the stories were told with enormous pleasure. They were to be told and retold and shared and giggled about.

Small acts of resistance go on every day. A student gives an essay to his father's secretary to type and she posts it back to the wrong university. 'I don't know how she could have done that, he says, she knew perfectly well which one I was at.' Occasionally they develop into something larger. It is not possible to predict when or where that 'something larger' will blow up, what it will be about or what its outcome will be. A boss may try to prevent a secretary ringing home after school to see if her child is all right. A secretary will experience difficulty working out her time after the baby is born in order to collect her maternity leave. Dress rules are enforced. Lunch or tea breaks are interfered with. A particularly nasty piece of sexual harassment is exposed. Someone is sacked unfairly. Someone else is bawled out and humiliated by an inconsiderate boss: 'Well I told him off in front of a couple of people in the office because he wasn't listening to what I was saying...and he yelled at me in front of someone and I did it back to him, so he said I had better go and get myself another job...And the girls had a meeting and they blackbanned his work...They were so loyal, they were wonderful.' Suddenly there is a stop-work, a series of blackbans, an organised protest. There is no necessary connection here with feminism: the least 'likely' people may become militant on an issue about which they feel strongly. Otherwise conservative secretaries will come to the defence of any of their number who has a childcare problem.

What is the relationship between these isolated outbreaks and organised feminism? Feminist secretaries do not create resistance, but arguably their presence creates the possibility of coordinating a series of isolated encounters into a larger struggle. In some workplaces struggles around the introduction of word processors, maternity and holiday leave, pay loadings and the like have been systematically fought. There is a large gap between isolated acts of resistance and the kind of campaign that would be necessary to win, say, a comparable worth case. Such a campaign could not be won without a core group who were willing to act on behalf of the larger group.

The time is ripe for the establishment of organisations like the American Nine to Five and Women Office Workers, which can build on the existing informal workplace networks. Such organisations could push the unions to run equal pay cases before the

Arbitration Commission and intervene directly on behalf of their members. The unions are short on qualified research staff and have not been able to give work value cases the careful preparation they deserve. If secretaries' skills are to be accurately measured, secretaries themselves will have to be actively involved in the process. Equal pay should not be conceived as a narrow material interest. Its achievement requires a thorough re-evaluation of women's skills and mounts a fundamental challenge to existing assumptions and frameworks, as well as to the 'masculine' economy which, it is claimed, cannot afford such a demand. It will not be won without a wider cultural politics that challenges the current discourses on gender.

The broader women's movement has publicised and politicised a number of issues that directly affect secretaries: notably stereotyping, sexual harassment, RSI, low wages and the lack of recognition of skills. While these issues have had isolated appeal they have not caught the imagination of secretaries as a whole. There have been all sorts of obstacles to a more systematic coordination of resistances among secretaries. Interwoven with and constructing the material realities of their lives are the discourses in which they have been inserted and which are notoriously difficult to disrupt. It is to be hoped that this book makes a contribution to that process.

Method

Research for the book falls into three categories. The first, the literature searches, collection of historical and statistical data and analysis of representations of secretaries in the mass media, requires no further elaboration. The second involved a study of secretarial training and was based largely on interviews with teachers and students. The third and major part involved interviews with a range of workers, both secretarial and non-secretarial, in a variety of workplaces. The method and the samples generated are described below.

We visited six TAFE and five private secretarial colleges in Sydney and NSW country areas. These were chosen to ensure that we had students from a range of socioeconomic and ethnic backgrounds. We sat in on classes in all subjects and ourselves took classes in 'individual development' in which we administered brief questionnaires and elicited wider group discussion. Students were then interviewed in groups of three for between 20 and 30 minutes. These interviews took place fairly early in the course. A smaller sample (30) of students were interviewed again near the end of their course and then followed into the workforce. Fifteen were interviewed a third time individually in their homes and asked to reflect on the value of the course. Teachers were interviewed separately for between 15 and 45 minutes. In all, we interviewed 90 students and 30 teachers from the TAFE system and 45 students and 15 teachers from the private colleges.

The rest of the interviews were carried out at a representative range of workplaces. Of 244 interviews, 72 were with employees in the public sector, 32 with unions, 96 with large corporations and 44 with small companies, agencies or partnerships. Since approximately 72 per cent of secretaries, typists and stenographers work in the private sector, the sample undoubtedly overrepresents unions and the public sector. However, it was less important to get a random sample than to ensure that a full range of people and workplaces was represented. The aim was to situate secretarial work in the activities of particular workplaces.

A number of organisations were approached and asked for their cooperation in setting up workplace interviews with secretaries, management and a selection of other workers who interacted with secretaries. A number of companies declined to participate, and frequently a personal contact provided a way in. The bulk of the sample (174) worked in nine organisations, scattered between head and regional offices. It was important to include a range of large and small, public and private, city, country and suburban workplaces, head and branch offices and different corporate cultures. Most of the interviews were carried out in Sydney and suburbs. A minority were done in Adelaide and the NSW country, to enable some account to be taken of regional differences.

I am satisfied that I have a representative sample across all the main industry groupings: mining, manufacturing, retailing, finance and so on, as well as the public sector. Education was chosen, not only because it is a large employer of secretaries, but to compare the kind of information that derives from going in 'cold' and that from an organisations with which we could claim some familiarity, had greater freedom to move around and select, and had our own 'gossip networks'. At all workplaces we requested varied samples but we had little control over the final selection. It is likely that the sample is biased towards the more articulate and confident, that 'troublemakers' were excluded, that those who wanted to avoid questioning on sensitive issues made themselves scarce on the days of the interviews, and that the subjects chosen were expected to be least critical of their workplace. We were told about these things often enough to take account of them. It is also the case that some with an axe to grind actively sought out interviews.

It was important to the study to include bosses, and boss—secretary pairs or other combinations were sought. Female bosses are disproportionately represented. Depending on one's definition, between a half and a quarter of the interviews were with secretaries. A selection of workers were interviewed in occupations with a secretarial component, as well as clerical and administrative workers who have dealings with secretaries. Casual and part-time secretaries, along with temporaries, are underrepresented in the sample since management are frequently loathe to grant them the time to be interviewed or are unable to see that they would have anything useful to say about the workplace. Since Aboriginal secretaries did not show up in large numbers in the workplace studies, Aboriginal organisations were approached and interviews conducted there with five women doing broadly secretarial work. Given the centrality of sexuality and gender to the themes of the book, additional numbers of feminists, lesbians, gay and heterosexual male secretaries were actively sought out via advertisement and personal contact. Twenty-eight 'volunteers' were thus contacted. These interviews were usually conducted in people's homes.

The interviews took 20—60 minutes and most were taped and transcribed. A minority declined to speak into the tape recorder and in these cases detailed notes were made. All interviews, except those with the volunteers, were carried out at work, in a private room. We had hoped to do a second interview at home but this proved to be beyond our resources. The two principal researchers carried out 60 per cent of the interviews while the remainder were done by three female research assistants. For the most part they were randomly allocated. In a majority of cases the principal researchers interviewed the top managers because it seemed politic to do so! A man interviewed a sample of eight bosses to see if that would generate different information. The differences were subtle rather than substantial.

The interviews are not easily quantifiable or directly comparable. Though the same areas have been covered in each, they follow an oral history format which provides the interviewee considerable scope in deciding which areas to focus on. We did not restrict the subject matter to work. Initially people were asked to start by talking about a typical day, leaving it entirely up to them what was included. Over time, our interests shifted or became more focused on the relation between different parts of their lives, on home and family, and their views on a range of political and social issues, and on their notions of 'good boss' and 'good secretary'. We became more interested in bosses and the ways in which the boss—secretary relation is constructed: at some points it looked as if we had turned it into a project on bosses rather than secretaries! The material in Chapters 2 and 3 thus draws mostly from interviews carried out in the second half of the project.

Sample Description

Interviewees by occupation	Number	Per cent
Top and middle management	54	22
Lower management	22	9
Clerical/administrative	18	7.5
Supervisory	9	3.5
Personal assistant	3	1.5
Secretary (1 boss)	63	26
Secretary (2+bosses)	29	12
Stenographer*	4	1.5
Typist	16	6.5
Word processor operator	6	2.5
Clerical assistant	20	8
Total	*244*	*100*

* This is based on the description by self and others. Many more of the secretaries, particularly in the public service, were officially designated 'stenographers'.

• *Method* •

	Higher secretarial	Lower secretarial
Sex		
Female	101	41
Male	6	1
Total	*107*	*42*
Age		
Under 20	1	10
20−24	13	12
25−29	21	5
30−34	18	5
35−39	14	5
40−49	26	3
50+	14	2
Total	*107*	*42*
Marital Status		
Single	30	17
Living with spouse	50	19
Separated, divorced,	21	
widowed, de facto	6	5
Homosexual	6	1
Total	*107*	*42*
Children		
None	52	19
Under 5	4	14
Schoolage only	28	7
Adults	16	4
Total	*107*	*42*

'Higher secretarial' includes personal assistants, secretaries and stenographers. 'Lower secretarial' includes typists, full-time word-processor operators and clerical assistants.

Bibliography

Abercrombie, N. and J. Urry (1983) *Capital, Labour and the Middle Classes* London: Allen & Unwin

A.C.I.B.S. (1985) *From Office Wife to Office Manager—new roles for tomorrow's secretaries* Report of a Seminar Sydney: Australian Council of Independent Business Schools, April

Bammer, G. (1986) 'Muscular-skeletal problems associated with VDU use at the Australian National University—A case study of changes in work practices' *Proceedings of the 1986 Annual International Ergonomics and Safety Conference*, Louisville, Kentucky, 12–14 June.

Barker, J. and H. Downing (1980) 'Word Processing and the Transformation of the Patriarchal Relations of Control in the Office' *Capital and Class* 10, Spring pp. 64–97

Barrett, M. and M. McIntosh (1982) *The Anti-social Family* London: Verso

Beechey, V. (1987) *Unequal Work* London: Verso

Benet, M.K. (1972) *Secretary: An Enquiry into the Female Ghetto* London: Sidgwick & Jackson

Benjamin, J. (1984) 'Master and Slave: The Fantasy of Erotic Domination' in A. Snitow et al. (eds) *Desire: The Politics of Sexuality* London: Virago

Black, M. and R. Coward (1981) 'Linguistic, Social and Sexual Relations' *Screen Education* 39, Summer

Blau, P.N. and M.M. Meyer, (1971) *Bureaucracy in Modern Society* New York: Random House

Braverman, H. (1974) *Labour and Monopoly Capital* New York: Monthly Review Press

Britten, N. and A. Heath (1983) 'Women, Men and Social Class' in Gamarnikow et al. *Gender, Class and Work*

Burton, C. et al. (1987) *Women's Worth. Pay equity and job evaluation in Australia* Canberra: AGPS

Byrne, R. (1982), Occupation—Secretary: an Historical Perspective, paper given to a seminar 'Secretarial Education: A New Direction' Chisholm Institute of Technology

——(1984) 'Powerless or Empowered? Secretarial Workers and Career Development Training' ANZAAS 1984.

——(1985) 'Secretaries and power' in M. Sawer (ed.) *Program for Change: affirmative action in Australia* Sydney: Allen & Unwin

Campioni, M. (1988) 'Bringing it All Back Home: Love and Hate in Lesbian Relationships' *Gay Information* 17, 18, pp. 11–17

Carroll, M.B. (1983) *Overworked and Underpaid* New York: Ballantine

Cass, B. (1978) 'Women's Place in the Class Structure' in E.L. Wheelwright and K. Buckley (eds) *Essays in the Political Economy of Australian Capitalism* vol. 3 Sydney: ANZ Book Co.

Cassedy, E. and K. Nussbaum (1983) *9 to 5: the Working Woman's Guide to Office Survival* London: Penguin

Chodorow, N. (1978) *The Reproduction of Mothering* Berkeley: University of California Press

• Bibliography •

Christie, A. (1953) *A Pocketful of Rye* London: Collins
——(1958) *Ordeal By Innocence* London: Collins
Clarke, J. and O'Leary, Z. (1969) *Girl Fridays in Revolt* Sydney: Alpha Books
Cockburn, C. (1983) *Brothers* London: Pluto
——(1986) *Machinery of Dominance* London: Pluto
Coffey, M. and D. Dunphy (1982) 'Towards the paperless office' *Work and People* 8, 3, pp. 3–9
Connell, R.W. et al. (1982) *Making the Difference* Sydney: Allen & Unwin
Connell, R.W. (1983) *Which Way Is Up? Essays on sex, class and culture* Sydney: Allen & Unwin
——(1987) *Gender and Power* Cambridge: Polity Press
Corish, R.C. (1960) *Tomorrow's Secretary* 2nd edn, Melbourne: Pitman
Creed, B. (1984) 'The women's romance as sexual fantasy: 'Mills & Boon'' in Women and Labour Publications Collective, *All Her Labours: Embroidering the framework* Sydney: Hale & Iremonger
Crompton, R. and G. Jones (1984) *White Collar Proletariat: Deskilling and Gender in Clerical Work* London: Macmillan
Crompton, R. and M. Mann (eds) (1986) *Gender and Stratification* London: Polity Press
Crompton, R. (1986) 'Women and the "Service Class"' in Crompton and Mann (eds) *Gender and Stratification*
Cuneo, C.J. (1985) 'Have women become more proletarianized than men?' *Canadian Review of Sociology and Anthropology* 22, 4, pp. 465–95
Davies, L. (1984) *Pupil Power: Deviance and Gender in School* London: The Falmer Press
Davies, M. (1982) *Woman's Place is at the Typewriter* Philadelphia: Temple University Press
Davis, D.J. (1966) Seventy-Five Years of Commercial Education in Victoria 1850–1925, M. Ed., University of Melbourne
Delphy, C. (1984) *Close to Home* London: Hutchinson
Delphy, C. and D. Leonard (1986) 'Class Analysis, Gender Analysis, and the Family' in Crompton and Mann (eds) *Gender and Stratification*
Doherty, M. (1980) 'An Historical Background to the Predominance of Women in Clerical Employment' *Second Women and Labour Conference Papers* Melbourne: Melbourne University
Dex, S. (1985) *The Sexual Division of Work* Brighton: Wheatsheaf
Dex, S. and L.B. Shaw (1986) *British and American Women at Work* London: Macmillan
Dowling, C. (1982) *The Cinderella Complex* Melbourne: Fontana
Duffy F. et al. (eds) (1976) *Planning Office Space* London: Architectural Press
Eisenstein, H. (1985) 'The Gender of Bureaucracy: Reflections on Feminism and the State' in J. Goodnow and C. Pateman (eds) *Women, Social Science and Public Policy* Sydney: Allen & Unwin
Elshtain, J.B. (1981) *Public Man, Private Woman* Princeton: Princeton University Press
Feldberg, R. and F.E. Glenn (1984) 'Male and female: job versus gender models in the sociology of work' in J. Siltanen and M. Stanworth *Women and the Public Sphere* London: Hutchinson
Fielding, J.E. (1972) *Secretarial Practice* Sydney: McGraw Hill

Fitzsimmons, K. (1980) 'The involvement of Women in the Commercial Sector 1850—1891' *Second Women and Labour Conference Papers* Melbourne: Melbourne University

Flax, J. (1978) 'The conflict between nurturance and autonomy in mother/ daughter relationships and within feminism' *Feminist Studies* 4, 2

Foskey, S. (1987), Pleasure, Pain and Patriarchy in the experience of RSI, Sociology Honours Research Essay, Macquarie University

Foucault, M. (1980) *The History of Sexuality* Volume 1 New York: Vintage

Gamarnikow, E. et al. (eds) (1983) *Gender Class and Work* London: Heinemann

Game, A. (1984) 'Affirmative Action: Liberal Rationality or Challenge to Patriarchy?' *Legal Services Bulletin* 9, pp. 253—57

Game, A. and R. Pringle (1983) *Gender at Work* Sydney: Allen & Unwin

——(1984) 'Production and consumption: Public versus private' in D.H. Broom (ed.) *Unfinished Business: Social Justice for Women in Australia* Sydney: Allen & Unwin

——(1986) 'Beyond *Gender at Work*: Secretaries' in N. Grieve and A. Burns (ed.) *Australian Women: New Feminist Perspectives* Melbourne: Oxford University Press

Gerth, H.H. and C.W. Mills (eds) (1958) *From Max Weber: Essays in Sociology* New York: Galaxy

Giddens, A. (1973) *The Class Structure of the Advanced Societies* London: Hutchinson

——(1979) *Central Problems in Social Theory* London: Macmillan

——(1984) *The Constitution of Society: Outline of the Theory of Structuration* Cambridge: Polity Press

Glenn, E.N. and R.L. Feldberg (1979) 'Proletarianization of Clerical Work: Technology and Organizational Control in the Office' in A. Zimbalist (ed.) *Case Studies in the Labor Process* New York: Monthly Review Press

Goffman, E. (1971) *The Presentation of Self in Everyday Life* Harmondsworth: Pelican

Gottfried, H. and D. Fasenfest (1984) 'Gender and Class Formation: Female Clerical Workers' *Review of Radical Political Economics* 16, 1, pp. 89—103

Grendt, E. (1982) *Report of 1979 Survey of Full time Secretarial Studies Students* Sydney: NSW TAFE

Griffin, C. (1985) *Typical Girls?* London: Routledge & Kegan Paul

Gutek, B.A. and V. Dunwoody (1987) 'Understanding Sex in the Workplace' in A.H. Stromberg et al. (eds) *Women and Work* (An Annual Review, Volume 2) Newbury Park: Sage

Hall, P. (1985) 'Technological change and the Social Organisation of Work' papers from seminar on *Technology and the Future of Women's Work* Sydney: WEAC

Hall, P. and C. O'Donnell (1988) *Getting Equal* Sydney: Allen & Unwin

Harding, S. (1986) *The Science Question in Feminism* Milton Keynes: Open University Press

Hargreaves, K. (1982) *Women at Work* Melbourne: Penguin

Haug, F. (1987) *Female Sexualization* London: Verso

Hawkins, G. (1982) *Resistance to School* Sydney: Inner City Education Centre

Hearn J. and W. Parkin (1984) 'Sex' at 'Work': methodological and other difficulties in the study of sexuality in work organizations, paper at British Sociological Conference, University of Bradford

——(1987) 'Sex' at 'Work': The Power and Paradox of Organisation Sexuality Brighton: Wheatsheaf Books

Hocking, B. (1987) 'Epidemiological aspects of "repetition strain injury" In 'Telecom Australia' Medical Journal of Australia 147, pp. 218–22

Hollway, W. (1984) 'Gender difference and the production of subjectivity' In J. Henriques et al. (eds) Changing the Subject London: Methuen

Hunt, J.W. and R.R. Collins (1983) Managers in Mid Career Crisis Sydney: Wellington Lane

Hunt, P. (1980) Gender and Class Consciousness London: Macmillan

Irigaray, L. (1985) This Sex Which is not One Ithaca, NY: Cornell University Press

James, B. (1986) 'Taking gender into account: feminist and sociological issues in social research' New Zealand Sociology 1, 1 pp. 18–33

Jarrett, J. (1983) History of Commercial Education in NSW, B. Ed. thesis, University of Sydney

Jones, H.P. (1967) History of Commercial Education in South Australia, MA. thesis, University of Adelaide

Kanter, R.M. (1975) 'Women and the Structure of Organizations: Explorations in Theory and Behavior' in M. Millman and R. Kanter (eds) Another Voice New York: Anchor

——(1977) Men and Women of the Corporation New York: Basic Books

Kingston, B. (1975) My Wife, My Daughter and Poor Mary Ann Melbourne: Nelson

Korda, M. (1972) Male Chauvinism! How It Works New York: Random House

Kuhn, A. (1984) 'Public versus private: the case of indecency and obscenity' Leisure Studies 3 pp. 53–65

Lees, S. (1986) Losing Out London: Hutchinson

Lockwood, D. (1986) 'Class, Status and Gender' in Crompton and Mann, (eds) Gender and Stratification

Lowe, G.S. (1987) Women in the Administrative Revolution Cambridge: Polity Press

Lloyd, G. (1984) The Man of Reason London: Methuen

Lucire, Y. (1986) 'Neurosis in the workplace' Medical Journal of Australia 145, October 6, pp. 323–27

MacDonald S. and Mandeville T. (1980) 'Word Processors and Employment' Journal of Industrial Relations 22, 2, pp. 137–48

McCrae S. (1986) Cross-Class Families Oxford: Clarendon Press

MacKinnon, C.A. (1979) Sexual Harassment of Working Women New Haven: Yale University Press

McNally, F. (1979) Women for Hire: A Study of the Female Office Worker London: Macmillan

Mann, M. (1973) Consciousness and Action among the Western Working Class London: Macmillan

——(1986) 'A crisis in Stratification Theory?' In Crompton and Mann (eds) Gender and Stratification

Manpower Research and Information Branch (1979) Word Processing and

Some Aspects of its Employment Impact in the Typing/Secretarial area, Department of Employment and Youth Affairs, Sydney, April

Marcuse, H. (1968) *One Dimensional Man* London: Sphere Books

Millett, K. (1972) *Sexual Politics* London: Abacus

Mitchell, J. (1975) *Psychoanalysis and Feminism* Harmondsworth: Penguin

Moran, P. (1984) Female Youth Culture and Attitudes to Education: a Focus on Social Relations in the School, paper presented at ANZAAS, ANU Canberra

O'Neil, J.P. (1970) *The Belconnen Office Complex* Canberra: AGPS

O'Neil, T. (1985) *Employment Prospects of Secretaries Stenographers*, Department of Employment and Industrial Affairs, Melbourne, October

Orbach, S. and L. Eichenbaum (1987) *Bittersweet* London: Century

Perkins T.E. (1979) 'Rethinking Stereotypes' in M. Barrett et al. (eds) *Ideology and Cultural Production* London: Croom Helm

Phillips, A. (1987) *Divided Loyalties: Dilemmas of Sex and Class* London: Virago

Philp, M. (1985) 'Michel Foucault' In Q. Skinner (ed.) *The Return of Grand Theory in the Human Sciences* Cambridge: Cambridge University Press

Poole, R. (1987) 'Rationality, Masculinity and Modernity' Sydney: paper read at the Femininity/Masculinity/Representation Conference, Sydney University, August

Porat, F. and M. Will (1983) *The Dynamic Secretary* New Jersey: Prentice Hall

Prandy, K. (1986) 'Similarities of life-style and occupations of women' in Crompton and Mann (eds) *Gender and Stratification*

Pringle, R. (1983) 'Women and consumer capitalism' in C.V. Baldock and B. Cass (eds) *Women, Social Welfare and the State in Australia* Sydney: Allen & Unwin

Pringle, R. and A. Game (1983) 'From Here to Fraternity: Women and the Hawke Government' *Scarlet Woman* 17, pp. 5–11

Rich, A. (1983) 'Compulsory Heterosexuality and Lesbian Existence' in Snitow et al. (eds) *Powers of Desire*

Ronalds, C. (1987) *Affirmative Action and Sex Discrimination* Sydney: Pluto

Rosaldo, M.Z. (1974) 'Woman, culture and society: a theoretical overview in M.S. Rosaldo and L. Lamphere (eds) *Woman Culture and Society* Stanford: Stanford University Press

Rose, J. (1986) *Sexuality in the Field of Vision* London: Verso

Rose, M. (1975) *Industrial Behaviour: Theoretical Development since Taylor* London: Allen Lane

Rubenstein, L. (1978) 'Women, Work and Technological Change' *Papers from First Women and Labour Conference* Sydney: Macquarie University

Rubery, J. (1978) 'Structured labour markets, worker organisation and low pay' *Cambridge Journal of Economics* 2, pp. 17–36

Rubin, G. (1984) 'Thinking Sex: Notes for a Radical Theory of the Politics of Sexuality' in Vance (ed.) *Pleasure and Danger*

Ryan, E. (1988) 'Equal Pay, Comparable Worth and the Central Wage Fixing System' *Australian Feminist Studies* 6 pp. 7–16

Samuel, L. (1983) 'The Making of a School-resister: A Case Study of Australian Working-Class Secondary Schoolgirls' in R.K. Browne and L.E. Foster, *Sociology of Education* 3rd edn, Melbourne: Macmillan

Schmertz, M.F. (ed.) (1961) *Office Building Design* New York: McGraw Hill

• Bibliography •

Schneider, B.E. (1984) 'The office affair: Myth and reality for hetero-sexual and lesbian women workers' *Sociological Perspectives* 27, 4, pp. 443–64

Scutt, J. (1983) *Even in the Best of Homes* Melbourne: Penguin

Segal, L. (1987) *Is the Future Female?* London: Virago

Sennett, R. (1981) *Authority* New York: Vintage Books

Sharpe, S. (1984) *Double Identity—The lives of Working Mothers* Harmondsworth: Penguin

Siltanen, J. and M. Stanworth (1984) *Women and the Public Sphere* London: Hutchinson

Silverman, D. (1970) *The Theory of Organisations* London: Heinemann

Silverman, K. (1984) 'Histoire d'O: The Construction of a Female Subject' in Vance (ed.) *Pleasure and Danger*

Smart, B. (1985) *Michel Foucault* London: Tavistock

Smith, D.E. (1983) 'Women, Class and Family' *Socialist Register* London: Merlin Press

A. Snitow et al. (eds) (1983) *Powers of Desire: The Politics of Sexuality* New York: Monthly Review Press

Softley, E. (1985) 'Word processing: new opportunities for women office workers?' in W. Faulkner and E. Arnold (eds) *Smothered by Invention* London: Pluto

Sokoloff, N.J. (1980) *Between Money and Love: The Dialectics of Women's Home and Market Work* New York: Praeger

Solly, E.H. et al. (1970) *The Secretary at Work* 3rd edn, Melbourne: McGraw Hill

Solly, E. and R. Byrne (1981) 'The Wilenski Report and Affirmative Action in New South Wales: Careers for Secretaries?' *Australian Commercial and Economics Teachers Association Conference* Canberra: Canberra College of Advanced Education

Sweet, R. (1983) *An Analysis of the Australian Labour Market for typists, Stenographers and Secretaries* NSW TAFE Counselling Research Unit, Sydney: AGPS

Taylor, S. (1983) 'Reproduction and Contradictions in Schooling: the Case of Commercial Studies' Brisbane: Brisbane CAE

Thompson, E.P. (1968) *The Making of the English Working Class* Harmondsworth: Penguin

Tiger, L. (1969) *Men in Groups* London: Nelson

Vance, C. (ed.) (1984) *Pleasure and Danger. Exploring Female Sexuality* Boston: Routledge & Kegan Paul

Vella, K. (1984) Tertiary Qualified Secretaries and Secretarial Work, MA thesis, Monash University

Wacjman, J. (1983) *Women in Control: Dilemmas of a Workers' Cooperative* Milton Keynes: Open University Press

Walby, S. (1986a) 'Gender, Class and Stratification: Towards a New Approach' in Crompton and Mann (ed.) Gender and Stratification

——(1986b) *Patriarchy at Work* London: Polity Press

Watson, S. (1986) *Housing and Homelessness: a Feminist Perspective* London: Routledge & Kegan Paul

Weeks, J. (1985) *Sexuality and its Discontents* London: Routledge & Kegan Paul

West, J. (1978) 'Women, sex and class' in A. Kuhn and A.M. Wolpe *Feminism and Materialism* London: Routledge & Kegan Paul

——(1982) 'New technology and Women's Office Work' in J. West (ed.) *Work, Women and the Labour Market* London: Routledge & Kegan Paul

Wills, S. (1986) *Review of General Staff Positions* Sydney: Macquarie University

Worksafe Australia (1986) *Repetition Strain Injury: A Report and Model Code of Practice* Canberra: AGPS

Wright, E.O. (1976) 'Class boundaries in advanced capitalist societies', *New Left Review* 98 pp. 3–41

——(1985) *Classes* London: Verso

Zaretsky, E. (1976) *Capitalism, the Family and Personal Life* London: Pluto

Index